The History and Theology of the Ecumenical Movement

The History and Theology of the Ecumenical Movement

A Postcolonial Reading

(In Commemoration of the 1700th Anniversary of the First Ecumenical Council at Nicaea)

Lalfakawma Ralte

Christian World Imprints

First Published in 2025 by

Christian World Imprints
Christian Publishing & Books from India
A-71 Group, Wazirpur Industrial Area
Delhi-110052
cwidelhi2017@gmail.com
www.ChristianWorldImprints.com
Phone: +91 11 41526079

ISBN: 978-93-6065-395-8

Printed in India.

Contents

Acknowledgement xv
Preface xvii

Chapter 1: The Term Ecumenical: Meaning, Origin, Re-Reading from a Postcolonial Perspective, Present-day Usage, and Significance 1

1.1. Meaning and Origin, and Re-Reading from a Postcolonial Perspective 1
1.2. Present-day Usage 9
1.3. Significance 10
1.3.1. Spiritual and Religious Context 10
1.3.1.1. Christian Unification and Harmony 10
1.3.1.2. Ecumenical Councils 11
1.3.1.3. Interfaith Dialogue 11
1.3.2. Broader Cultural Context 11
1.3.2.1. Unity Across Divisions 11
1.3.2.2. Global Perspective 12
1.3.2.3. Bridge-Building 12
1.3.2.4. Cultural and Historical Impact 12
1.3.3. Modern Application 12

Chapter 2: Biblical and Theological Foundations of Ecumenism 13

2.1. The Tower of Babel 13
2.2. The Unity of Pentecost - Overcoming the Division of Babel (Acts 2:1-12) 14
2.3. The Body of Christ Unites All People 15
2.4. Divine Imperative for Ecclesiastical Unity 15
2.5. The Role of the Holy Spirit in Ecclesial Cohesion 16
2.6. Postcolonial Reading of Melchizedek: An Ecumenical Prototype 16
Conclusion 17

Chapter 3: Division of the Church in the First and Second Millennium 19
3.1. Division in the Early Church 20
3.1.1. Localised Issues 20
3.1.2. Broader Challenges within the Church 20
3.1.3. Montanism 21
3.1.3.1. Background 21
3.1.3.2. Origin of Montanism 21
3.1.3.3. Features of Montanism 22
3.1.4. Manichaeism 23
3.1.5. Gnosticism 24
3.1.5.1. The Gnostics: The Birth of Religious Philosophy 24
3.1.6. Monarchianism 26
3.1.6.1. An Examination of Early Christological Controversies 26
3.1.7. Arianism 27
3.1.8. Macedonianism 28
3.1.9. Nestorianism 29
3.1.10. Eutychianism 30
3.1.11. East and West Division/The Great Schism of 1054 31
3.1.11.1. Linguistic Divergence 31
3.1.11.2. Political Dynamics 31
3.1.11.3. Eastern Universalism 31
3.1.11.4. Western Universalism 31
3.1.11.5. Theological Contrasts 32
3.1.12. Iconoclastic Controversy 32
3.1.12.1. First Iconoclasm (726–787) 32
3.1.12.2. Second Iconoclasm (814–842) 32
Conclusion 33
Chapter 4: Ecumenical Movement 35
4.1. Evangelical and Missionary Movements of the 19th Century 35
4.1.1. Interdenominational Unity in the Context of the Evangelical Movement 35
4.1.1.1. Pietism 35
4.1.1.2. Evangelical Awakening 37
4.1.1.2.1. The First Great Awakening (1725-1750) 37
4.1.1.2.2. The Second Great Awakening (1825-1835) 38

4.1.1.2.3. The Third Great Awakening (1857-1858) 38
4.1.1.3. Voluntary Movements and Student Christian 40
Movements 40
4.1.1.3.1. Young Men's Christian Association 40
4.1.1.3.2. Young Women's Christian Association 40
4.1.1.3.3. Student Volunteer Movement (S.V.M.) 41
4.1.1.3.3.1. Roles of Women in S.V.M. 41
4.1.1.3.4. Modern Missionary Movements 42
4.1.1.3.4.1. The Society for Promoting Christian Knowledge (SPCK) 43
4.1.1.3.4.2. The Danish-Halle Lutheran Mission 43
4.1.1.3.4.3. Baptist Missionary Society 43
4.1.1.3.4.4. The London Missionary Society (1795) 44
4.1.1.3.4.5. The American Board of Commissioners for Foreign Missions 44
4.1.1.3.4.6. Interdenominational Cooperation in Germany 44
4.1.1.3.4.7. The Swedish Missionary Society 45
4.1.1.3.4.8. The Church of Scotland 45
4.1.1.3.4.9. The Basel Mission 45
4.1.1.3.4.10. Zenana Missions 47
Conclusion 47
Chapter 5: World/International Missionary Conferences 49
5.1. The World Missionary Conference at Edinburgh (1910) 50
5.1.1. The Context 50
5.1.2. Title 50
5.1.3. The Conference 51
5.1.3.1. Representation at the Conference 51
5.1.4. The Eight Commissions 53
5.1.5. The Impacts of WMC 54
5.1.6. Postcolonial Reading of the IMC 54
5.2. Life and Work and Faith and Order Movements 56
5.2.1. Life and Work 56
5.2.2. Faith and Order 58
5.2.2.1. Origin 58

5.2.2.2. Preliminary Meeting 59
5.2.2.3. First World Conference Lausanne 1927 59
5.2.2.4. Second World Conference Edinburgh 1937 61
5.2.2.5. Final Meeting, Amsterdam 61
5.2.3. Impacts of Life and Work and Faith and Order on the Modern Understanding of Christian Unity 62
5.2.3.1. The Life and Work Movement: A Practical Approach to Christian Unity (1925–1948) 62
5.2.3.1.1. Impact on Contemporary Christian Unity 62
5.2.3.2. Doctrinal Unity in the Faith and Order Movement (1910s–1948) 63
5.2.3.2.1. Effects on Contemporary Unity 63
5.2.4. International Missionary Conference at Crans in 1920 64
5.3. International Missionary Council (IMC) 1921-1961 65

Chapter 6: World Council of Churches 69
6.1. Beginning and Development of WCC 69
6.2. The Basis 72
6.3. Assemblies of WCC 73
6.3.1. First Assembly: Amsterdam, Holland, 1948 73
6.3.2. Second Assembly: Evanston, 1954 74
6.3.3. Third Assembly: New Delhi, 1961 75
6.3.4. Fourth Assembly: Uppsala, Sweden, 1968 75
6.3.5. Fifth Assembly: Nairobi, Kenya, 1975 76
6.3.6. Sixth Assembly: Vancouver, 1983 76
6.3.7. Seventh Assembly: Canberra, 1991 77
6.3.8. Eighth Assembly: Harare, Zimbabwe, 1998 77
6.3.9. Ninth Assembly: Porto Alegre, Brazil, 2006 77
6.3.10. Tenth Assembly: Busan, South Korea, 2013 78
6.3.11. Eleventh Assembly: Karlsruhe, Germany, 2022 78
6.4. Postcolonial Reading of the WCC 79
6.4.1. Colonial Heritage and Eurocentrism 79
6.4.2. Mission and Empire's Legacy 79
6.4.3. Global South Involvement and Participation 80
6.4.4. Philosophy of Emancipation and Equity 81
6.4.5. Ecumenical and Intercultural Cooperation 82
Conclusion 82

Chapter 7: Continental Ecumenical Movements 85
7.1. Christian Conference of Asia 86
7.2. Ecumenical Association of Third World Theologians (EATWOT) 89
7.2.1. Aims and Objectives of Eatwot 92
7.2.2. Key Themes in EATWOT Theology 92
7.2.3. Notable Theologians in EATWOT 93
7.2.4. EATWOT and Indian Contextual Theology 94
7.2.5. EATWOT and Northeast Indian Theology 95
7.2.6. EATWOT's Legacy and Ongoing Relevance 96
7.3. Church Auxiliary for Social Action (CASA) 96
Conclusion 98
Chapter 8: Key Concepts in Ecumenism (Exploring Terms that Shape Christian Unity and Dialogue) 99
8.1. Comity 99
8.1.1. Meaning 99
8.1.2. Cooperation and Unity in Mission Fields 100
8.1.3. Benefits and Challenges of Comity 100
8.1.4. Benefits 101
8.1.4.1. Newbegin's Articulation 101
8.1.4.2. Comity Fosters Solidarity among Christians 101
8.1.4.3. It Minimises Resource Duplication 102
8.1.4.4. It Encourages Collaborative Engagement 102
8.1.4.5. It Strengthens the Global Witness 102
8.1.4.6. It Improves Resource Sharing 102
8.1.4.7. It Promotes Harmonious Coexistence 102
8.1.5. Challenges of Comity in the Ecumenical Movement 102
8.1.5.1. Negotiations on Theological Authenticity 102
8.1.5.2. Opposition from Denominations 102
8.1.5.3. Concerns Regarding Justice 102
8.1.5.4. Restrictions on Missionary Efforts 102
8.1.5.5. Risk of Superficial Harmony 103
8.1.5.6. Cultural and Contextual Challenges 103
8.2. Wider Ecumenism 103
Conclusion 110
Chapter 9: Different Models of Church Unity 111
9.1. Cooperative Action 112
9.2. Organic Union 112

9.3. Conciliar Fellowship 116
9.4. Intercommunion 120
9.5. Spiritual Model 121
Chapter 10: Ecumenism in Northeast India (Tribal Ecumenism): Trials and Emerging Ecumenical Trajectories 123
10.1. The Emergence of Christianity in Northeast India 123
10.1.1. Mizoram 123
10.1.2. Arunachal Pradesh 124
10.1.3. Meghalaya 125
10.1.4. Manipur 127
10.1.4.1. The Establishment of the Arthington Aborigines Mission 127
10.1.4.2. The Establishment of the Welsh Presbyterian Mission 128
10.1.5. Tripura 129
10.1.6. Nagaland 131
10.1.7. Assam 132
10.2. Attempts at the Formation of Church Union in Northeast India 133
10.3. Challenges to Church Union Negotiations (A Period of Trials) 135
10.3.1. Doctrinal Factors 135
10.3.2. Influence of Ultra-Conservative Theology 136
10.3.3. Communalism 136
10.3.4. Form of Worship 136
10.3.5. Ecclesiastical Organisations 136
10.3.6. Ecclesiastical Rituals and Lifestyle 136
10.3.7. Churches' Internal Problems and Splits 137
10.3.8. Denominational Ecumenism 137
10.4. The North East India Christian Council (NEICC) 137
10.4.1. Common Project 139
10.4.2. Strengths of NEICC 139
10.4.3. Weaknesses of NEICC 139
10.5. Relationship between Roman Catholic and Protestant Churches 140
10.6. Emerging Ecumenical Trajectories 140
10.6.1. From the Institutional to the Mystical 141
10.6.2. From the Centre to the Margins 142
Chapter 11: National Ecumenical Movements 145
11.1. National Council of Churches in India (NCCI) 145
11.1.1. The Function of the National Christian Council 147

11.1.1.1. The National Movement and the NCC 147
11.1.1.2. NCC and Evangelism and Mission 148
11.1.1.3. Church-Centric Focus within the Council 148
11.1.2. Critique of the National Council of Churches in India 148
11.2. The National Christian Council of Sri Lanka 148
11.3. Myanmar Council of Churches 150
11.3.1. An Overview 150
11.3.2. Background Context 151
11.3.3. Membership Criteria 151
11.3.4. Mission & Ecumenism Department Purpose 151
11.3.5. Strategic Plans 152
11.3.6. Vision and Mission 152
11.3.7. Objectives 152
11.3.8. Myanmar Ecumenical Institute (M.E.I) 153
11.3.9. Purpose 153
11.3.10. Plans 153
11.4. Criticism of the Myanmar Council of Churches 153
11.4.1. Perceived Insufficient Advocacy 153
11.4.2. Concerns Regarding Religious Freedom 153
11.4.3. Government Alignment 154
11.4.4. Internal Divisions and Unity Issues 154
11.4.5. Impact of Colonial History 154
Chapter 12: Roman Catholics and Protestant Churches 155
12.1. Pre-Vatican Relationship 155
12.1.1. Historical Context 155
12.1.2. Catholic Attitude toward Protestants 156
12.1.3. Protestant Views of the Catholic Church 156
12.1.4. Vatican (1962–1965): A Turning Point 157
12.1.4.1. Key Documents 158
12.1.4.2. Changes in Theology 159
12.1.4.3. Shifts in Attitude 159
Conclusion 159
Chapter 13: Indian Expressions of Ecumenism 161
13.1. Formation of National Missionary Council 161
13.2. South India United Church (SIUC) 164
13.3. The Church of South India 166
13.3.1. Challenges 168

13.3.1.1. Recognition of Episcopal Authority 168
13.3.1.2. Personal Jealousies 169
13.3.1.3. Problems Identified by Bishop Chellappa 169
13.3.2. Towards Wider Union 169
13.3.3. Worship 170
13.3.4. Women in the Church 170
13.3.5. Statement on Baptism 171
13.4. The Church of North India 171
13.4.1. Round Table Conferences 171
13.4.2. Issues and Challenges 174
13.5. Communion of Churches in India 175
13.5.1. Aims and Objectives of the Communion 176
13.5.2. Challenges 178
13.6. United Theological College 179
13.6.1. Mission of the College 179
13.6.2. Theological Courses of Ecumenical Nature Offered at UTC 180
13.6.3. Ecumenical Ecclesial Exposure 181
13.6.4. Intensive Field Education 181
13.7. Ecumenical Christian Centre 183
13.7.1. ECC's Programmes 184
13.7.2. Contributions to Nation-Building and Social Change 186
13.7.3. The Indian School of Ecumenical Theology (ISET) 186
13.7.4. ECC Neighbourhood Interactive Forum 187
13.8. Christian Medical College and Hospital, Vellore 188
13.8.1. Hospital Network 188
13.8.2. Mission and Vision 189
13.8.3. Motto 189
13.8.4. Department of Community Health 190
13.8.5. Rural Unit for Health and Social Affairs (RUHSA) 190
13.8.6. Low Cost Effective Care Unit & Shalom Family Medicine Centre 190
13.8.7. The Department of Ophthalmology 191
13.8.8. College of Nursing Community Health (CONCH) 191
Conclusion 191

Chapter 14: Council of Churches in Mizoram 193
14.1. Mizoram's Ecclesiastical History can be Broadly Categorised into 4 Distinct Periods 194

14.1.1. The First Period (1894-1948) 194
14.1.2. The Second Period (1949-1983) 194
14.1.3. The Dark Period (1884-2010) 194
14.1.4. The Brighter Period (2011-2023) 195
14.2. First Business Session 197
14.3. Inauguration of the Council of Churches in Mizoram 197
14.4. Mission Statement 198
14.5. Membership 198

Chapter 15: Women in the Ecumenical Movement 199
15.1. Theological Contributions 200
15.1.1. Letty M. Russell 200
15.1.2. Mercy Amba Oduyoye 200
15.1.3. Kwok Pui Lan 201
15.2. Administrative Role 202
15.3. Equity Work 202
15.4. Fostering Down-to-Earth Movement 203
15.5. Historical Study of Women's Engagement in the Ecumenical Movement 203
15.6. The Zenana Mission 205
15.7. A Postcolonial Reading of the Contributions of Women in the Ecumenical Movement 206
Conclusion 208

Chapter 16: Edinburgh 2010 211
16.1. An Overview 211
16.2. The Conference 212
16.3. Hopes Beyond Edinburgh 2010 215
16.4. Postcolonial Reading of Edinburgh 2010 216
16.4.1. Edinburgh 1910s Legacy: Persistence and Disintegration 216
16.4.2. Western Domination 217
16.4.3. Representation and Counterfeiting 217
16.4.4. Colonial Shadows and Missiological Vocabulary 218
Conclusion 218

Bibliography 221

Acknowledgement

My thanks are due to God, whose boundless grace has bestowed upon me the strength, time, space, and opportunity to pen this book. This endeavour would not have come to fruition without God's unwavering presence and gentle guidance.

I thank my beloved wife, Mathani, who has been my steadfast anchor and source of encouragement throughout this journey. Her unwavering support and quiet confidence in me have been instrumental in completing this work. With her, I express my gratitude to our precious daughters - Ainam, Zualtei, Felfeli, and Faith - whose love, laughter, and presence infuse my life with joy and purpose. They, along with Mathani, transform our house into a true home, and their companionship has made this writing journey both deeply rewarding and inspiring.

To the esteemed readers of this publication, I extend my sincere gratitude for your interest in exploring the themes of Christian unity and ecumenical reflection. I hope that within these pages, you will uncover both historical significance and spiritual depth. May your hearts be increasingly receptive to embracing and accommodating others through the teachings of Jesus Christ. I wish you a meaningful and rewarding reading experience.

Happy reading!
Warm regards

Lalfakawma Ralte
UTC, Bangalore, 2025

Preface

The pursuit of unity among the diverse traditions within the Christian faith constitutes a significant theological and missional endeavour in contemporary society. Central to this initiative is the ecumenical movement, which aspires to achieve more than mere structural agreements; it seeks to promote a deeper communion based on shared beliefs, mutual respect, and a collective testimony to the Gospel amidst a fragmented world. This book examines the meaning, development, and various expressions of ecumenism, delineating its theological foundations, historical progressions, institutional frameworks, and contemporary challenges. It commences with a comprehensive exploration of the term "ecumenical," tracing its origins, evolution, and reinterpretation in both postcolonial and present contexts.

This foundational work equips readers with an understanding of the spiritual and biblical vision that undergirds the call for Christian unity. The book provides an innovative interpretation of ecumenism, positing that early Christian writers inherited Roman concepts of territorial claims, thereby linking their religious endeavours to the broader narratives of power, unity, and universality associated with Roman ideals. Throughout church history, the work examines the causes and repercussions of ecclesial divisions that occurred in the 1st and 2nd millennia. It emphasises crucial events from the 19th and 20th centuries, such as the Edinburgh 1910 Conference, the establishment of the World Council of Churches, and the emergence of both continental and national ecumenical organisations, all of which have significantly influenced the modern ecumenical consciousness.

In particular, this book offers a contextual analysis of ecumenism in Northeast India, focusing on the region's unique ecclesial landscape, tribal identities, mission histories, and the evolving trajectories toward unity in the face of doctrinal, cultural, and communal challenges. Additionally, it evaluates national movements in South and Southeast Asia, assessing the strengths and criticisms of institutions such as the National Council of

Churches in India, the National Christian Council of Sri Lanka, and the Myanmar Council of Churches.

Beyond the discussion of institutions, the book addresses fundamental concepts such as wider ecumenism, comity, conciliarism, and intercommunion, exploring various models of church union that range from organic to spiritual. It also acknowledges frequently overlooked contributors, particularly women who have played significant roles in the ecumenical movement, and invites fresh perspectives that have emerged from events such as the Edinburgh 2010 Conference.

With a robust integration of theology, history, culture, and contextual realities, this book encourages readers to perceive ecumenism as an ongoing process rather than a completed project. It embodies a journey from division to dialogue, from institutional frameworks to spiritual fellowship, and from mainstream narratives to insights from marginalised voices. This work serves as both a historical reference and a compelling call for renewed commitment to the visible unity of the Body of Christ in the contemporary world.

Sincerely,

Lalfakawma Ralte
United Theological College
Bangalore

Chapter 1

The Term Ecumenical
Meaning, Origin, Re-Reading from a Postcolonial Perspective, Present-day Usage, and Significance

1.1. Meaning and Origin, and Re-Reading from a Postcolonial Perspective

The term "ecumenical" denotes a sense of universality or generality regarding extent, influence, or application. This term is derived from the Greek word *oikos* or *oikumene,* originally referring to the entirety of the inhabited earth in a geographical context. Visser't Hooft elucidates the various implications and meanings of the term "ecumenical" in the following manner:[1]

a) pertaining to or representing the whole (inhabited) earth;
b) pertaining to or representing the whole of the (Roman) empire,
c) pertaining to or representing the whole of the Church,
d) that which has universal, ecclesiastical validity,
e) pertaining to the worldwide missionary outreach of the Church,
f) pertaining to the relations between and the unity of two or more Churches (or Christians of various confessions);
g) that quality or attitude which expresses the consciousness of and desire for Christian unity.

---

[1] Willem Adolf Visser't Hooft, "The Word 'Ecumenical' Its History and Use," in *A History of the Ecumenical Movement 1517-1948*, 3rd ed., edited by Ruth Rouse, Stephen Charles Neil (Geneva: WCC, 1993), 735. Hereafter cited as Visser't Hooft, "The Word 'Ecumenical.'"

During the 5th century B.C.E., the term *oikumene* was initially limited to a secular context, designating the territories inhabited by the Greco-Roman Empire. This designation identified the regions under Greco-Roman influence and established a cultural dichotomy, distinguishing the "civilised" world from the lands occupied by what the Greeks and Romans termed "barbarians."

Over time, the meaning of *oikumene* expanded to encompass areas beyond those occupied by the Greeks, ultimately representing the entirety of the inhabited world. This broader definition is notably evident in the works of the philosopher Aristotle, who employed the term in this inclusive manner. The Roman Empire's extensive reach, particularly as it expanded eastward, enabled it to dominate territories previously governed by the successors of Alexander the Great.

The Romans possessed a distinct conception of *oikumene*; their worldview extended the notion of empire to encompass any area that contained inhabitants, thereby asserting their imperial authority over these regions. This perspective was reflected in the cultural practices of Rome and Roman-occupied Greece, where various athletic events were organised to celebrate the empire, collectively referred to as the *oikumenia*. In this framework, the emperor acted as master and benefactor, serving as a unifying figure for the *oikumene*.

As stated earlier, the term *oikumene*, derived from the Greek word οἰκουμένη, refers to the known world and delineates the geographical and political boundaries of Roman imperial authority during the extensive conquests of the empire across diverse territories and populations. As Rome expanded, its understanding of geographical limits evolved, mirroring a concurrent expansion of its political and military power. The Latin expression *orbis terrarum*, translating to "circle of lands," further underscores the breadth of Roman ambition and control over extensive regions. This imperial endeavour transcended mere territorial acquisition; it fundamentally centred on the consolidation of power and influence[2] over various cultures and societies.

The territorial claims associated with the *oikumene* are deeply interconnected with Rome's political objectives. Historian Yann Le Bohec emphasises that the Romans regarded the *oikumene* as a mechanism to establish and uphold their dominance over the known regions of the world. In his analyses, Nicolet references the ancient historian Polybius, who famously asserted, "All the known regions of the *oikumene* are now under

[2] See Gladson Jathanna, *Decolonising Oikumene* (Delhi: ISPCK, 2020), 3. Hereafter cited as Jathanna, *Decolonising*.

Roman control."[3] This declaration highlights the magnitude of Roman territorial claims at the zenith of its power, illustrating how the empire not only expanded its geographical boundaries but also shaped the political landscape of the Mediterranean and beyond. Thus, the concept of *oikumene* serves as a crucial framework for understanding the complexities of Roman imperial ideology and its enduring impact on world history.

The Romans were often referred to as the "lords of the *oikumene*," a term that encompassed the known world and highlighted their dominance over vast territories. Roman emperors were not just rulers but also symbolically "tread their feet" upon the *oikumene*, signifying their authority over all inhabited lands. One notable example is General Pompey, who celebrated his military conquests with extravagant trophies. Among these was a massive monument richly adorned and inscribed with the phrase "a trophy of the inhabited world" (*oikumene*),[4] that communicated the magnitude of his victories and the extension of Roman influence. Prominent emperors such as Julius Caesar and Augustus also sought to reinforce their connections to the *oikumene* through various acts and public monuments. Caesar, for instance, expanded Rome's boundaries through military campaigns in Gaul and beyond, while Augustus, as the first emperor, established a lasting legacy by promoting stability and prosperity throughout the empire. These representations not only reflect the emperors' triumphs but also symbolise the wider imperial perspective[5] and their deep-rooted affiliation with the Roman Empire's ideology of conquest and civilisation.

Christianity emerged during the expansive period of the Roman Empire, which significantly influenced its early development and outreach. The term *oikumene* reflects the Roman imperial vision of a unified world under Roman governance, where the idea of a global community was promoted. This concept of *oikumene* not only underscored the geographic extent of the Empire but also shaped the way the early Christians perceived their mission. By adopting this terminology, early Christian writers effectively linked their religious activity to the broader narratives of power, unity, and universality characteristic of Roman ideals, thus framing their message within a familiar cultural and political context.[6] This connection

---

[3] As cited in Jathanna, *Decolonising*, 3.

[4] See Barbara R. Rossing, "(Re)-claiming Oikumene?: Empire, Ecumenism, and the Discipleship of Equals," in *Walk in the Ways of Wisdom: Essays in Honour of Elisabeth Schuessler Fiorenza*, edited by Shelly Matthews, et.al. (Harrisburg, London, New York: Trinity Press International, 2003), 76.

[5] See Jathanna, *Decolonising*, 3, 4.

[6] Cf. Jathanna, *Decolonising*, 4.

illustrates how early Christianity navigated its identity and outreach against the backdrop of a dominant and interconnected world order.

A poignant illustration of this can be found in the Gospel of Luke, which states that a census was to be conducted throughout the *oikumene* (Luke 2:1).[7] Different translations of this verse reinforce this understanding of *oikumene*, with renderings such as "the entire Roman world" in the New International Version (NIV) and "all the world" in the King James Bible, underscoring its global significance.[8] This connotation persists in other passages, including Acts 17:6, Acts 11:28, and Acts 19:27, where the activities of Paul and Silas are described as having upturned the world. Additionally, Matthew 24:14 refers to a vast arena for the dissemination of Christ's teachings, while Hebrews 2:5 contrasts the present situation with a future *oikumene*, implying the advent of the Kingdom of Heaven.

As Christianity began to spread throughout both the Eastern and Western regions of the Roman Empire, a new and dynamic community of Christian churches emerged. This burgeoning community exhibited numerous common elements that fostered a sense of belonging among its members. Early Christians regarded each other as brothers and sisters, transcending local identities to unite in a shared faith. By the 2nd century, this phenomenon gave rise to the concept of the catholicity of the Church, which defined both the universality and unity of the Christian body.

This notion of catholicity was rooted not only in communal bonds but also in the structure of episcopacy, which conferred spiritual authority through apostolic succession - an unbroken line of leadership traced back to the original apostles. Furthermore, it encompassed dogmatic principles asserting that ultimate truth could only be attained within the Church, conceived as a singular entity with various local communities, akin to the sun, one and undivided, emanating multiple rays of light throughout the world.

The term *oikumene* received formal ecclesiastical recognition in 381 CE, following its mention at the Council of Constantinople, where it was referred to in the context of the Council of Nicaea as an "ecumenical synod." This designation conferred upon the term a significant label, one that implied acceptance as authoritative and valid across the entirety of the Christian Church.[9] Origen, an influential early Christian theologian, utilised the term *oikumene* to denote the inhabited world. Through his theological

---

[7] See Ninan Koshey, "The Ecumenical Movement in Asia," in *History of Ecumenical Movement: Issues, Challenges and Perspectives*, edited by Watimongla Jamir (West Bengal: SCEPTRE, 2014), 3.

[8] See Visser't Hooft, "The Word 'Ecumenical,'" 736.

[9] See Visser't Hooft, "The Word 'Ecumenical,'" 736.

reflections, he articulated a profound understanding of the soul as a barren desert - a state that is profoundly transformed when filled with the divine presence of God. Origen posited that the *oikumene* becomes vibrant and alive when it embraces Christ and welcomes the Holy Spirit. He viewed it as encompassing individuals who had deviated from sin but were ultimately restored through the redemptive power of Jesus Christ.

Eusebius, another prominent church historian and theologian, interpreted the concept of *oikumene* in two prominent ways. He suggested that the church of God itself constitutes the *oikumene*, founded on the unblemished foundation represented by Jesus Christ, who is described metaphorically as the uncracked and solid stone. In various contexts, Eusebius expanded this notion by equating the *oikumene* with the entire world, portraying it as filled with the transformative power of the Saviour, within which the Gospel of Christ was proclaimed and disseminated.

As theological thought progressed, the 7th century theologian Maximus the Confessor provided a dualistic perspective of the earth, envisioning it as divided between Paradise and the *oikumene*. He asserted that Christ had united these two realms, establishing a singular earth that is not fragmented into disparate parts. This unity emphasises that the *oikumene*, sanctified and unified with Paradise, resonates with the divine purpose. Maximus posited that Christ's appearances to his disciples after the resurrection serve as a testament to this oneness of the earth.

Initially, the term *oikumene* bore a missionary connotation, referring to a field for spreading the new faith. As Christianity expanded throughout the known world, the term evolved to symbolise the Church itself. Ultimately, both the Church and the *oikumene* were revered as analogous to Paradise, given that Christ had inseparably unified these entities through his divine mission.

Coming back to *oikumene* as a reference to the Roman Empire, following the transfer of the Empire's capital to Constantinople, the Roman Empire retained significant influence over the Western territories for an extended period. Constantine posited that the God who created the universe also guided the Roman Emperor, conferring upon him the charge of the *oikumene*, or Roman Empire. He thought of himself as the greatest in the religious and political domain, as he was the *pontifex maximus*.[10] This assertion of sovereignty over the entirety of the Roman Empire persisted, particularly during the reign of Justinian, who sought to restore substantial portions of the Western Empire.

---

[10] See Harold Drake, "The Emperor as a Man of God: The Impact of Constantine the Great's Conversion on Roman Ideas of Kingship," in *Historia*, vol. 35, (1 Jan., 2016), 3.

As a result, the Christian Emperor in Constantinople consciously viewed himself as the successor of a universal emperor and as a representative of the Christian Church, which was intrinsically linked to the *oikumene*. The concept implied that the entire world, or *oikumene*, delineated the ideal - or actual - boundaries of his Empire, influencing the overarching objectives of his governance. In this framework, the emperor was seen as sovereign over the *oikumene*, while the bishop of Constantinople was regarded as the presiding authority of the unified Church.

In response to the Arian controversy, which caused considerable discord within the Church, Constantine took decisive action by convening a representative council at Nicaea in Bithynia.[11] He ensured a wide invitation for bishops to attend, providing transportation and financial support for their participation. The gathering included most Eastern bishops, with acknowledgement of Western representation as well. Although the synod did not initially proclaim itself as ecumenical, the term became associated with it in subsequent discourse. Eusebius, reflecting this shift, began to employ the adjective "ecumenical," committing to the notion that Constantine had assembled an "ecumenical synod." To Eusebius, the term *oikumene* not only mentioned the Church but also its correlation with the Roman Empire. Athanasius echoed similar sentiments, closely identifying the *oikumene* with the Church.

According to Raj Bharat Patta, the prophetic mission of Jesus is notably absent from the Nicene Creed, which was formulated during the reign of Emperor Constantine. The creed does not reference either his entry into Jerusalem or the Kingdom of God that Jesus proclaimed and exemplified. Furthermore, it fails to articulate Jesus' transformative liberating mission in response to the social inequalities and unjust systems prevalent during his time. Instead, what emerges is a high Christology[12] that serves to legitimise existing centres of power. Clatworthy rightly says, "What Christian emperors needed was a theology that approved of their rule, their warmongering, their economic exploitation and their suppression of dissent."[13]

According to Rohan Gideon, the Council of Nicaea, convened in 325 CE under the auspices of Emperor Constantine, aimed to establish a definitive orthodoxy within Christianity and to promote uniformity across the burgeoning faith. The Council's motto, "One God, one Lord, one faith,

---

[11] See Anil J. T. Couto, *May They All be One: Ecumenism in Catholic Perspective* (Bangalore: Conference of Catholic Bishops of India, 2021), 34. Hereafter cited as Couto, *May They All be One*.

[12] See Raj Bharat Patta, "Nicene Creed: A Dalit-Decolonial Reading," in *The New Guardian*, 8/1 (March, 2025), 2. Hereafter cited as Patta, "Nicene Creed."

[13] As cited in Patta, "Nicene Creed," 3.

one church, one empire, one emperor," encapsulates the prevailing attitude of homogenisation that the leaders sought to enforce. Rohan emphasises that throughout history, there have been numerous instances where emperors have leveraged their political authority and personal agendas to sway the outcomes of complex theological and philosophical debates. This manipulation often led to the marginalisation of dissenting voices; those who dared to challenge the established norms were frequently branded as heretics.[14] Consequently, they faced exile and were ostracised from both governmental and religious institutions, illustrating the significant consequences of deviation from the orthodox trajectory that the Council sought to impose.

John Chrysostom notably referred to St. Paul as "The Apostle of the *oikumene*," thereby attributing titles such as "ecumenical teacher" or "teacher of the *oikumene*" to distinguished Fathers of the Church. The title "ecumenical teacher" was conferred upon St. John Chrysostom by Theodosius II, reflecting his role as a spiritual leader for the entire Christian world. Notable figures such as Basil the Great, Gregory of Nazianzus, and John Chrysostom were duly recognised by the Orthodox Church as esteemed teachers of the *oikumene*.[15] This title continued to be ascribed in the 7th century to Stephanos, further solidifying its significance in ecclesiastical contexts.

The term "ecumenical" possesses a significant historical context, particularly highlighted during the intense theological and political contention between Rome and Constantinople in the 6th century. During this period, various patriarchs, in conjunction with the Pope, at times utilised the honorary title of "ecumenical." Notably, Patriarch John the Faster claimed this title as exclusive to the Patriarchate of Constantinople, thereby fundamentally altering its implications. Pope Gregory the Great firmly opposed this interpretation, emphasising that "ecumenical" should encapsulate its meaning of *universalis*.[16] This disagreement likely arose from a misunderstanding regarding the term's significance. Originally, the title aimed to underscore the unique role and esteemed position of the Patriarch of Constantinople, whose See was synonymous with the capital of the Byzantine Empire. In this capacity, the term redefined the concept of the

---

[14] See Rohan Gideon, "Why Revisiting the Process of Nicene Creed is Important," in *The New Guardian*, 8/1 (March, 2025), 4, 5.

[15] See Stephen Mackenna, "The Saintly Scholars of the Church," in *The Ecclesiastical Review*, (August, 1942), 127-134.

[16] Meaning "universal."

oikumene, intertwining the notion of the empire with that of the inhabited world.[17]

With the eventual decline and fall of the Byzantine Empire, the political ramifications of the term diminished, shifting the focus toward its religious implications. This transition resolved the longstanding conflict between the Christian and secular interpretations of the term, which had been fluctuating since the New Testament era. Consequently, the universal Church began to be identified as the *oikumene*.

Throughout the 19th century and into subsequent periods, the term continued to be employed within its traditional context, encompassing geographical and ecclesiastical definitions. For instance, the 1900 Ecumenical Mission Conference held in New York sought to represent the entirety of the inhabited world rather than the universal Church. During this time, the term was more narrowly interpreted in a strictly geographical sense. Nevertheless, the connotation of the term referring to the entire global Church in its various manifestations persisted. Originally designated as the Third Ecumenical Conference of 1910, the Edinburgh Mission Conference subsequently dropped this designation in 1908. This modification, likely influenced by Anglican perspectives, stemmed from concerns that "ecumenical" might be inappropriate for a conference that did not encompass the Roman Catholic or Orthodox Churches.[18]

As Jathanna observes, contemporary ecumenical discussions, including the esteemed Edinburgh Conference of 1910, prominently feature an expansionist ecumenical framework reminiscent of a Roman model. Notably, the Edinburgh 1910 discourse consistently urged European mission organisations to pursue this agenda, often disregarding alternative viewpoints, irrespective of their genuine intentions. The concept of "mission" has historically been intertwined with territorial imperialism. An analysis of history reveals that absolute claims invariably reflect imperialistic ambitions, which seek to encroach upon and assimilate diverse external cultures into a singular way of life.[19] This trend is not exempt from ecumenical initiatives.

The report generated by the first commission at the Edinburgh Conference, titled "Carrying the Gospel to all the non-Christian world," was regarded as the "most significant commission of the conference" among the various submissions. The Western imperial concept of *oikumene*, which aims to impose Western rationality on non-Western contexts, is unmistakably present in the reports produced by the commissions. Jathanna contends

---

[17] See Visser't Hooft, "The Word 'Ecumenical,'" 736.

[18] See Visser't Hooft, "The Word 'Ecumenical,'" 737.

[19] See Jathanna, *Decolonising*, 9.

that the terminology employed during the conference distinctly conveys a perception that the West is the architect of human history, whereas the non-West and the Other are relegated to a position of passive recipients.[20] The Edinburgh Conference of 1910 effectively established a pronounced sense of 'Otherness' in its characterisation of the beliefs of people of other faiths and global cultures.

The Oxford Conference of 1937 played a key role in expanding the understanding and popularity of the term, articulating a definition that underscored the historical unity of the Church and positing that ecumenical expressions reflect a community of Christians united in their confession of one Lord.[21] The term has since been applied in both its classical sense - addressing issues concerning the Church as a whole - and in more contemporary interpretations that emphasise the importance of the Church's wholeness and the relationships among various Christian denominations.

1.2. Present-day Usage

The diverse responses to the evolving landscape of the organised ecumenical movement, particularly as represented by the World Council of Churches (WCC), have profoundly influenced contemporary interpretations. In a foundational statement from 1951, the WCC delineated its understanding of the term *oikumene*, or "ecumenical." This term, originating from its Greek roots, is intended to encompass all dimensions of the church's mission to disseminate the Gospel on a global scale. Therefore, it addresses the concepts of unity and mission from a worldwide perspective;[22] however, maintaining the inherent dynamic tension within this term remains a complex challenge.

Initially, the Roman Catholic Church expressed significant reservations regarding this new interpretation but later embraced it, with a focus on unity. The Decree on Ecumenism from the Second Vatican Council, issued in 1964, clarifies that the phrase "ecumenical movement" pertains to initiatives and activities designed to promote Christian unity. For Roman Catholics, the *Unitatis Redintegratio* reorients ecumenism by emphasising Christ as the sole source and centre of ecclesial communion, rather than a theology of a "return to Rome"[23] as the centre of Church unity.

The Decree on Ecumenism articulates that the Holy Spirit actively invites all Christians to participate in meaningful ecumenical efforts to foster unity among diverse Christian traditions. While every believer is encouraged to contribute to this dialogue, certain individuals are called specifically to

---

[20] See Jathanna, *Decolonising*, 12, 13.

[21] See Visser't Hooft, "The Word 'Ecumenical,'" 739-740.

[22] See Brown, *Ecumenical*, 17, 18.

[23] See Couto, *May They All be One,* 142.

dedicate their lives and ministries to this important work. The document emphasises that complete unity within the Church cannot be achieved solely through human initiatives or efforts; our shortcomings and differences often hinder this goal. In practice, our ability to worship together as we deeply desire is significantly challenged by the longstanding theological, liturgical, and doctrinal differences that exist between Catholicism and other Christian denominations, such as differing views on the sacraments, authority of scripture, and interpretations of core beliefs.

However, amidst these divisions, we must understand that true unity is ultimately a gift from God, a work of grace that transcends our human limitations. We are reminded of the prayer that Jesus offered in John 17, where he earnestly sought the oneness of all believers: "that they may all be one, just as you, Father, are in me, and I in you." This prayer is not only a theological foundation for ecumenism, but also a continual call for commitment to reconciliation and deeper fellowship within the Body of Christ. Thus, we are encouraged to trust in this divine promise and actively participate in the journey toward greater unity, honouring both our differences and shared faith in Christ.

The Orthodox Churches have participated in the ecumenical movement since its inception, terming it "ecumenism in time" while adopting a critical viewpoint. From the Orthodox standpoint, the primary objectives of ecumenical exploration include the reintegration of the Christian intellect, the restoration of Apostolic tradition, and the manifestation of a comprehensive Christian vision that resonates throughout history.

Nevertheless, the ongoing conflict and even animosity between advocates of the social dimension of ecumenism and those who prioritise the spiritual or ecclesial aspect have complicated efforts to reconcile these two scriptural perspectives. Recently, there has been a growing call for "wider ecumenism" or "macro-ecumenism," which seeks to expand the ecumenical movement to incorporate other religious and cultural traditions beyond the Christian community, particularly as expressed by churches in Asia and Latin America.

1.3. Significance

The ecumenical movement, also known as ecumenism, carries substantial significance across multiple domains, especially in religion, culture, and collaborative efforts.

1.3.1. Spiritual and Religious Context

1.3.1.1. Christian Unification and Harmony

The term "ecumenical" within the framework of Christianity signifies a series of initiatives and movements aimed at fostering unity among the various denominations that compose the Christian faith. This movement endeavours to bridge the gaps arising from doctrinal differences, variations in liturgical practices, and distinct organisational structures among churches. The ecumenical movement encompasses a diverse array of Christian traditions, including but not limited to Catholicism, Orthodoxy, and Protestantism. Through the promotion of dialogue and understanding, ecumenical efforts aspire to establish a more cohesive Christian witness in the world.

1.3.1.2. Ecumenical Councils

Ecumenical councils are significant assemblies that comprise church leaders, theologians, and ecclesiastical representatives who convene to deliberate on major theological and doctrinal issues pertinent to the faith. A notable example is the Council of Nicaea, convened in 325 CE, which addressed the fundamental question regarding the nature of Christ concerning God. This council ultimately led to the formulation of the Nicene Creed, a foundational declaration of Christian belief that continues to be recited in numerous Christian liturgies today.[24] These councils not only shape theological understanding but also seek to achieve consensus among diverse Christian communities.

1.3.1.3. Interfaith Dialogue

Interfaith dialogue pertains to structured conversations and initiatives designed to foster mutual understanding, respect, and collaboration among individuals and groups from various religious traditions. While this term typically encompasses dialogues focused on promoting unity within Christianity, it also extends to broader efforts involving religions such as Judaism, Islam, Buddhism, Hinduism, and others. Such dialogue is essential for cultivating peaceful coexistence and addressing shared ethical concerns in an increasingly pluralistic society.

1.3.2. Broader Cultural Context

1.3.2.1. Unity Across Divisions

The concept of unity across divisions signifies a commitment to inclusivity, collaboration, and harmony among diverse groups, whether in the realms of religion, politics, social matters, or cultural identities. It emphasises the importance of identifying common ground and working collectively toward shared objectives, despite inherent differences. This approach encourages respect for diverse perspectives and fosters environments conducive to dialogue.

---

[24] See Couto, *May They All be One*, 142.

1.3.2.2. Global Perspective

The notion of a global perspective entails recognising the interconnectedness of humanity and understanding that many challenges, including poverty, conflict, and environmental degradation, transcend national and cultural boundaries. It highlights the necessity for collective action and collaboration on a global scale to effectively address these pressing challenges. This perspective promotes a sense of shared responsibility among individuals and communities worldwide.

1.3.2.3. Bridge-Building

The ecumenical movement advocates for cooperation, tolerance, and shared objectives across various divides, thereby enabling individuals and groups to collaborate effectively despite their differences. This bridge-building engenders a spirit of camaraderie and shared purpose, which can result in constructive outcomes in both religious and secular contexts.

1.3.2.4. Cultural and Historical Impact

The ecumenical movement has significantly influenced theological discussions and global conversations surrounding peace, reconciliation, and mutual respect among differing faiths and ideologies. Its historical impact is evident in numerous religious reforms and movements that strive to address divisions and promote understanding through a shared commitment to core values.

1.3.3. Modern Application

In contemporary contexts, the principles of the ecumenical movement remain highly relevant as they inform dialogues about global cooperation on pressing issues, such as climate change, social justice, and human rights. The emphasis on collaborative endeavours underscores our shared human responsibilities and the moral imperative to work collectively towards creating a more just and sustainable world for all.

Chapter 2

Biblical and Theological Foundations of Ecumenism

The pursuit of unity among diverse Christian denominations, commonly referred to as ecumenism, transcends mere institutional objectives and is deeply rooted in Scripture and theological reflection. The biblical narrative consistently reveals a profound theme of God's desire for human connection and reconciliation, even amidst human divisions and fragmentation. From the disintegration of uniformity at the Tower of Babel to the inclusive outpouring of the Holy Spirit at Pentecost, Scripture presents a vision of unity that honours diversity and fosters mutual understanding. Fundamental theological principles - such as the unity of the Body of Christ, the interrelationships within the Trinity, and the unifying action of the Holy Spirit - serve as robust foundations for ecumenical dialogue. These scriptural insights, when analysed through theological and postcolonial lenses, establish a critical framework for envisioning Christian unity not as mere uniformity, but as a vibrant and diverse harmony under the lordship of Christ.

2.1. The Tower of Babel

The concept of unity in the biblical narrative is intricately illustrated in the story of the Tower of Babel found in Genesis 11. In this passage, humanity, united in purpose, endeavours to construct a monumental tower that reaches the heavens. Their motivation is clearly articulated in their desire to "make a name for ourselves" (Gen. 11:4). This ambition, however, carries a colonial and dominating undertone, suggesting a problematic impulse toward self-aggrandisement and control rather than collaboration and coexistence. The preceding chapter (Gen. 10) emphasises a diverse humanity, comprised of various families and nations, each with its unique language and culture (Gen. 10:5).

This context highlights the rich tapestry of linguistic and cultural groups that existed before the Babel incident, illustrating that there were already established political and social structures in place. The actions of the Babel builders display a significant disregard for the myriad perspectives of those "others" living in proximity to them. This lack of consideration for alternative viewpoints underscores a critical flaw in their unified pursuit. In contemplating this narrative, it is pertinent to draw from the insights of postcolonial theorist Gayatri Spivak. She profoundly remarks that "intellectuals must attempt to disclose and know the discourse of society's other."[25] This perspective urges a deep reflection on the importance of understanding and respecting the voices and experiences of marginalised groups, which the builders of Babel failed to acknowledge. The story serves as a potent reminder of the necessity for inclusivity and the appreciation of diversity in our quest for unity, especially in the context of ecumenism, where the goal is to foster dialogue and collaboration among different faith traditions.

2.2. The Unity of Pentecost - Overcoming the Division of Babel (Acts 2:1-12)

The narrative of Pentecost illustrates a profound moment in Christian history where the curse of Babel is magnificently lifted. During this event, individuals from diverse nations and cultures - Jews, Gentiles, and proselytes - miraculously understood the Gospel in their languages. This phenomenon not only displays the inclusivity of God's message but also highlights God's divine intention to restore peace and unity within humanity through Christ. A statement called "Communicating Credibly," which comes out of the Vancouver Assembly of the World Council of Churches, states that it is the Spirit that leads[26] us from the discord of Babel to the ecumenism of Pentecost.

The outpouring of the Holy Spirit serves as a powerful catalyst that unites believers from various backgrounds, contrasting starkly with the division that arose at Babel, where human arrogance and self-sufficiency led to a scattering of languages and peoples. Ecumenism emerges as a

[25] Gayatri C. Spivak, "Can the Subaltern Speak?" in *Postcolonialism, Critical Concepts, Vol. IV*, edited by D. Brydon (London and New York: Routledge, 2000), 1424-1477.

[26] See Pradip Thomas, *An Ecumenical Wordsmith: the Writings of T. K. Thomas*, (Tiruvalla: Christava Sahitya Samithi, 2002), 34. Hereafter cited as Thomas, *An Ecumenical Wordsmith*.

vital movement that endeavours to foster reconciliation among Christians, emphasising the work of the Holy Spirit rather than relying solely on human efforts. This approach mirrors the unity exemplified at Pentecost, reinforcing the idea that true harmony among believers transcends denominational boundaries. The emphasis is placed on shared faith and common mission, advocating that the Body of Christ is stronger together, thereby promoting a culture of mutual understanding and collaboration.

2.3. The Body of Christ Unites All People

In Ephesians 2:14-16, the Apostle Paul articulates how Jesus Christ has decisively broken down the walls that separate people, particularly between Jews and Gentiles. By his sacrificial death, Christ abolishes the enmity that existed due to cultural and religious barriers, creating a unified people of God. Jesus Christ, thc Son of God, chose to descend to earth and experience life as a human, intimately walking among men and women. In doing so, he embraced the full spectrum of human experience - joy, sorrow, struggle, and triumph. This profound act of humility not only exemplified his love and compassion but also established him as the ultimate model of unity for all people. By bridging the divine and the human, Jesus demonstrated how we can live in harmony with one another, transcending divisions of race, gender, and social status. His life and teachings inspire us to seek connection, understanding, and grace in our relationships with each other.[27] This radical inclusiveness calls the Church to embody this unity, urging members not to let doctrinal differences lead to division. Instead, the focus is redirected toward the common identity found in Christ, enhancing the holistic vision of the Church as a single body.

2.4. Divine Imperative for Ecclesiastical Unity

The New Testament articulates a fundamental principle of Christian theology - the essential unity of believers within the Church. Particularly notable is Jesus' intercessory prayer in John 17:21, wherein he implores: "That they all may be one, as you, Father, are in me, and I in you, that they also may be in us, that the world may believe that you sent me." This plea for unity transcends mere ecclesiastical aspirations; it reflects a divine archetype inherent to the nature of God. The theological foundation for Christian cooperation is deeply intertwined with the intra-Trinitarian relationship of the 3 persons in the Trinity - an eschatological model that the Church is called to embody in its communal existence.

Furthermore, this metaphor vividly illustrates the profound interdependence and interconnectedness among believers, highlighting the

[27] See Thomas, *An Ecumenical Wordsmith*, 37.

vital importance of each individual's contribution to the overall growth and health of the body.[28] Scholars like Gordon Fee and others emphasise the organic unity inherent within the body of Christ, underscoring the necessity of recognising and valuing each believer's distinct gifts and roles.[29] Their insights remind us that the flourishing of the Church relies on the harmonious collaboration and appreciation of these unique attributes, fostering a rich and vibrant community that enhances its collective mission and purpose. This metaphor underscores that the Church's unity is not merely a philosophical ideal but a theological necessity, addressing the pervasive fragmentation evident in diverse denominational expressions and doctrinal divergences.

2.5. The Role of the Holy Spirit in Ecclesial Cohesion

Integral to Christian doctrine is the belief in the Holy Spirit as the unifying agent within the Church. The Spirit operates as a reconciler of conflicts, facilitating understanding among the heterogeneity that characterises the Christian community. The ecumenical movement advocates for collaborative discourse among disparate Christian traditions, underscoring the significance of pluralism within the ecclesial body. It posits that various denominations and theological perspectives can coexist while pursuing a collective unity in Christ. Each tradition brings forth unique charisms - gifts instantiated by the Holy Spirit - which not only enrich individual congregations but also enhance the church's overarching mission to witness effectively to the world. Collectively, these diverse charisms - whether teaching, healing, service, or leadership - constitute a dynamic and vibrant tapestry of faith, reflecting the richness of divine creation and the overarching teleological purpose of the Church.

2.6. Postcolonial Reading of Melchizedek: An Ecumenical Prototype

Melchizedek is introduced within the biblical narrative as "the Priest of God Most High," a figure of considerable significance who embodies the archetypal priesthood.[30] F. L. Horton illustrates that Melchizedek's unique role transcends specific religious identities, highlighting his position as a foundational priestly figure. In a crucial encounter, he receives Abraham, presenting him with bread and wine, gestures rich with spiritual and communal symbolism, and blesses him in the name of God Most-High.

---

[28] See Jose Prakash, "Jesus Tradition in Paul and Pauline Circle: Pauline Understanding of Church (Ecclesiology)," www.academia.edu/115679991/Pauline_Understanding_of_Church_Ecclesiology_ (04 March 2025).

[29] See George Shillington, *The New Testament in Context* (New York: T&T Clark, 2008), 38-40.

[30] See F. L. Horton, *The Melchizedek Tradition* (England: Cambridge University Press, 1976), 158.

Notably, the biblical texts do not specify Melchizedek's denominational affiliation, thereby leaving his religious tradition ambiguous. This ambiguity prompts intriguing considerations regarding his universal significance; there is no explicit indication of whether he subscribes to Orthodox, Catholic, or Protestant beliefs. Joseph A. Fitzmyer S.J. describes Melchizedek as "the High Priest of the Cosmic religion,"[31] emphasising that his role extends beyond sectarian confines.

The characterisation of Melchizedek as a "High Priest of the cosmic religion" imbues him with substantial ecumenical relevance, perpetually directing attention to the ministry of Jesus Christ, who is proclaimed as King and Priest forever. This notion resonates with the call for unity within the Church and the broader human community. In Colossians 1:19, the cosmic Christ acknowledged in the Christological hymn further illustrates a divine reality that transcends the royal and priestly attributes associated with Melchizedek. Thomas notes that Melchizedek's role appears to precede the covenant with Abram and subsequently with Abraham, suggesting that the profound truth of God's sovereignty encompasses the entirety of creation.[32] This theological framework posits that Melchizedek is not merely a pagan priest but a figure through whom God's covenantal love is expressed. His blessings upon Abram, while conveying gratitude to the God who selected Abram, serve to challenge exclusivist or sectarian interpretations of salvation.

As Thomas elaborates, Melchizedek's distinctive position radically subverts any narrow concept of divine election, establishing him as a pivotal figure in discussions of universal salvation and community.[33] Consequently, Melchizedek emerges as an essential symbol of ecumenical affirmation, representing a bridge that connects diverse faiths under the acknowledgement of a singular divine authority, an invitation to seek unity amidst the diverse tapestry of human spirituality.

Conclusion

The biblical and theological principles that undergird ecumenism assert that unity is not an aspirational goal but rather a divine mandate intrinsically linked to God's nature and intention for the Church. The narratives and theological reflections from Babel to Pentecost, from the Epistle to the Ephesians to the figure of Melchizedek, underscore a continuous call for

---

[31] Joseph A. Fitzmyer S.J., *Essays on the Semitic Background of the New Testament* (USA: Sources for Biblical Study & Society of Biblical Literature and Scholars Press, 1974), 243.

[32] See Thomas, *An Ecumenical Wordsmith*, 58.

[33] See Thomas, *An Ecumenical Wordsmith*, 58, 59.

reconciliation, inclusion, and mutual enrichment. Despite the existence of doctrinal distinctions, the testimony of Scripture and the movement of the Holy Spirit encourage the Church to transcend its historical divisions and to embody the unity for which Christ fervently prayed. Authentic ecumenism does not negate diversity; rather, it directs diversity toward a shared mission of love, justice, and witness to the world. By embracing this vision, the Church serves as a foretaste of the reconciled humanity that God wishes to achieve for all of creation.

Chapter 3

Division of the Church in the First and Second Millennium

The history of Christianity encompasses a rich and intricate narrative characterised by profound faith, global mission, and a remarkable trajectory of expansion. However, it is equally defined by significant internal conflicts and divisions. From its inception, the Church encountered substantial theological, ecclesiastical, and cultural challenges that spurred the emergence of diverse doctrinal beliefs and schismatic movements. The first and second millennia witnessed a multifaceted evolution of these divisions, beginning with localised disagreements regarding interpretations of Scripture and doctrine that escalated into major controversies, ultimately reshaping the structures and theological frameworks of the Church.

Early so-called heretical movements such as Montanism, which emphasised new prophetic revelations and a stringent moral code; Gnosticism, which proposed a dualistic worldview and questioned the inherent goodness of the material world; Arianism, which contested the nature of Christ's divinity; and Nestorianism, which maintained a distinct separation between Christ's divine and human natures, exemplify the intense struggles of early Christians to articulate and defend Orthodox beliefs amid competing interpretations. These theological debates were not merely of an academic nature; they carried significant social and political implications, influencing community identities and church governance.

The interplay of overarching political dynamics, particularly the increasing influence of the Roman Empire and later the Byzantine Empire, alongside linguistic diversification, contributed to the widening rifts within the Church. The culmination of these complexities manifested in the Great Schism of 1054, a critical event that irrevocably divided Christianity into Eastern (Orthodox) and Western (Catholic) branches. This schism did not arise from a singular dispute; it was the result of centuries of escalating ecclesiastical tension, which included differing practices - such as the use of leavened versus unleavened bread in the Eucharist - as well as varying theological emphases, particularly concerning the nature of the Holy Spirit and the authority of the papacy.

In the Eastern Church, the iconoclastic controversies of the 8th and 9th centuries further intensified internal tensions. These debates concerning the veneration of icons revealed the profound connection between theology and imperial power, as various factions within the Church aligned themselves with imperial authorities or local resistance against iconoclasm. The controversies prompted significant theological reflections on the nature of Christ and the role of images in worship, mirroring broader cultural shifts and theological disputes.

This chapter examines the significant controversies and doctrinal conflicts initiated with the Apostolic Council in Acts 15 and culminating in the Great Schism of 1054, while analysing how these events reflect the evolving identity of the Christian Church and its endeavours to uphold orthodoxy amid diversity.

3.1. Division in the Early Church

3.1.1. Localised Issues

In the nascent Christian community, various localised misunderstandings emerged. Notably, Euodius and Syntyche experienced conflict within the Philippian congregation (Philippians 4:2). Additionally, factions arose among followers of Paul, Cephas (Peter), and Apollos, leading to divisions highlighted in 1 Corinthians 3:3-4. Furthermore, Diotrephes exhibited a claim to superior ecclesiastical authority over fellow church members (3 John). Although these disputes were contained within specific communities,[34] they did not jeopardise the overall unity of the Church.

3.1.2. Broader Challenges within the Church

The conflict depicted in Galatians 2:11-14 illustrates a significant tension regarding Jewish customs and the integration of Gentile believers. The episode involves a confrontation in Antioch where Peter, having dined with Gentile Christians, refrained from associating with them upon the arrival of Jewish Christians from Jerusalem. Paul's public admonishment of Peter

[34] See O. L. Snaitang, *A History of Ecumenical Movement: An Introduction* (Bangalore: BTESSC, 2016), 18. Hereafter cited as Snaitang, *A History*.

reflects the necessity of upholding the Gospel's unifying message; Peter's withdrawal not only undermined the inclusive nature of salvation through faith in Christ but also risked deepening the divide between Jewish and Gentile Christians (Galatians 2:16).

The Apostolic Council described in Acts 15 represents a pivotal moment in resolving whether Gentile converts should adhere to Jewish customs, specifically the requirement of circumcision, for salvation. The council concluded that imposing the entirety of Jewish legalism on Gentile believers was unnecessary and that redemption is attained through grace via faith in Jesus Christ. Acts 15 serves as a framework for ecclesiastical dispute resolution, emphasising that maintaining unity requires mutual respect, understanding, and commitment to the fundamental tenets of the Gospel over mere conformity. The council's decision underscores the importance of contextualising the Gospel in ways that are sensitive to diverse theological and cultural backgrounds.

3.1.3. Montanism

3.1.3.1. Background

Early Christians maintained Messianic aspirations by confirming their trust in Jesus' return after his death. But, as the wait grew longer, the church's chiliastic passion waned, and secularisation increased.[35] The fire that had fuelled the Christian Church's growth began to fade as the church's prosperity grew.[36] The bishops' authority grew,[37] causing some church members to be uneasy with them. It was in this setting that the Montanists rose to proclaim Christ's impending return and the arrival of the New Jerusalem on earth. As they resisted the growing authority of bishops and nominal Christian life, they met with opposition from the Roman Catholic Church.

3.1.3.2. Origin of Montanism

Due to a discrepancy between the two references of Eusebius and Epiphanius, determining Montanist origins is difficult. Eusebius documented that Montanus began his prophecy amid Marcus Aurelius' reign, which was about 171 CE. He recorded that the spread of his movement started in 177.[38] Epiphanius determined the origins of Montanism nineteen years

---

[35] See H. N. Bate, *History of the Church to A.D. 325*, 2nd ed. (London: Rivingtons, 1943), 63. Hereafter cited as Bate, *History*.

[36] See F. F. Bruce, *The Spreading Flame* (Exeter: Paternoster Press, 1964), 219.

[37] See David Christie-Murray, *A History of Heresy*. (Oxford: O.U.P., 1990), 33.

[38] See Butler, *The New Prophecy*, 14.

after Antoninus Pius[39] became emperor, which was about 157 CE.[40] To reach a consensus, R. A. Knox argued that Epiphanius recorded Montanus' prophetic activity beginning in 157 CE, and Eusebius referred to the movement's spread in the 170s.[41] Timothy David Barnes, on the other hand, snubbed such a deal. He reviewed the narratives of the two early historians. He rejected Epiphanius' chronology and backed Eusebius' claim that Montanism began around 170 CE.[42] Other scholars, on the other hand, believed that the appearance of Montanist ideas in the West by 177 CE implied an earlier date. As a result, while Frederick C. Klawiter questioned Epiphanius, he also rejected Eusebius and offered a date of around 165 CE.[43] Early Montanism's history points to an earlier rather than a later date. Looking at these discussions, we may conclude that Montanus began prophesying in the year 157 CE, and by 171 CE, the movement had spread to Rome.

3.1.3.3. Features of Montanism

Montanism derived its name from its founder, Montanus.[44] Their movement was popularly known as the New Prophecy.[45] The movement was cradled in Phrygia (now modern Turkey). The most significant places of the New Prophecy were Ardabau, Pepuza, and Tymion. Montanus renamed Pepuza, prominent in the prophecies of Christ's return, Jerusalem[46] to assemble his disciples into one place. Montanism grew from Pepuza to Rome and North Africa.[47]

Montanus immediately drew followers, including female members Maximilla and Priscilla, who provided most of the movement's prophetic activity.[48] Much has been made of the prophecy attributed to Priscilla that

---

[39] He was a Roman Emperor from the year 138 to 161.

[40] See Butler, *The New Prophecy*, 14.

[41] See Butler, *The New Prophecy*, 14.

[42] See Butler, *The New Prophecy*, 14.

[43] See Butler, *The New Prophecy*, 14.

[44] See William Tabbernee, *Fake Prophecy and Polluted Sacraments Ecclesiastical and Imperial Reactions to Montanism* (Leiden, Boston: Brill, 2007), xxix. Hereafter cited as Tabbernee, *Fake Prophecy.*

[45] See Rex D. Butler, *The New Prophecy and New Visions: Evidence of Montanism in the Passion of Perpetua and Felicitas* (Washington D.C.: The Catholic University of America Press, 2006), 9. Hereafter cited as Butler, *The New Prophecy.*

[46] See Butler, *The New Prophecy*, 10. See also Robert Bradshaw, "Montanism: Heresy Montanism: Heresy or Healthy Revival?" NDLI: Montanism: Heresy or Healthy Revival? (iitkgp.ac.in.) (22 Nov. 2021).

[47] See Tabbernee, *Fake Prophecy*, xxx.

[48] See Butler, *The New Prophecy*, 10.

the New Jerusalem would descend on Pepuza in Phrygia,[49] which was a rural area. That was where followers of Montanus stayed as one community. In response to the purportedly sinful secularisation of the Catholic Church,[50] Montanists' eschatological chiliasm sought a heavenly ethic,[51] which is in contrast with the earthly one.

When it became clear that the Montanist ideology was an attack on the Catholic religion, Asia Minor's bishops convened synods and condemned the Montanists in 177 CE.[52] In the East, Montanism persisted until Emperor Justinian I (who reigned from 527 to 565 CE) enacted harsh legislation against it,[53] effectively destroying it, though some traces are thought to have lingered into the 9th century[54] and beyond.

3.1.4. Manichaeism

The birthplace of Mani (216–274) was Mesopotamia. He was of Persian ancestry and had some Parthian Arsacid blood in his veins when he was born in the early 3rd century. He emerged as a prophet in 242 CE, motivated by what he claimed to be a supernatural revelation.[55] He wrote the 7 volumes that made up his church's canon in Aramaic while travelling widely, including to India. In the 7th century, Manichaeism made its way to China.

He held that Zoroaster and Jesus were among the forerunners who had received divine inspiration. Ideas of Zoroastrian, ancient Babylonian, Jewish, and Christian origins were included in his theory.[56] Mani believed that Jesus was the Parent's unwavering light, bringing the truth from heaven to earth. He thought that Jesus was a divine being who came among people, even though he was not born of a woman. In his opinion, Jesus had not

---

[49] See Christine Trevett, *Montanism: Gender, Prophecy, and the New Authority* (U.K.: Cambridge University Press, 1996), 77. Hereafter cited as Trevett, *Montanism.*

[50] See Kenneth Scott Latourette, *A History of Christianity* (New York, Evanston and London: Harper & Row Publishers, 1953), 138. Hereafter cited as Latourette, *A History of Christianity*.

[51] See Frederick C. Klawiter, "The New Prophecy in Early Christianity: The Origin, Nature and Development of Montanism A.D. 165–220" (Ph.D. dissertation, University of Chicago, 1975). Hereafter cited as Klawiter, "The New Prophecy."

[52] See Klawiter, "The New Prophecy," 57.

[53] See Bate, *History*, 57.

[54] For example, Kenneth Scott Latourette believes that Montanism expressed itself in many forms until the Reformation. See Latourette, *A History of Christianity*, 786.

[55] See Kenneth Scott Latourette, *A History of the Expansion of Christianity, Vol. I, The First Five Centuries* (New York and London: Harper & Brothers Publishers, 1937), 351. Hereafter cited as Latourette, *A History of the Expansion.*

[56] See Latourette, *A History of the Expansion*, 351.

truly been crucified. He claimed that, as promised by Jesus, he was the *Paraclete*[57] or that the *Paraclete* spoke through him.

A complex cosmogony that describes the world's past, present, and future circumstances forms the basis of the central Manichaean teaching of the profound dualism of spirit and matter, light and darkness. Jesus the Light (one of various Jesus figures) and the Light- Nous are among the divinities, emissions of the Father of Excellence, who battle the forces of Darkness that terrorise human minds.

Equipped with human properties, the Manichaean elect worked for the liberation of the divine light in two significant ways: they preached and disseminated the words of truth in order to instil enlightenment in the human mind, and they daily consumed light-containing vegetarian food by which light was released through digestion. This required regular purification through fasting, prayer, hymn singing, and confession.

3.1.5. Gnosticism

3.1.5.1. The Gnostics: The Birth of Religious Philosophy

The term "Gnosticism" is derived from the Greek word "gnosis," which translates to "knowledge." However, the Gnostics provided a specific interpretation of this term, signifying a unique form of revealed knowledge that was essential for the salvation of human souls. Gnosticism was not a singular, cohesive religion; it refers to a diverse array of religious attitudes and movements that flourished in the early centuries of the Common Era.

Tracing the origins of Gnosticism is challenging, but one identifiable Gnostic school emerged in Alexandria, Egypt, featuring prominent thinkers such as Basilides and Valentinus during the mid-2nd century CE. Additionally, Marcion represents a significant school of Gnostic thought.[58]

A fundamental principle of Gnosticism is its inherent dualism, which delineates a stark division between 2 deities: a God of light and a malevolent power of darkness. Within this belief system, the presence of intrinsic evil in the material world is pervasive. A generalised definition of 'Gnosticism' positions it as a religious phenomenon wherein salvation is contingent upon knowledge.[59] The material world is perceived to contain remnants of a divine realm, albeit a fragmented and distant one; as Valentinus articulated, "Just

---

[57] See Latourette, *A History of the Expansion*, 352.

[58] See Ronald H. Nash, *Christianity and the Hellenistic World* (Michigan: Zondervan Publishing House, 1984), 213. Hereafter cited as Ronald H. Nash, *Christianity and the Hellenistic World.*

[59] See Ronald H. Nash, *Christianity and the Hellenistic World,* 215.

as the image is less than the distant face,"[60] the world is deemed inferior to the living aeon.

Theological perspectives held by Gnostics reflect a sombre view of the cosmos. They categorically rejected the material world, deeming even the beauty of nature inadequate for fulfilling their spiritual quest. They perceived an inherent evil within nature, attributing a diabolic principle to it.[61] This opposition to the material world and the creator deity resulted in the adoption of at least two contrasting ethical frameworks. Some Gnostics embraced an ascetic lifestyle, seeking to renounce bodily pleasures, including food, drink, and sexual relations. Conversely, others championed libertinism, arguing that the God who created the universe, as represented in the Old Testament, was not the saviour who imparts knowledge (gnosis), and should thus be defied by contravening his virtues and laws. Most Gnostics contended that an individual's salvation or condemnation was independent of their actions.[62] Other heretical movements, such as Marcionism, Montanism, Docetism, and Ebionism, align closely with Gnostic thought.

Gnosticism is regarded as a significant threat to the Church, merging elements of Hellenistic and Oriental traditions. It posits an account of Christian doctrine intended for an elite group who are drawn to imaginative speculation and the aura of secrecy surrounding it.

Key characteristics of Gnosticism include: i) a dualistic framework contrasting God with matter, and the God of light against the God of matter; ii) the existence of intermediary beings, referred to as Eons, which are emanations of divine light that together with God constitute a realm of light, devoid of matter; iii) the narrative where one of the Eons, the Demiurgus, was cast out of the realm of light and subsequently created the material universe, leading to a revolt against God; iv) the belief that human beings' souls are fragments of the divine light trapped in matter, constantly striving for liberation, with "gnosis" serving as the esoteric knowledge that facilitates this endeavour.

Christian concepts increasingly became interpreted through Gnostic frameworks. In Gnostic theology, salvation is perceived as a product of esoteric knowledge, which Gnostics regarded as superior to the understanding held by the general populace.[63] They categorised human beings into 3 distinct classes: *pneumatic* (spiritual individuals), *psychic*

---

[60] As cited by Jules Lebreton, S.J. and Jacques Zeiller, *Heresy and Orthodoxy* (USA: Macmillan Company, 1962), 35.

[61] See Walter Nigg, *The Heretics* (New York: Alfred A. Knopf, 1962), 29.

[62] See Elizabeth Clark and Herbert Richardson, *Women and Religion* (New York: Harper & Row Publishers, 1977), 38.

[63] See Latourette, *A History of the Expansion*, 30, 31.

(those straddling the spiritual and worldly realm), and *somatic* (worldly individuals, who are ultimately destined for damnation). Pneumatics are considered already saved, while psychics may occupy a state of uncertainty. Gnosticism rejects traditional concepts such as original sin, the incarnation, and redemption. For Gnostics, Christ is seen as a benevolent Aeon who descended into the material realm to impart secret knowledge to the captive particles of light, guiding them towards salvation. They deny the notion of Christ having a true physical body, positing instead that he only appeared to be corporeal, thus negating both his death and resurrection. The possession of secret knowledge is believed to be restricted to a select few who possess certainty regarding their salvation. They transcend the physical realm and mortality, belonging to a distinguished class characterised as spiritual beings. In contrast, ignorant Christians are viewed as inferior, oriented towards material pleasures and necessitating rigorous ascetic practices. Pagans, categorised as the 3rd class of humanity, are perceived as possessing no potential for salvation.

3.1.6. Monarchianism

3.1.6.1. An Examination of Early Christological Controversies

Monarchianism was a significant theological movement in early Christianity that sought to affirm the unity of God in the face of the emerging Trinitarian framework, which increasingly delineated the 3 distinct persons of the Trinity. Proponents of Monarchianism contended that the articulation of the Trinity posed a potential threat to monotheism, suggesting that it could dilute the oneness of God by introducing the notion of multiple divine persons.

This movement primarily emerged in response to various interpretations that positioned Jesus Christ as the incarnation of the Logos, effectively presenting him as a secondary divine being, or veered into tritheism, the belief in 3 separate gods. Monarchianists aimed to address the theological tensions arising from the established roles of God as Creator, the dual nature of Jesus as both divine and human, and the presence of the Holy Spirit, advocating for a more stringent interpretation of God's singularity[64] and sovereignty in the Christian faith.

This movement can be categorised into 2 principal forms: Modalistic Monarchianism (Modalism) and Adoptionistic Monarchianism (Adoptionism).

Modalistic Monarchians posited that the 3 persons in the Godhead represent not distinct persons but varying "modes" or manifestations of the singular divine essence. They maintained that God manifested in different roles across redemptive history: as the Father (Parent) during creation, the

---

[64] See Latourette, *A History of Christianity,* 143.

Son in the incarnation, and the Holy Spirit in the sanctification process. Key figures include theologian Sabellius, who was most prominently associated with Modalism, leading to the term Sabellianism.

This view was deemed heretical by orthodox Christians as it undermined the personal distinctions within the Godhead, which were more clearly articulated in the Nicene definition of the Trinity established at the Council of Nicaea in 325 CE. Despite condemnation, Modalism continued to influence some Christian communities for several centuries.

Adoptionistic Monarchians asserted that Jesus was not inherently divine at birth but was a human individual adopted by God into sonship. They contended that Jesus, born of Mary and Joseph, was endowed with divine authority and identity, typically at the moment of his baptism. Theodotus of Byzantium and later Paul of Samosata were notable proponents of this viewpoint. Adoptionism was also classified as heretical for denying the pre-existence and eternal divinity of Christ, thus jeopardising the unity of his dual natures, an essential aspect of later Christological formulations.

Both forms of Monarchianism emerged in response to early Christian debates regarding the nature of divinity attributed to Christ and God. Monarchian proponents reacted against the perceived threat to monotheism posed by the diversification of the Godhead found in Trinitarian doctrine. Monarchianism is interconnected with significant Christological debates, especially concerning the relationship between Christ's divine and human natures within a monotheistic framework.

The early Church formally rejected both Modalism and Adoptionism as heresies. The condemnation of Modalism clarified the doctrine of the Trinity, affirming the 3-personed nature of the Godhead, while the rejection of Adoptionism reinforced the doctrine of Christ's eternal divinity. The discussions at the Council of Nicaea, 325 CE, included critiques of Modalism, leading to the formulation of the Nicene Creed, which categorically declared Christ as "of one substance with the Father," thereby directly opposing both Modalistic and Adoptionistic interpretations.

In conclusion, Monarchianism constituted an essential movement addressing the theological tensions of the early Church as it grappled with articulating the unity of God amidst challenges from developing Trinitarian doctrine. However, both Modalist and Adoptionist solutions were ultimately deemed incompatible with orthodox Christian notions of God's nature and Christological identity.

3.1.7. Arianism

In the year 325 CE, 300 bishops from all around the Christian world travelled to Nicaea to discuss a new doctrine called Arianism, the crisis brought on by the new teachings that emerged around 323 CE. It claimed that Jesus was a perfect being, created from nothing, prone to fall, and that the name "God" in the Bible for Jesus was merely a metaphor[65] for God.

The reason underlying the teaching of Arius is that God, who is eternal, is to be understood as too pure to appear on the earth. Therefore, God produced Christ the Son out of nothing as the first and greatest creation.[66] On 30th May 325, the Council of Nicaea convened in the imperial summer residence in Nicaea. There were bishops from Egypt, Palestine, Syria, Asia Minor, Persia, the Caucasus, Greece, Africa, Spain, Gaul, and Italy, as well as from the region between the Danube and the Aegean.[67] There was unanimous condemnation of Arius' theology. The actual problems were still to come.

3.1.8. Macedonianism

After Arius was condemned, Emperor Constantine recalled him in 334 CE and welcomed him to court. Arius died in 336 CE, and Constantine passed away in 337 CE. Following Constantine's death, the Arian party began proposing alternatives to the Nicene formula. One of Constantine's sons, Constantius II, became the sole ruler of the empire in 350 CE, vigorously promoting Arianism through councils and enforcing it with significant violence. Valens, a co-emperor in the East, was a staunch follower of Arianism and continued the policies of Constantius, resulting in the persecution of Catholics.

Over time, the bishops recognised the necessity of articulating the doctrine of *homoousios* to safeguard the Church from the insidious influence of Crypto-Arians. This assertion became imperative as the presence of Crypto-Arianism threatened to undermine orthodox beliefs. During this period, Bishop Macedonius advanced the doctrine known as Macedonianism, which contended that the Holy Spirit was not coeternal with the other two persons in Trinity, but rather a created being akin to angels. This perspective was widely regarded as Crypto-Arian in nature, causing considerable consternation among the faithful.

After Valens was killed in a conflict with the Goths, a Catholic general from Spain named Theodosius took his place. This opened up an opportunity to restore traditional Church beliefs. For the first time in 50 years, the decisions made at the Council of Nicaea could finally be fully implemented throughout the Eastern Church.

---

[65] See Philip Hughes, *The Church in Crisis: A History of the Twenty Great Councils* (London: Burns & Oates, 1961), 11, 12. Hereafter cited as Hughes, *The Church in Crisis.*

[66] See Couto, *May They All be One*, 35.

[67] See Hughes, *The Church in Crisis,* 20.

The First Council of Constantinople in 381 CE, convened by Emperor Theodosius I, concluded this ongoing struggle. It condemned Bishop Macedonius and his doctrine of Macedonianism, which taught that the Holy Spirit was not eternal. The Council of Constantinople, attended by 150 bishops,[68] condemned Macedonianism.

3.1.9. Nestorianism

Alexandria and Constantinople had previously established a stable relationship with Rome. However, following the death of Atticus in 424 CE, his successor - a senior cleric - skillfully navigated the various factions within the capital, appeasing the clergy, monastic communities, and imperial authorities alike. This equilibrium was abruptly disrupted with Nestorius's appointment in April 428. He urged the Emperor to eradicate the residual heretical elements that persisted in Constantinople, invoking his ecclesiastical authority to tackle what he perceived as theological deviations. Nestorius asserted that the Virgin Mary should be referred to as *Christokos*, meaning "Bearer of Christ," rather than *Theotokos*, or "Mother of God." This theological distinction led him to prohibit the use of the term *Theotokos* altogether. His stringent enforcement of this decree incited significant unrest within the city,[69] igniting a series of conflicts and theological disputes that ultimately extended beyond the borders of the empire.

Nestorius maintained that only the human aspect of Jesus Christ experienced suffering and crucifixion, explicitly rejecting formulations such as "God suffered" or "God was crucified."[70] His views not only challenged foundational concepts of salvation and the idea of divine immanence but also cast doubt on the doctrine of the Incarnation. He characterised Christ as a human being who was divinely inspired rather than as one who was ontologically generated by God.[71] This perspective has significant implications for Christological discourse and the understanding of the dual nature of Christ in theological frameworks.

Cyril publicly condemned Nestorius and subsequently authored a letter in February 430 expressing his astonishment at Nestorius's actions, which he believed were unsettling the faith of the believers. In response, Nestorius launched an attack on Cyril. The Emperor convened a General Council of the Church to resolve the dispute between the Churches of Constantinople and Alexandria, anticipating that the council would serve as a venue for the trial of Cyril on charges of heresy. When the Council of Ephesus convened

---

[68] See Hughes, *The Church in Crisis*, 31.

[69] See Hughes, *The Church in Crisis*, 36, 37.

[70] See Couto, *May They All be One*, 35.

[71] See Couto, *May They All be One*, 35.

on 7th June 431, it culminated in the decision to depose Nestorius[72] from his position as Bishop of Constantinople.

The Nestorian schism and the subsequent separation of the Byzantine Church from the Assyrian Church of the East emerged as a direct result of the censure issued by the Council of Ephesus. In distinguishing itself from other ancient Eastern churches, the Assyrian Church of the East has been labelled as "Nestorian" in Western contexts due to its persistent allegiance to Nestorius and its refusal to classify him as a heretic. The outcome of the Council of Chalcedon further entrenched the divisions within the Byzantine Church, which grappled intensely with the Christological controversy surrounding the nature of Christ - whether he possessed one divine nature (Monophysitism) or a dual nature, both divine and human (Dyophysitism).[73] This theological rift has had lasting implications for Christian ecclesiology and inter-church relations.

3.1.10. Eutychianism

Eutyches was a prominent figure who supervised 300 monks in a monastery. Due to his long life of asceticism, the Emperor held him in high esteem. Eutyches believed he was facing a resurgence of Nestorianism, a theological position he opposed. He insisted that Christ's 2 natures were entirely merged into a single divine essence at the time of his incarnation. When called to appear before the court, he refused to acknowledge that the incarnate God possessed two natures (*physis*). Cyril seemed to interpret the Greek word *physis* as being similar to the Latin word *persona*, which means "person." However, most Greek theologians would have understood *physis* to mean "nature" (*natura*) rather than "person."[74] Eutyches emphasised solely the divine aspect of Christ while denying his humanity.

The Council of Chalcedon, held in 451 CE in the city of Chalcedon (present-day Kadıköy, Turkey), was convened at the request of Emperor Marcian, with the consent of Pope Leo I. Both the Roman Catholic Church and the Eastern Orthodox Church recognise this council as the 4th of the first 7 ecumenical councils. The Chalcedonian Definition, produced by the council, affirmed that Jesus Christ is one person with two natures: fully human and fully divine. This definition refuted the Monophysite viewpoint, which asserted that Christ had only one divine nature. According to the definition, Christ's two natures coexist "without confusion, without change, without division, without separation." As a result, Eutyches was declared a heretic by the Council.

---

[72] See Hughes, *The Church in Crisis*, 47.

[73] See Couto, *May They All be One*, 35.

[74] See Hughes, *The Church in Crisis*, 56.

3.1.11. East and West Division/The Great Schism of 1054

The Eastern Greek Church, based in Constantinople, and the Western Latin Church, based in Rome, sustained their communion for an extended period despite underlying tensions. However, cultural, ecclesiastical, and theological divergences increasingly led to mutual rejection rather than acceptance. The factors contributing to the East-West Schism can be categorized as follows:

3.1.11.1. Linguistic Divergence

The Roman Empire's bifurcation under Emperor Diocletian in the 3rd century resulted in the establishment of the Eastern Roman Empire (Byzantine Empire) and the Western Roman Empire. This division fostered a linguistic rift, with Greek predominating in the East and Latin in the West, catalysing the gradual estrangement of the 2 regions.

3.1.11.2. Political Dynamics

The fragmentation of the Empire prompted the patriarchs of Rome, Alexandria, Antioch, Constantinople, and Jerusalem (the Pentarchy) to delineate their spheres of influence. Despite being regarded as "first among equals," the Pope of Rome lacked definitive authority over other patriarchs. The Western Church asserted its ecclesiastical preeminence and the legitimacy of its claims over the Eastern Churches. Notably, the Eastern Council of 867 formally repudiated Roman oversight of the Episcopal dioceses of Constantinople, reinforcing its policy of non-recognition.[75]

3.1.11.3. Eastern Universalism

With Emperor Constantine's establishment of Constantinople as the new capital, he engaged deeply in ecclesiastical matters, convening councils and enforcing their decrees empire-wide. This integration of church and state characterised the Eastern Church's relationship with regional cultures, allowing local churches to retain their distinctive identities amidst a broader Orthodox framework.

3.1.11.4. Western Universalism

In contrast, the West began to manifest imperialism imbued with theological nuances, leading to a deliberate ecclesiastical distancing from secular authority. The fear of political entanglement propelled the elevation of the Church's status in Rome, where the consolidation of papal leadership diminished local church identities. Consequently, the rise of a universal Church ideology overshadowed regional expressions of faith.

---

[75] See Snaitang, *A History,* 23.

3.1.11.5. Theological Contrasts

The political instabilities of the period exacerbated doctrinal differences between the Eastern and Western churches. By 700 CE, with the rise of Islam, the patriarchates of Antioch, Alexandria, and Jerusalem experienced a marked decline in influence, while Rome augmented its spiritual authority. This power shift strained Constantinople's historic perspectives, compelling it to confront Islamic challenges with diminishing support from Rome, which increasingly focused on missionary endeavours.

A pivotal theological contention arose with Charlemagne's introduction of the *filioque* clause into the Nicene Creed, which inflamed the schism. The Eastern Orthodox Church contested the Western stance that the Holy Spirit proceeds from the Son, arguing that this claim lacks scriptural basis. The Western tradition countered that, while not directly articulated in Scripture, implicit indicators justify the inclusion of the *filioque*.

The schismatic rift escalated dramatically on 16th June 1054 CE, when Cardinal Humbert, representing Pope Leo IX, excommunicated Patriarch Michael Cerularius of Constantinople. This excommunication, rooted in the Pope's unilateral endorsement of the *filioque* addition to the Nicene-Constantinopolitan Creed, marked a significant moment in the deepening divide[76] between the 2 traditions.

3.1.12. Iconoclastic Controversy

Between the 8th and 9th centuries, the Byzantine Empire faced a major disagreement called the Iconoclastic Controversy. This argument was about the use of icons - pictures used in Christian worship. Different interpretations of the First Commandment's ban on idolatry sparked this debate. The spread of Islam, which opposed religious images, also played a role.

3.1.12.1. First Iconoclasm (726–787)

In 726, Emperor Leo III ordered the destruction of religious images to prevent idolatry. His son, Constantine V, supported this decision. Monks and other defenders of icons disagreed, arguing that icons were not idols but revered images. These supporters, known as iconophiles, believed that pictures could help teach and deepen people's connection to God. They pointed to early Christian traditions that allowed images as long as they did not promote idolatry.

3.1.12.2. Second Iconoclasm (814–842)

In 814, Emperor Leo V reinstated the ban on icons after a brief restoration by the Second Council of Nicaea in 787. Empress Theodora ended

[76] See Couto, *May They All be One*, 40.

iconoclasm in 842, restoring the use of icons in what is now called the Feast of Orthodoxy in Eastern Orthodox Christianity. As the Roman Catholic Church continued using religious images, the disagreement widened the divide between it and the Eastern Orthodox Church.

Conclusion

The divisions within the Church during the 1st and 2nd millennia illuminate both the vibrancy and fragility of Christian thought and community in the context of doctrinal complexity, imperial influence, and cultural diversity. The controversies surrounding Montanism, Gnosticism, Arianism, and other such movements were not mere transient theological aberrations; they reflected the Church's ongoing struggle to delineate and defend its core beliefs amid rapidly evolving contexts.

The Great Schism of 1054, rooted in centuries of theological and institutional divergence, institutionalised a profound and lasting division within Christianity between Roman Catholic and Eastern Orthodox traditions. Contributing factors such as linguistic divergence, contrasting ecclesial structures, and differing theological emphases shaped this schism and established distinct ecclesial identities that persist today.

Furthermore, the iconoclastic debates underscored the intricate relationship between theology and political authority in the Byzantine context, highlighting the interconnection between faith and governance. These historical episodes not only illuminate the processes that fractured Christian unity but also invite contemporary reflection on their lasting theological, cultural, and ecumenical implications for the Church today. By critically engaging with these historical divisions, the modern Church is called not only to acknowledge its fragmented past but also to actively pursue pathways toward reconciliation and unity, grounded in a shared faith and mutual respect among its diverse traditions.

Chapter 4

Ecumenical Movement

The 19th century represented a significant period of transformation in Christian history, characterised by widespread evangelical revivals and the advent of modern missionary initiatives that transcended denominational boundaries. These developments laid a crucial foundation for the contemporary ecumenical movement. Central to these initiatives was a shared evangelical zeal and an increasing recognition of the imperative for Christian unity in mission efforts. Drawing inspiration from earlier spiritual awakenings and pietistic movements, this era witnessed an unprecedented rise in interdenominational collaboration through voluntary organisations, student Christian groups, and missionary societies. Although these collaborative endeavours were rooted in Protestant traditions, they reflected a burgeoning conviction that the universal call of the Gospel necessitated a unified Christian witness. These initial expressions of ecumenism not only contributed to the advancement of global missions but also sowed the seeds for more structured and formal ecumenical developments in the following century.

4.1. Evangelical and Missionary Movements of the 19th Century

4.1.1. Interdenominational Unity in the Context of the Evangelical Movement

4.1.1.1. Pietism

To Pietism, Christianity became first and foremost a personal and individual experience and a way of life. All Christians who had the experience of being saved lived in spiritual unity, whatever church they might belong to. It refused any kind of identification of a particular confession with the Church of Christ, and it did not see the necessity of organic or visible unity.[77] It was within the Pietistic tradition that evangelical renewal grew up and that in turn gave rise to great youth movements and missionary enterprises from which the pioneers of contemporary ecumenism emerged.

The German Lutheran Church's Philip Jacob Spener (1635–1705) emerged as a prominent figure in the pietistic movement, which sought to revitalise and deepen the personal faith of Christians. Spener championed the idea that true Christianity requires a profound transformation of the heart and life, emphasising that mere attendance at church services and the rote recitation of written prayers are insufficient for genuine faith. His vision of spirituality encouraged believers to engage actively with their faith, fostering a more intimate relationship with God. In 1670, the ecumenical movement began to take shape, marked by the establishment of the *Collegia Pietatis*, a network of small gatherings known as converticles. These meetings provided a supportive environment for individuals, offering companionship and community, as well as opportunities for Bible study, prayer, and the sharing of personal testimonies.[78] This initiative not only strengthened the spiritual lives of participants but also laid the groundwork for future developments in Christian unity and interdenominational dialogue, reinforcing the importance of personal piety and mutual encouragement among believers.

Count Nikolaus Ludwig von Zinzendorf (1700–1760) emerged as a steadfast champion of pietism and a pioneering figure in the movement toward Protestant ecumenism. He profoundly understood the inseparable bond between love and piety, even when doctrinal differences and theoretical disputes emerged among various traditions. As the guiding leader of the Moravian Church, Zinzendorf served not only as a theological reformer but also as a visionary social architect. His fervent desire was to cultivate an inclusive ecumenical Protestant community that transcended denominational barriers. On his idyllic estate in Saxony, he provided refuge for Moravian exiles and established a vibrant Moravian community that became an example of spiritual renewal. Zinzendorf's dedicated disciples spread the message that salvation was solely rooted in the atoning sacrifice of Christ, a sharp departure from the Halle Pietists, who emphasised the necessity of penitential sorrow.[79] His efforts laid the groundwork for a

[77] See Couto, *May They All be One*, 84.

[78] See Snaitang, *A History,* 42, 43.

[79] See Gillian Lindt, "Nikolaus Ludwig, count von Zinzendorf, German religious leader," www.britannica.com/biography/Nikolaus-Ludwig-Graf-von-Zinzendorf (18 March 2025).

transformative approach to faith that prioritised heartfelt devotion over rigid adherence to dogma.

John Wesley and August Hermann Franke emerged as significant figures within the Pietistic movement, each leaving an indelible mark on its evolution. Both deeply embraced the core principles of pietism, cultivating a profound understanding of God's transformative salvation and the idea of new life in Christ. Followers of the Pietistic movement shared a tapestry of experiences and theological insights, woven together by fundamental tenets that emphasized heartfelt repentance, the power of regeneration, and the pursuit of holiness. Their faith was characterised by a commitment to Bible-centred teaching, fervent prayer, and dedicated fasting, creating a rich environment for spiritual growth and community.[80] Through these shared practices, individuals united in their quest for a more profound relationship with God and a deeper expression of their faith.

4.1.1.2. Evangelical Awakening in Europe and North America in the 18th and 19th centuries contributed towards ecumenical awareness, especially among leaders of Protestant churches.

4.1.1.2.1. The First Great Awakening (1725-1750)

The leaders of this Awakening were Jonathan Edwards (1703-1758), Gilbert Tennent (1703-1764), and George Whitefield (1714-1770). The significance of the First Great Awakening is that it sparked American liberation and a new nation.[81] To put it differently, engaging in a spiritual revival stimulated a political awakening as studied as follows.

He started his first continental tour in 1740,[82] from Boston, Massachusetts, to Savannah, Georgia. He opposed the religious hierarchy in his church and preached that religious revival must free one from the clutches of religious conservatism.[83] Timothy Cutler is pleased to report that "Whitefield encouraged laity in the colonies to turn against their proper leaders and question established religious beliefs and customs."[84]

Another great leader of the Awakening was Gilbert Tennent. People remember him for his blazing persuasions to sinners. Traditionalistic Presbyterians attacked him as he stood against rigid traditions. Tennent's

[80] See Snaitang, *A History,* 43.

[81] See Jim Wallis, *The Great Awakening Reviving Faith and Politics in a Post-Religious Right America* (New York: HarperOne, 2008), 2.

[82] See Kamrath, "George Whitefield," 1.

[83] See Kamrath, "George Whitefield," 1.

[84] Gardiner H. Shattuck, "Whitefield, George," *Encyclopedia of American Religious History, Fourth Edition*, Facts On File, 2018. *American History*, online.infobase.com/Auth/Index?aid=280813 &itemid=WE52& articleId=194202 (18 April 2020).

assaults on the majority arrived at their height in 1740 when in his Nottingham Sermon, he blamed his antagonists[85] as hypocrites.

4.1.1.2.2. The Second Great Awakening (1825-1835)

The most popular leaders of the Second Great Awakening were revivalists such as Charles Grandison Finney (1792-1895) and Jonathan Blanchard (1811-1892). This Awakening had its theme the appeal for the emancipation of slavery. Finney asserted that religious revival must produce social change. Blanchard, too, fought the institution of slavery through a religious revival. He established a journal, called the "Presbyterian of the West," later changed to the "Herald and Presbyter."[86] He attended the 1843 World Anti-Slavery Convention in London as a representative of the Ohio State Anti-Slavery Society. The convention named him its American Vice President.[87]

As this religious awakening fought for the eradication of slavery and other social evils like child labour, historian Michael Kazin observes, "From the Second Great Awakening in the 1820s to the 1920s, there was a period where social movements were infused with the evangelical spirit."[88] Christians led the abolitionist movement, helped and supported proposals to organise unions. They struggled to secure voting rights for women.[89] This awakening also brought to the scene Christian feminism with leaders such as Lucy Stone, Angelina, and Sarah Grimke.[90] All these were possible only because of the spiritual awakening.

4.1.1.2.3. The Third Great Awakening (1857-1858)

After the effects of the Second Awakening shrunk, Americans started to lose their religious life again. Since America advanced economically, people ran after temporal possessions rather than God. The number of church members declined downhill, and worldliness stole peoples' hearts.[91] Several Christian groups, who knew that America needed another revival, prayed that God

---

[85] See Gilbert Tennent, "American Presbyterian Clergyman," https://www.britannica.com/ biography/ gilbert-tennent" (5 June 2020).

[86] See "Jonathan Blanchard (abolitionist)," https://infogalactic.com/info/Jonathan_Blanchard_ (abolitionist) (8 June 2020). Hereafter cited as "Jonathan Blanchard."

[87] See "Jonathan Blanchard," 1.

[88] Jim Wallis, *The Great Awakening Reviving Faith and Politics in a Post-Religious Right America* (New York: HarperOne, 2008), 8. Hereafter cited as Wallis, *The Great Awakening.*

[89] See Wallis, *The Great Awakening*, 8.

[90] See Wallis, *The Great Awakening*, 2.

[91] See J. Edwin Orr, *The Event of the Century: The 1857-1858 Awakening* (Wheaton: International Awakening Press, 1989), 7.

would intervene in the peoples' lives and revive them again[92] with the Holy Spirit.

Meanwhile, a Dutch Reformed Church in Manhattan employed Jeremy Lanphier (1809-1898) as a church worker. His assignment was to visit church members as well as to revive their spiritual vitality.[93] He rented a prayer room at Fulton Street and sent out 22,000 leaflets inviting people to join him in prayer. The date he set for the prayer meeting was 23rd September 1857. When the time came, ten men turned up. By October, he had to shift to a larger building owing to the increase in membership.[94] Surprisingly, on 10th October 1857, the Bank of Pennsylvania collapsed, followed by the distortion of the wide-ranging banking structure of the United States. The catastrophe brought disintegration to many thousands of people in New York, Philadelphia, Boston, and the other manufacturing cities. That caused financial panic to hit America. Railways went broke, factories were padlocked, and the New York stock market shattered.[95] Unemployment escalated drastically.

That led various kinds of people to fall on their faces, praying to God. Capitalists, entrepreneurs, businessmen and church-goers of numerous cities, like New York, Chicago, St. Louise, Cleveland, San Francisco, Southern California, and many more, got on their knees. Churches had to open their sanctuaries for noon and evening prayers. A reporter who visited different churches was able to count more than six thousand persons praying on one day alone.[96] As these worried souls tried to find solace at the prayer meetings, the Holy Spirit worked mightily,[97] causing the Third Great Awakening of America. One distinct feature of this Awakening was that ordinary members led the prayer meetings[98] instead of pastors.

J. Edwin Orr, a revival historian, approximated that 10,00,000 souls gave their lives anew to God. To put it differently, regenerations amounted

---

[92] See "The Great Awakening of 1857-1858," https://www.smithworks.org/revival/1857.html (8 June 2020).

[93] Cf. C. Lianzuala, "America Khawmualpuia Harhna," *Harhna: Mizoram Revival Centenary Souvenir, 1906-2006* (Aizawl: Synod Revival Committee, 2006), 120. Hereafter cited as Lianzuala, "America Khawmualpuia Harhna."

[94] See "Jeremy Lanphier and the Prayer Revival," https://christianhistoryinstitute.org/it-happened-today/9/23/ (9 June 2020). Hereafter cited as "Jeremy Lanphier and the Prayer Revival."

[95] See Derrick Bowman, "The Third Great Awakening in America," fpcurrent.com/third-awakening/ (8 June 2020). Hereafter cited as Bowman, "The Third Great Awakening."

[96] See "Jeremy Lanphier and the Prayer Revival," 1.

[97] See Bowman, "The Third Great Awakening," 1.

[98] Cf. Lianzuala, "America Khawmualpuia Harhna," 121.

to more than 3 per cent of the nation's population during 1858-1859.[99] The Awakening impacted Harvard, Yale, and Princeton Universities in which several university students became born again in Christ,[100] giving their lives to him. As many as a 1,50,000 soldiers enlisted their names[101] in the church.

The Modern Missionary Movement or Protestant Era, for some, started as early as 1792, when William Carey urged his listeners to "expect great things from God," and to "attempt great things for God." After that famous sermon, many enthusiasts founded missionary societies to recruit missionaries.

4.1.1.3. Voluntary Movements and Student Christian Movements

4.1.1.3.1. Young Men's Christian Association

It was founded by George Williams in London in 1844. It was an interdenominational lay movement. It spread to Boston in the US in 1851. The YMCA is a globally recognised entity committed to cultivating a compassionate society anchored in the principles of justice, love, peace, and reconciliation, with the overarching goal of promoting the well-being of all creation. It functions as a youth-oriented, membership-driven voluntary organisation that embraces individuals from a variety of faith backgrounds, including but not limited to Christianity and other religions. The mission of the YMCA is to facilitate the holistic development of individuals across spiritual, mental, and physical dimensions. It places a strong emphasis on the values of inclusivity and equality, striving to eliminate disparities related to caste, colour, gender, or race. Through its diverse programs and initiatives, the organisation aims to foster an environment that ensures equitable access to opportunities for personal growth and community engagement.

4.1.1.3.2. Young Women's Christian Association

It was organised in England in 1854. It found an immediate response from American women and subsequently secured its foothold there. The Y.M.C.A. and Y.W.C.A. expanded their influence significantly on a global scale, promoting an ethos of inclusivity that embraced individuals from a wide array of denominational backgrounds. During this period, young adults across Europe and elsewhere sought a profound spiritual engagement, leading to a deep integration of their daily lives with their faith.[102] Many reported transformative experiences with Jesus, which significantly

---

[99] Cf. Mathew Backholer, *Revival Fires and Awakenings: Thirty-Six Visitations of the Holy Spirit* (United Kingdom: Faith Media, 2009), p. 63.

[100] See Lianzuala, "America Khawmualpuia Harhna," 121.

[101] See Lianzuala, "America Khawmualpuia Harhna," 122.

[102] See Snaitang, *A History*, 46.

reshaped their religious identities. This vibrant milieu was characterised by the formation of active prayer cells, engaging Bible study cohorts, and dynamic social clubs, where participants from diverse backgrounds congregated. These groups facilitated a supportive community framework that not only inspired individual members but also guided them through a collective spiritual journey. The atmosphere of these gatherings was marked by energetic participation and a palpable sense of belonging, culminating in the cultivation of deep interpersonal connections and communal spiritual growth.

4.1.1.3.3. Student Volunteer Movement (S.V.M.)

In 1886, the Student Volunteer Mission for Foreign Missions (SVM) was established to mobilise American college and university students for overseas missionary service. Its mission extended beyond recruitment to encompass the promotion and support of the overall missionary enterprise. Notable founders included Luther D. Wishard, C. K. Ober, Robert Wilder, D. L. Moody, and John R. Mott, among others. During this period, approximately 1 in every 37 college students signed a declaration expressing their intent to commit their lives to disseminating the Gospel in foreign regions.

The SVM subsequently became an essential element of the Student Christian Movement (SCM), which originated in Great Britain and Ireland in 1898. The SCM sought to unify Christian students globally for evangelisation and humanitarian service. Leadership included figures such as Tissington Tatlow, William Temple, V. S. Azariah, Joseph H. Oldham, Nathan Soderblom, John R. Mott, and W. A. Visser't Hooft. These individuals played a significant role in shaping ecumenical thought and action throughout the 20th century.

4.1.1.3.3.1. Roles of Women in S.V.M.

Despite their indispensable contributions to the Protestant missionary movement, the narratives of women involved in these efforts have frequently been marginalised or overlooked. Women played pivotal roles in various mission organisations, often taking on significant responsibilities; however, they were not afforded the same recognition or treatment as their male counterparts, highlighting the gender disparities that permeated this domain. A prominent figure in this context was Grace Wilder, who, alongside her brother Robert Wilder, ardently advocated for an expansive missionary movement within colleges to recruit more volunteers for labour in overseas mission fields.[103] Their efforts aimed to galvanise support and participation

[103] See Ruth Rouse, Stephen Neill, eds., *A History of the Ecumenical Movement, Vol. I – 1517-1948*, 3rd revised ed. (Geneva: WCC, 1948), 35. Hereafter cited as Rouse, *A History.*

among students, recognising the pressing need for dedicated workers in the mission field.

Among the various missions, the SVM emerged as a significant contributor, comprising some of the most effective missionaries of the time. This organisation employed a widely-accepted missionary framework known as "women's work for women," which specifically encouraged the involvement of women in missionary tasks. Mary Fullerton, a notable figure of her time, was among the group of women who ventured to India during the 19th century. This era was characterised by deeply entrenched societal prejudices regarding the role of women. Dominant stereotypes painted young women as calm, submissive, and largely defined by their willingness to embrace self-sacrifice and self-denial. These women, often motivated by millennialist expectations, were depicted as fervently dedicated to the task of converting those deemed 'heathens.' For them, this missionary endeavour represented not just a personal mission but the most crucial issue of their time. Missionary Lucile Dooley profoundly reflected this sentiment, stating, "No sacrifice is to be considered [too great] in such a call." Many of these women, including Fullerton, expressed an unwavering commitment to their cause. One could sense their passion and resolve through statements like, "I am entirely willing, nay, eager, to go,"[104] highlighting their determination to contribute to what they viewed as an essential spiritual mission. Their fervour and conviction to effect change in the world around them shed light on the complex interplay of gender, religion, and societal expectation during this transformative period in history.

This approach stemmed from the belief that only female missionaries could adequately address the needs of women in foreign cultures. Cultural norms in many regions prohibited male missionaries from directly interacting with native women, reinforcing the necessity for female missionaries to outreach and provide care. For instance, in specific areas of China and India, male missionary physicians were not permitted to treat women, further emphasising the critical need for women in the missionary workforce. This unique dynamic not only facilitated the engagement of women in missions but also played a vital role in meeting the spiritual and physical needs of women in the communities they served.

4.1.1.3.4. Modern Missionary Movements

As Christian members who experienced spiritual transformation joined together in fellowship, they began Bible study and met on regular basis.

---

[104] As cited in Frederick J. Heuser, "'Woman's Work for Woman,' Cultural Change, and the Foreign Missionary Movement," in *The Journal of Presbyterian History (1997)*, 75/2, 1997, pp. 119–30.

They shared the same burden for the salvation of others. These developments paved the way for the emergence of Missionary Movements in Europe and North America.

4.1.1.3.4.1. The Society for Promoting Christian Knowledge (SPCK)

The Pietistic influence played a significant role in the establishment of this society in England in 1699. Its primary objective was to promote Christian literature to enhance religious understanding, as well as to appoint clergy for members of the Anglican Communion residing in the American colonies. In its formative years, its efforts toward ecumenical collaboration for missionary initiatives in India were notably impactful.

4.1.1.3.4.2. The Danish-Halle Lutheran Mission

The Danish-Halle Mission, established in 1705, emerged as a direct result of Frankie's dedication to providing thorough missionary training to the students at the University of Halle. This initiative laid the groundwork for significant missionary efforts in the 18th century. Among the first fruits of this endeavour were Bartholomew Ziegenbalg and Henry Pluetschau, two notable figures who, influenced by the principles of Pietism cultivated in Halle, ventured to South India as Protestant missionaries in 1706.[105] Their pioneering work not only marked the beginning of Protestant missions in the region but also had a profound impact on the Christian community and indigenous culture, setting the stage for subsequent evangelical efforts in the area.

4.1.1.3.4.3. Baptist Missionary Society

William Carey of the Baptist Missionary Society was a product of the Evangelical Awakening. He was a great-grandson of the founder of the BMS.[106] During the Baptist Ministers' meeting in 1785, William Carey suggested that the church should start doing something in reaching out the Gospel to people of other faiths. His suggestion was rejected outright by the words of John Ryland, who said, "Young man, sit down! You are an enthusiast. When God pleases to convert the heathen, he'll do it without consulting you or me."[107] The underestimation, however, did not put off Carey's intense desire.

---

[105] See Woba James, *History of Christianity in India: A Reader* (Delhi: Christian World Imprints, 2019), 51. Hereafter cited as Woba James, *History of Christianity.*

[106] See Brian Stanley, *The History of the Baptist Missionary Society 1792-1992* (Edinburgh: T&T Clark, 1992), 285.

[107] See Greg Strand, "William Carey: An Enquiry Into the Obligations of Christians," https://blogs.efca.org/strands-of-thought/post/William-Carey-An-Enquiry-Into-the-Obligations-of-Christians (19 April 2025).

Following the publication of "An Enquiry into the Obligations of Christians to Use Means for the Conversion of the Heathens" and his sermon on Isaiah 54:2, "Expect great things from God, attempt great things for God,"[108] one saw the birth of the Baptist Missionary Society in 1792. The dawn of Modern Protestant Missions can be said to have begun in 1792. William Carey's mission to India started in 1793. Though there had been missionary efforts in England and Holland-Germany long before the inauguration of the Baptist Missionary Society, they lacked commitment to world evangelisation.

Most Protestant churches in Europe and North America realised the urgent need for evangelisation and quickly began to form missionary societies by following Carey's example and copied the organisational pattern he had established. Notable amongst those that emerged in the process were the London Missionary Society (1795); the Church Missionary Society (1799); the Church Missions to the Jews (1809), and the Wesleyan Methodist Missionary Society (1817). They were from England. The American Board of Commissioners for Foreign Missions (1810); the Basel Society (1815) in Germany; Swedish Missionary Society (1835) were the other societies formed to promote evangelisation.

4.1.1.3.4.4. The London Missionary Society (1795)

The organisation was established in response to William Carey's initial correspondence from India. A defining characteristic of this society is its interdenominational nature, which promotes a noteworthy inclusivity aimed at evangelising individuals across the globe. Congregationalists, Dissenters, Presbyterians, and Evangelical Anglicans collaborated to create this cooperative entity. Members collectively adopted the designation "Christian," expressing a desire to transcend their distinct ecclesiastical identities.[109]

4.1.1.3.4.5. The American Board of Commissioners for Foreign Missions

It was an organisation with high cooperative involvement from various Protestant Christians and churches in the US. Its early inclusiveness and interdenominational vision for worldwide mission had brought admirable fruit of Christian unity.

4.1.1.3.4.6. Interdenominational Cooperation in Germany

Unlike the development in England, where most mission societies were organised denominationally, the situation in Germany was somewhat

---

[108] See Woba James, *History of Christianity*, 61.

[109] See Snaitang, *A History*, 53.

different. Missionary agencies were organized from the regional perspective irrespective of denominational affiliations.

4.1.1.3.4.7. The Swedish Missionary Society

It contributed much to interdenominational awareness and understanding. Its initial development witnessed the inclusion of Lutherans, Moravian Brethren, Swedish and English Wesleyans. The Society supported financially other missionary societies like the Basel Missionary Society, the London Missionary Society, the Wesleyan Missionary Society and the Moravian Brethren.

The growing rise of interdenominational collaboration in the 18th century and in the early 19th was highly creditable but the sudden growth of denominational consciousness by the middle of the 19th century had led to the withdrawal of practical cooperative endeavours. However, their search for unity was still alive in their vision and thinking as they began to explore broad and flexible ways of missionary involvement. That subsequently led to the ushering in of the ecumenical International Missionary Council in the 20th century.

4.1.1.3.4.8. The Church of Scotland

The first missionary for the Church of Scotland in India was Alexander Duff, born on April 26, 1806. He significantly influenced later missionary endeavours by supporting higher education. Before arriving in Calcutta (May 1830), Duff survived two disasters. There, he founded an English-language school for Muslims and Hindus while incorporating Western scientific ideas that were at odds with traditional religious beliefs, such as Bible studies.

The Calcutta Review was co-founded in 1844 by Duff, who later served as its editor from 1845 to 1849 before relocating to Scotland. He was appointed to serve as the moderator of the Free Church assembly in 1851, but in 1856, the Bengal army fought for independence from the British colonial government, and he went to India. The government's plan was criticised in The Indian Mutiny: Its Causes and Results (1858). Duff declined the vice chancellorship at the University of Calcutta in 1863 because of his poor health. In 1873, after his return to Scotland, he was once more selected to preside as moderator of the Free Church assembly.

4.1.1.3.4.9. The Basel Mission

Switzerland was the home of the Basel Mission, a Christian missionary organisation. It operated from 1815 to 2001, when it entrusted the operational job to Mission 21, which was established in that year.

The society's original goals were to be Protestant yet non-denominational. Due to worries about what would happen if Napoleon were successful in capturing Basel, both Basel Calvinists and Württemberg Lutherans signed a sacred pledge to construct the seminary if Basel was spared. The outcome was the Basel mission. The Reverend Nikolaus von Brunn served as the society's first president.

In 1815, the German Missionary Society was established as a mission. The Basel Evangelical Missionary Society, then the Basel Mission, were later the names of the mission. In 1816, the association erected a school to educate Dutch and British missionaries. Since then, the mission has conducted operations in Russia and the Gold Coast (Ghana) starting in 1828, India starting in 1834, China starting in 1847, Cameroon starting in 1886, Borneo in 1921, Nigeria starting in 1951, and Latin America and the Sudan starting in 1972 and 1973.

On 18th December 1828, the Basel Mission Society, coordinating with the Danish Missionary Society, sent its first missionaries, Johannes Phillip Henke, Gottlieb Holzwarth, Carl Friedrich Salbach and Johannes Gottlieb Schmid, to take up work in the Danish Protectorate at Christiansborg, Gold Coast. On 21 March 1832, a second group of missionaries, including Andreas Riis, Peter Peterson Jäger, and Christian Heinze, the first mission doctor, arrived on the Gold Coast only to discover that Henke had died four months earlier.

A major focus for the Basel Mission was to create employment opportunities for the people of the area where each mission is located. To this end, the society taught printing, tile manufacturing, and weaving, and employed people in these fields. The Basel Mission tile factory in Mangalore, India, is such an endeavour. The organisation gave a high priority to uplifting the role of native women, and used women missionaries as role models of what Christian womanhood ought to be.

In West Africa, the Basel Mission had a small budget and depended on child labour for many routine operations, such as daily household chores. The children were pupils in the mission schools who split their time between general education, religious studies, and unpaid labour. The Basel Mission made it a priority to alleviate the harsh conditions of child labour imposed by slavery and the debt bondage of their parents.

The Basel Mission initially tried to print evangelical material in Bombay, but this was laborious. In 1841, Gottfried Weigle obtained a printing press from Bombay and brought it back to Mangalore in 1842 with two Marathi printing assistants. The printing press was named as Basel Mission Press. In 1842, they published a Kannada pamphlet by Moegling and made 1500 copies. The next item was Christian Greiner's Tulu translation of St. Matthew's Gospel. In July 1843, the press began the first Kannada newspaper called "Mangalur-samachar," edited by Hermann Moegling. Two issues a month were produced until February 1844, after which it was printed in Bellary.

4.1.1.3.4.10. Zenana Missions

The zenana missions were outreach programmes created in British India, originally meant to convert women to Christianity. Starting in the middle of the 19th century, they sent female missionaries into Indian women's homes, including the private areas of houses, known as zenana, that male visitors were not allowed to see. Gradually, these missions expanded from purely evangelical work to providing medical and educational services. Hospitals and schools were established by these missions.

The Zenana missionaries had expanded their work by the 1880s, opening schools to teach girls the fundamentals of the Christian religion. This initiative also included home visits, the opening of segregated women's wards in normal hospitals, and the creation of women's hospitals. To attract female doctors, one organisation, the Zenana Bible and Medical Mission, encouraged Indian women to pursue medical education while also pushing female doctors from Europe to travel to India to convert them. As a result, the Zenana missions in India somewhat lessened the male prejudice against colonial medicine.

The Zenana missions increased their focus on healthcare in the 1930s. Beatrice Marian Smyth inaugurated the Elizabeth Newman Hospital. This 60-bed facility provided care for men, women, children, and residents of Kashmir, India, who needed blood transfusions, childbirth, and anaemia treatment.

The Church of England Zenana Missionary Society, a British Anglican missionary organisation founded in 1880 and involved in sending missionaries to mission stations in nations like India in the 19th and 20th centuries and late Qing dynasty China beginning in 1884, was inspired by the work of the Baptists. In addition to Meerut, Jabalpur, Calcutta, and Amritsar in North India, Zenana missionaries also established offices at Trivandrum, Palamcotta (Sarah Tucker College), Masulipatnam, and Madras in South India.

Conclusion

The evangelical and missionary movements of the 18th and 19th centuries played an essential role in shaping both the theological and practical foundations of the ecumenical movement. Through shared experiences of revival, collective mission initiatives, and the establishment of voluntary and student-led organisations, Christians from various denominational backgrounds identified common ground in service, spirituality, and purpose. Although the mid-19th century experienced a resurgence of denominationalism that obstructed some collaborative activities, the enduring vision of unity remained vibrant.

These early movements not only demonstrated the effectiveness of cooperative mission work but also set the stage for institutional forms of ecumenism, including the International Missionary Council. Consequently, the legacy of the evangelical and missionary movements of the 19th century continues to inspire and influence ecumenical efforts within the contemporary Christian landscape.

Chapter 5

World/International Missionary Conferences

The missionary conferences and spiritual movements of the 18th and 19th centuries culminated in the landmark World Missionary Conference convened in Edinburgh, Scotland, in 1910. This event marked a significant turning point for both the missionary movement and the ecumenical agenda, as it symbolised a concerted effort among mission leaders to unify missionaries, indigenous leaders, and mission organisations to advance global evangelism. Recognised as the inaugural World Missionary Conference, Edinburgh 1910 set a precedent for subsequent international assemblies of its kind throughout the 20th century.

The 19th century offers numerous examples of interdenominational and international cooperative ventures, foreshadowing and laying the foundation for those of the 20th century. The period after 1860 discloses a growing momentum toward all that is associated with the World Missionary Conference at Edinburgh in 1910. There were the efforts of missionary leaders through conferences, councils, and other cooperative means to meet an ever-growing need for integrated planning and effort.[110] On the other hand, limited communications, determination to maintain denominational prestige, and inability to achieve effective organisation confined these efforts within a small area geographically and denominationally.

A notable achievement stemming from the Edinburgh conference was the establishment of the International Missionary Council (IMC) in 1921.

---

[110] See William Richie Hogg, *Ecumenical Foundations: A History of the International Missionary Council and its Nineteenth Century Background* (New York: Harper and Brothers Publishers, 1952), 16. Hereafter cited as Hogg, *Ecumenical.*

The IMC emerged as one of the most influential Christian organisations of its time, uniting church leaders from diverse global contexts. It played a crucial role in driving significant missiological research and supporting the creation of national councils of churches in regions newly evangelised.

5.1. The World Missionary Conference at Edinburgh (1910)

Edinburgh 1910 is now recognised as a fundamental event in the history of modern missionary collaboration, marking the beginning of a new era in the church's outreach efforts. This conference is celebrated as a significant chapter, where missionary societies first engaged in cooperative activities and established organised frameworks for joint missions, setting a precedent for future collaboration.

5.1.1. The Context

The Centenary Missions Conference, held in London from 9-19th June 1888, is esteemed as the first major missionary conference in history. This landmark event brought together representatives from 139 different Protestant denominations, totalling 1,579 participants from various regions, including Europe, North America, South America, and Africa. This ecumenical meeting not only aimed to promote the gospel and the concept of "civilisation" but also showcased a concerted effort to unify Protestantism across denominational lines.

Following this, the next significant global missionary conference unfolded at Carnegie Hall in New York City, from 21st April to 1st May 1900. With astonishing attendance numbers reaching nearly 2,00,000 individuals, this gathering became the most heavily attended missionary conference of its time. It featured prominent figures such as President William McKinley and New York Governor Theodore Roosevelt, who highlighted the cultural significance of missionary endeavours. The conference also underscored the complex relationship between missionary work and imperialism, reflecting the prevailing ideology of the "white man's burden," where Western nations sought to impose their values and cultural frameworks on other countries in the name of "civilising" them. This period marked a transformative moment in the history of missions, intertwining religious motives with broader geopolitical objectives.

5.1.2. Title

The guiding principle of the Protestant Christian Missionary organisation during this pivotal period was encapsulated in the stirring motto, "The Evangelisation of the World in This Generation." This phrase became the cornerstone of the conference, shaping the discussions and infusing the atmosphere with a profound sense of duty and urgency among its participants. The World Missionary Conference, formally titled "Conference to Consider Missionary Problems in Relation to the Non-Christian World," aimed to foster a spirit of collaboration among Protestant missionaries. While attendees came from diverse backgrounds and did not adhere to a unified liturgical practice, there was a strong underlying desire for unity in their mission. The conference served as a crucial platform for examining strategies and sharing insights on how best to engage with people of various living faiths, emphasising the importance of cooperation[111] in the noble endeavour of spreading their message.

5.1.3. The Conference

From 14-23rd June 1910, the historic Edinburgh Missionary Conference convened within the hallowed halls of the University of Edinburgh. The event was presided over with dignity by Lord Balfour of Burleigh, a renowned former Unionist cabinet minister and an esteemed member of the Church of Scotland. Among the impressive attendees was the Archbishop of Canterbury, who delivered a thoughtful address that resonated throughout the gathering. Each evening was dedicated to illuminating discussions, where an array of distinguished Christian leaders took to the stage to share their insights.

Among them were Bishop Charles H. Brent, the passionate Sherwood Eddy, the Archbishop of York, Cosmo Gordon Lang, R. Wardlaw Thompson, Pastor Henry Ussing, the eloquent Robert E. Speer, and the insightful Henry Sloane Coffin, each contributing to the rich tapestry of theological dialogue. The representation of "missionary churches" was notably diverse; it included the notable K. Ibuka, President of Mejji Gakuin, Rev. V. S. Azariah, a luminary from India, and Tasuku Harada, President of Doshisha University in Japan. A highlight of the conference came on Thursday evening, 23rd June, when the inspirational John R. Mott captivated the audience[112] with his presentation.

5.1.3.1. Representation at the Conference

In a remarkable display of commitment, 160 Protestant mission societies or boards sent forth an impressive assembly of 1,200 representatives to partake in this pivotal conference. The organisers, while keenly aware of the differing ecclesiastical beliefs and customs, chose to set aside these concerns in favour of a united mission - to evangelise regions that had yet to hear the gospel of Jesus Christ. Implicitly, attendees found common ground

[111] See T. V. Philip, *Edinburgh to Salvador: Twentieth Century Ecumenical Missiology: A Historical Study of the Ecumenical Discussions on Mission* (Delhi: ISPCK, 1999), 27.

[112] See Hogg, Ecumenical, 123.

in acknowledging the authority of the Bible, the unique salvation offered through Christ, the urgent need of the world for a Saviour, and a collective duty to undertake global missions. In stark contrast to earlier gatherings such as the London Conference of 1888 and the New York Conference of 1900, which welcomed anyone with a passion for the cause, the Edinburgh Conference served primarily as a consultative assembly. Participation was granted exclusively to individuals nominated by their respective organisations or the Executive Committee. Among the 1,200 delegates were representatives from 41 Continental European societies, counting 170 delegates, alongside 46 British societies, which contributed over 500 delegates. The American societies contributed a notable 500 delegates or more as well, while the remaining 26 delegates hailed from far-off lands in Australia and South Africa.[113] This congregation of leading theologians, administrators, and historians of Protestant missionary work was poised to shape the future of global missions.

Notable figures such as Gustav Warneck (who, regrettably, was unable to attend due to illness but contributed a paper), Dr. Julius Richter, the revered Moravian Bishop from Herrnhut, Count von Moltke, C. Mirbt of Marburg, K. Meinhof, Lord Balfour of Burleigh, V. S. Azariah, Tasuku Harada, Seth Low, Charles Harford, Sir Andrew H.L. Fraser, Sir Mackworth Young, Michael E. Sadler, C. M. J. Parkin and the illustrious Sir John Kennaway were all represented among the esteemed attendees.[114]

Roman Catholic and Eastern Orthodox missionary organisations, however, were notably absent from the dialogue. Prominent activists such as Joseph Oldham of the Student Christian Movement and the fervent American Methodist lay leader John R. Mott, who spearheaded both the World Student Christian Federation and the Student Volunteer Movement for Foreign Missions, also made their mark.

While members of newer churches constituted less than 2% of the attendees, their presence was significantly more pronounced at Edinburgh 1910 than in previous ecumenical missionary conferences. Delegates included eight representatives from India, one from Burma, three from China, one from Korea, and four from Japan. However, it is noteworthy that there were no representatives from Africa or the Pacific Islands or Indonesia,[115] regions rich in tribal or animist religious traditions.

The absence of African voices at this critical conference underscores a troubling fact: the conference did not merely overlook the contributions

[113] See Friesen, Missionary, 24.

[114] See W. H. T. Gairdner, Edinburgh 1910: An Account and Interpretation of the World Missionary Conference (Edinburgh and London: Oliphant, Anderson and Ferrier, 1910), 53.

[115] See Friesen, Missionary, 27.

of African Christians; it reflected a broader paternalistic mindset within the mission agencies, which mirrored the prevailing social norms of Western society at the time. The "Animistic Religions" inquiry only garnered a single response from a female participant, while Commission IV included just one woman, neglecting the vital perspectives of women in these discussions. Stanley Friesen astutely observed that the organisational structure of the conference, particularly regarding Africa, revealed an underlying patronising attitude consistent with many sectors of Western culture in that era.[116]

5.1.4. The Eight Commissions

In the spring of 1908, a distinguished International Committee of 18 members was constituted from Western nations to delineate the framework for a crucial conference. This multidisciplinary assembly of experts is committed to formulating a comprehensive agenda and managing the complex logistics necessary for a successful convening. To facilitate an in-depth analysis of pertinent issues, eight strategic topics were identified as central themes for discussion. In alignment with these topics, a dedicated commission was established to produce critical conference materials aimed at elucidating each subject area. Over the following two years, committee members engaged in a robust interchange of ideas, utilising extensive correspondence to foster a collaborative atmosphere. They developed meticulously designed questionnaires, systematically gathered and organised a substantial dataset, and synthesised their findings into analytical reports that were subsequently published. The various commissions involved included:

1) Carrying the Gospel to all the Non-Christian World.
2) The Church in the Mission Field.
3) Education about the Christianization of National Life.
4) Missionary Message in Relation to the Non-Christian World.
5) The Preparation of Missionaries.
6) The Home Base of Missions.
7) Missions and Governments.
8) Co-operation and the Promotion of Unity.

After the Conference wrapped up, a 9th volume was released, showcasing the most significant speeches and proceedings. This compelling collection captures the essence of the event and the impactful voices that shaped it.[117]

---

[116] See Friesen, Missionary, 30.

[117] See B. M. Thomas, "Edinburgh 1910 and The International Missionary Council (IMC), with Special Reference to the IMC as Means of Involving Asian and African Christians in Ecumenical Movement up till 1961," https://www.academia.edu/19351072/Edinburgh_1910_and_the_IMC (1 May 2025). Hereafter cited as B.M. Thomas, "Edinburgh 1910."

5.1.5. The Impacts of WMC

5.1.5.1. For upcoming ecumenical movement leaders like John R. Mott, Joseph Oldham, V. S. Azariah, Charles H. Brent, and others, the Edinburgh Conference served as an exceptional training ground.[118]

5.1.5.2. A fresh feeling of Christian camaraderie was established in Edinburgh. A diverse range of nationalities, races, and ecclesiastical beliefs were represented, or there had been a broad representation of global Christianity.[119] In Christ, however, a connection had been found that went beyond all boundaries.

5.1.5.3. The Faith and Order Movement, one of the two groups of organisations that resulted in the creation of the WCC, also began to take root in Edinburgh.[120]

5.1.5.4. Through the Continuation Committee, the Conference outlined strategies for future unity and collaboration. The Continuation Committee elected Joseph H. Oldham as its secretary and John R. Mott as its president.[121]

John R. Mott visited several nations and spoke with local officials and missionaries. Translating goals of the Edinburgh Conference in 1910 on areas of cooperation was the goal. By publishing the *International Review of Mission*, J. H. Oldham made the work stronger.[122] The effort was interrupted by the unexpected start of World War I. Nevertheless, the Committee put the World Missionary Conference's desire into practice once the war ended.

5.1.5.5. The International Missionary Council was established in 1921 as a significant development resulting from the World Mission Conference. Its primary objective was to foster greater understanding among diverse Protestant groups and to encourage active participation in global evangelisation initiatives.

5.1.6. Postcolonial Reading of the IMC

According to Jathanna, the landmark event in 1910 in Edinburgh served as a critical and persistent reminder for European mission organisations

---

[118] See Kenneth Scott Latourette, "Ecumenical Bearings of the Missionary Movement and the International Missionary Council," in A History of the Ecumenical Movement 1517-1948, edited by Ruth Rouse and Stephen Charles Neil (London: SPCK,1954), 360. Hereafter cited as Latourette, "Ecumenical Bearings."

[119] See B. M. Thomas, "Edinburgh 1910," 5.

[120] See Latourette, "Ecumenical Bearings," 361.

[121] See "Mott, John R. (1865-1955) Missions and ecumenical statesman," https://www.bu.edu/missionary/biography/l-m/mott-john-r-1865-1955/ (1 May 2025).

[122] See Snaitang, A History, 101.

regarding their historical commitment to expanding their empires. This expansion often came at the expense of recognising and respecting opposing viewpoints, despite the organisations' stated intentions of goodwill and service. The term "mission" is inherently laden with significant imperial connotations, suggesting that these efforts were not merely about spiritual outreach but were intertwined with broader ambitions of territorial and ideological control.[123] As M. P. Joseph argues, this terminology implies an assumption of an exhaustive understanding of divine truth that others are expected to accept and conform to. This belief in possessing absolute knowledge of God, combined with the drive to impose a singular version of truth upon a richly diverse world, formed the very foundation of modern missionary endeavours.[124] It was perceived as justifiable to eliminate differing perspectives in the name of virtue and civilisation.

The initial commission report, aptly titled "Carrying the Gospel to All the Non-Christian World," emerged as one of the most vital findings of the conference, encapsulating the essence of the discussions held. These reports unveil the deeply entrenched Western imperial mindset, which was not merely focused on spiritual outreach but also committed to global conquest and the imposition of Western rationality and values. This imperial project was heavily influenced by the philosophies of the European Enlightenment, which championed reason and empirical evidence often at the expense of traditional knowledge systems and practices of non-Western societies.

Such missionary initiatives, despite their earnest dedication, were executed with a startling lack of awareness about the cultural and epistemological richness they sought to overshadow. These historical examples illustrate that the objectives of Christian ecumenism, while framed under the banner of spiritual unity and cooperation, closely mirrored the Roman Empire's efforts to legitimise its dominance over other cultures and societies.[125] The parallels are not merely coincidental but reflect a broader pattern of how religious fervour has, at times, fuelled imperial aspirations, leading to the marginalisation of diverse worldviews in the name of a purportedly higher moral and civilisational calling.

---

[123] See Jathanna, *Decolonising*, 8, 9.

[124] See M. P. Joseph, "Revisiting the Edinburgh Conference in the Context of Globalisation," in *Witnessing in Context, Essays in Honour of Eardly Mendis*, edited by Monica J. Melanchton and George Zachariah (Tiruvalla: CSS, 2007), 153.

[125] See Jathanna *Decolonising*, 10, 11.

5.2. Life and Work and Faith and Order Movements

5.2.1. Life and Work

The Life and Work Movement emerged as a significant response to the influence of the Edinburgh Conference. This conference notably inspired Bishop Nathan Soderblom of Sweden to seek ecumenical cooperation in addressing social issues. Although efforts for interdenominational Christian collaboration to support the poor had begun in 19th century Germany, Soderblom had a twofold vision for this movement: to promote Christian social reforms and to foster unity among Christian denominations.[126]

The context of the First World War, along with various societal upheavals and national conflicts, severely disrupted peace and human interactions. In this challenging environment, it became essential for ecumenical leaders to gather, deliberate, and strategise about promoting international peace, unity, and rehabilitation. In 1907, a group of Christian leaders from England, Germany, and the United States came together, sharing a common goal of upholding Christian principles in a rapidly changing world. This collaboration resulted in the formation of the World Alliance of the Churches for Promoting International Friendship in 1914, which later adopted a new name: the World Alliance for Promoting International Friendship via Churches.[127]

In furthering this vision, Soderblom organised a conference focused on the Church's engagement with social and international issues. Held in Geneva from 9-12th August 1920, this meeting laid the groundwork for the World Conference on Life and Work, which took place in Stockholm from 19-29th August 1925. The preliminary conference in Geneva in 1920 sought to avoid divisive discussions on theology and doctrine, instead focusing on practical matters.[128] The Stockholm conference, attended by over 600 delegates, marked a significant milestone for the Life and Work Movement and was largely orchestrated by Soderblom.

Delegates were primarily appointed by their churches, with strong representation from Orthodox traditions. The event fostered a sense of Christian fellowship that transcended denominational differences and national conflicts. A notable slogan of the participants was, "doctrine divides, service unites,"[129] reflecting the movement's commitment to collaborative action over doctrinal arguments.

---

[126] See Snaitang, A History, 114.

[127] See Snaitang, A History, 115.

[128] Robert McAfee Brown, *The Ecumenical Revolution: an Interpretation of the Catholic-Protestant Dialogue*, (London: Burns & Oates, 1969), 30. Hereafter cited as Brown, The Ecumenical.

[129] See Brown, The Ecumenical, 30.

The conference addressed a range of critical issues, including the Church's responsibilities within the context of divine providence, the Church's engagement with economic and industrial challenges, the social and moral obligations incumbent upon the Church, the Church's role in international relations, educational initiatives related to the Church, and strategies for inter-church cooperation and federative efforts.

Support for the movement stemmed from various Orthodox leaders, including the Patriarchs of Jerusalem and Alexandria, as well as substantial contributions from figures like Bishop William Temple and other British church leaders. The objective of the conference was to forge unity among churches and Christians while raising awareness of pressing global, social, and industrial issues of the era. Central to the movement was its emphasis on Christian service, successfully identifying actionable strategies to cultivate greater unity for service, thereby fostering collaboration among diverse churches to assist those impacted by conflicts. Additionally, the movement played a significant role in advocating for a global framework aimed at conflict prevention and the resolution of international tensions.

In 1928, the Life and Work Movement established its headquarters in Geneva, engaging with various organisations, including the International Missionary Council's Department of Social and Economic Research, the League of Nations, the International Labour Office, and the European Central Bureau for inter-church aid. The second Congress of the Life and Work Movement took place in Oxford from 12-16th July 1937, with 435 attendees, including 30 delegates from younger churches. Discussions at these meetings revolved around the Church's societal roles, community engagement, and church-state relations. While theological studies foundational to the Life and Work Movement emphasised concepts such as the Christian understanding of humanity and the Kingdom of God, other groups explored issues related to education, economic structures, and international relations.[130]

The expansion of topics addressed represented a significant shift in recommendations emanating from the conferences. The initial slogan, "doctrine divides, service unites," was deemed insufficient, leading to recognition that discussions on church-state relations could not be divorced from doctrinal considerations. Consequently, the Oxford conference proposed a merger between the Life and Work Movement and the Faith and Order Movement, intending to create a World Council of Churches. This proposal was accepted, resulting in a synthesis of the two movements and the establishment of the World Council of Churches as an international

---

[130] See Oldham, ed. *Foundations of Ecumenical Social Thought* (Philadelphia: Fortress Press, 1966), 211.

ecumenical entity.[131] Following this integration, the formal procedures for establishing the council were initiated during the movement's meeting in Utrecht on 13th May 1938, which ultimately charged the newly formed Provisional Committee of the World Council of Churches with the responsibility of advancing the movement's objectives.

5.2.2. Faith and Order

The Edinburgh World Missionary Conference of 1910 deliberately left out the concern on matters pertaining to Faith and Order and did not deal with it. Such concern led to the genesis of the Faith and Order movement. This is a movement that rose with the sole aim of calling the churches to the goal of visible unity in one faith and one Eucharistic fellowship. It led many churches from all over the world into a theological dialogue related to faith and practice to manifest their unity.

5.2.2.1. Origin

The origin of the proposal to hold a World Conference on Faith and Order can be associated with the World Mission Conference, Edinburgh 1910. Towards the close of the Edinburgh Conference, Bishop Charles Brent of the Protestant Episcopal Church in the United States spoke about the new vision, i.e., the vision of a united Church. The Church appointed a commission in October 1910[132] to make necessary preparations.

The commission to work for the cause was duly appointed and elected the Bishop of Chicago (C.P. Anderson) as President and Robert Gardiner as Secretary. Various commissions were appointed, and cooperative committees were organised in the U.S. and Britain. There was a good response from the churches in the U.S. By 1913 CE, 30 commissions, following the pattern of Edinburgh 1910, had been appointed, representing various Churches throughout the world. John R. Mott addressed the Advisory Committee of the various commissions in March 1914 and outlined further opportunities for Faith and Order preparation in Europe and the Near East. The North American Preparatory Conference was formed in 1916, where efforts were made to prepare various subjects to be discussed in the World Conference, and representatives were deputed to Churches in different countries[133] for the same purpose.

---

[131] See Brown, The Ecumenical, 31.

[132] See Snaitang, A History, 120.

[133] See B. M. Thomas, "Ecumenicity of the Faith and Order Movement up to the Lund Meeting," https://www.academia.edu/19351003/Ecumenicty_of_the_Faith_and_Order_Movement_up_to_the_Lund_Meeting (3 May 2025). Hereafter cited as B. M. Thomas, "Ecumenicity."

5.2.2.2. Preliminary Meeting

During 12-20th August 1920, Church leaders from 40 nations representing 70 autonomous Churches gathered in Geneva. Bishop Charles Brent presided over the meeting. Three things were achieved in this meeting:[134]

a) A Continuation Committee was appointed, consisting of 51 members from different churches and nations with the duty of carrying on the work of preparing a World Conference on Faith and Order, fixing its date and choosing a place for it to meet.[135] In other words, responsibility from the American Protestant Episcopal Church was passed on to the newly appointed interdenominational and international committee.[136]
b) It brought the Orthodox Church into the movement.[137]
c) Some German Church leaders were present, though they initially refused the invitation, and a beginning was made towards securing German co-operation. A Continuation Committee from the Geneva meeting met at the Stockholm 1925 Conference on Life and Work and decided to have the World Conference on Faith and Order in 1927 at Lausanne for 3 weeks.

5.2.2.3. First World Conference Lausanne 1927

The First World Conference on Faith and Order was held on 3rd August 1927 at Lausanne, Switzerland. There were 385 men and 9 women. They came from 108 churches - Lutheran and Reformed, Old Catholic, Orthodox, Anglican, Methodist, Congregational, Baptist and Disciples. Africa, America and Europe were well represented, but only 2 nationals and some missionaries were from Asia. Bishop Brent was the president of the Conference, and A. E. Garvie was deputy Chairman. The agenda for the Conference was based on the following sections:[138]

1) The Call to unity.
2) The Church's message to the world -- the Gospel.
3) The Nature of the Church.
4) The Church's common confession of faith.

---

134 See Snaitang, A History, 121.

135 See Kuncheria Pathil, *Models in Ecumenical Dialogue* (Bangalore: Dharmaram Publications, 1981), 39.

136 See Snaitang, A History, 121.

137 See B.M. Thomas, "Ecumenicity," 2.

138 Odair Pedroso Mateus, "Faith and Order from Lausanne 1927 to Nicaea 2025: A Century of World Conferences," https://www.academia.edu/Faith_and_Order_from_Lausanne_1927_to_Niocaea2025:_A_Century_of_World_Conferences (3 May 2025). Hereafter cited as Mateus, "Faith and Order."

5) The Church's ministry.
6 The Sacraments, and
7) The Unity of Christendom in Relation to Existing Churches.

A series of discussions were made regarding these 7 sections of the agenda. Since the delegates came with their own theological beliefs and practices, the discussions were not easy. There were more disagreements than agreements. There were acceptance and protest, calm and heated debates throughout the Conference. But "the fact that they had come together on a mission to express their views on doctrinal issues was a great achievement in the history of Christianity,"[139] says Dr. Snaitang.

From 4-6th August, daily plenary sessions were held with a central focus on topics related to faith. Attendees were organised into three groups, each concentrating on a specific faith issue. Their primary task was to document both the "evident level of fundamental agreements" and the "significant points of disagreement" that emerged between Monday, 8th August, and Wednesday, 10th August. On 11th August, the groups presented their findings during plenary sessions,[140] creating a comprehensive overview of the discussions.

The sessions on faith topics spanned a total of seven working days. Following this, another series of morning sessions was conducted from 12-15th August, addressing subjects numbered 5 through 7. Participants were again assigned to groups, this time, focusing on the 3 "order" subjects during the afternoons of the same period. The discussions regarding these subjects took place on 17-18th August. Subsequently, the second draft of all section reports was reviewed in plenary meetings on 19-20th August. Notably, the "order" subjects were covered in less than five working days.[141]

By 20th August, reports of the first 6 sections were accepted for transmission to the Churches. But the 7th section met with difficulties. It was referred to the Continuation Committee; the final revision appeared as an appendix to the Lausanne report. The Orthodox Church declared that they would accept only the 2nd section, i.e., "The Church's message to the world - the Gospel." However, their declaration did not make any difference to their practical participation in the Conference as they continued to take full share in all the discussions. When the Lausanne Conference came to an end, the full Conference had unanimously adopted a statement on "The Call to Unity" prepared by the officers of the Conference and the chairmen and secretaries of the 6 sections. The Conference had become a spiritual fellowship, manifestly the work of the Spirit of God.

---

139 See Snaitang, A History, 122.

140 Mateus, "Faith and Order."

141 Mateus, "Faith and Order."

5.2.2.4. Second World Conference Edinburgh 1937

On 3rd August 1937, the Second World Conference on Faith and Order convened in Edinburgh, featuring delegates from 123 churches. The assembly included 15 members of the Continuation Committee, 344 delegates, and 84 alternates, along with 53 members of the Youth Group and eight conference guests. Canon Hodgson was appointed as the conference secretary, and William Temple, the Archbishop of York, was selected as its president.[142] Unfortunately, the German Evangelical Church was unable to send a delegation due to the German government's refusal to issue passports.[143] The Commission's reports, developed over several years, were concurrently discussed in four sections of the conference, addressing various topics. They are:

1) The Grace of our Lord Jesus Christ.
2) The Church of Christ and the Word of God.
3) The Church of Christ: Ministry and Sacraments.
4) The Church's unity in Life and Worship.

When the last section was dealt with - "Church's Unity in Life and Worship," there was some friction which arose solely on one point - the proposal of the formation of the WCC. By 18th August, the whole report had been completed and was accepted for presentation to the Churches. Responding to the proposal by the Life and Work movement, the Edinburgh Conference appointed a Committee of 60 persons to examine and report on the proposal. After a long and at times heated debate, they agreed to unite Faith and Order with the movement for Life and Work, to form a Council of Churches. This decision led to the formation of the World Council of Churches (WCC) in 1948.

5.2.2.5. Final Meeting, Amsterdam

On 21st August 1948, the continuation committee of the World Conference on Faith and Order convened for its final meeting in Amsterdam. During this session, the committee reviewed a proposed constitution for the Faith and Order Commission of the World Council of Churches (WCC), which was subsequently submitted to the central committee for final approval. The Faith and Order Commission of the WCC was established by members of the continuity committee formed in Edinburgh in 1937. This commission was organised around the core principles that the Faith and Order movement

---

142 See Snaitang, A History, 123.

143 See B. M. Thomas, "Ecumenicity," 4.

had advocated for nearly four decades.[144] Following the 1948 meeting, the Commission on Faith and Order continued the efforts of the Faith and Order movement,[145] sustaining its mission and objectives within the WCC framework.

5.2.3. Impacts of Life and Work and Faith and Order on the Modern Understanding of Christian Unity

Two vital components of the early ecumenical movement that profoundly influenced contemporary notions of Christian unity, both in theological discourse and practical application, are the Faith and Order movement and the Life and Work movement, which thrived between 1925 and 1948. While each movement possesses its unique characteristics, together they provided complementary insights that have had a lasting impact on modern ecumenical thought and laid the essential groundwork for the formation of the World Council of Churches in 1948.

5.2.3.1. The Life and Work Movement: A Practical Approach to Christian Unity (1925–1948)

This movement concentrated on the critical importance of Christian witness in the wider world, advocating for collaboration in service and the active application of social ethics as a practical expression of faith. The 1925 Stockholm Conference, convened by the visionary Nathan Söderblom, marked a turning point for this movement, bringing together diverse Christian voices in a historic dialogue on the necessity of cooperative action.[146] The Life and Work movement postulated that engaging in shared Christian action did not require uniformity in theological beliefs. This inclusive approach underscored the notion that moral, political, and social challenges - ranging from combating racism to pursuing economic justice and fostering peace - could be effectively confronted through collective endeavours within the Christian community. It highlighted the indispensable role of the church in advocating for public witness and emphasised the Christian duty to face societal issues head-on.

5.2.3.1.1. Impact on Contemporary Christian Unity

The Life and Work Movement played an instrumental role in fostering cooperation among various churches, even in the face of doctrinal

---

[144] See Tatlow Tissington, "The World Conference on Faith and Order," A History of the Ecumenical Movement (1517-1948), edited by Ruth Rouse and Stephen Neill (Philadelphia: The Westminister Press,1986), 431ff.

[145] See Gunther Gassmann, "Faith and Order." In Dictionary of the Ecumenical Movement, edited by Nicholas Lossky (Geneva: WCC, 1991), 411-412.

[146] See Brown, The Ecumenical, 30.

differences. It introduced the empowering principle of "unity in diversity," a concept that has become a cornerstone of modern ecumenism. The movement's strong emphasis on service and mission as vital components of unity has continued to resonate through the WCC's mission and vision.

In summary, the Life and Work Movement was crucial in advancing the cause of Christian unity, focusing on practical collaboration and social ethics. Its rich legacy has significantly shaped the ecumenical landscape for generations, encouraging a faith rooted in action and community engagement.

5.2.3.2. Doctrinal Unity in the Faith and Order Movement (1910s–1948)

The Faith and Order Movement, which emerged in the early 20th century, was marked by significant events such as the Lausanne Conference in 1927 and the Edinburgh Conference in 1937. The movement primarily focused on the convergence of theology and ecclesiology, aiming to reconcile various theological differences, especially those related to ecclesiology, ministry, and sacraments. This initiative encouraged meaningful theological dialogue among Protestant, Catholic, and Orthodox churches, emphasising the importance of outward fellowship grounded in theological agreement as a key element of genuine unity.[147]

5.2.3.2.1. Effects on Contemporary Unity

The Faith and Order Movement highlighted the importance of harmonious religious discussions and paved the way for influential documents, including the landmark 1982 statement on Baptism, Eucharist, and Ministry (BEM). It underscored that thorough, patient religious conversations are more valuable than mere surface-level agreements, advocating for a deeper understanding and exchange of ideas among different Christian traditions.

The BEM document, officially released by the World Council of Churches' Faith and Order Commission, is commonly known as the 1982 Statement on Ministry, Eucharist, and Baptism. It is often referred to as the Lima Document, as the concluding phrase was ratified in a city in Peru. The primary objective of the document is to articulate a unified understanding among Christian churches concerning three fundamental components of faith and practice: ministry, baptism, and the Eucharist.[148]

The document positions baptism as the inaugural step into the Body of Christ, thereby incorporating individuals into the Church. It underscores the significance of a singular baptism for the forgiveness of sins and affirms that

---

[147] See Brown, The Ecumenical, 32, 33.

[148] See William H. Lazareth, Nikos Nissiotis, Baptism, Eucharist and Ministry, Faith and Order Paper No. 111, (Geneva, World Council of Churches, 1982), https://archive.org/details/wcc/fops2.118 (5 May 2025).

baptism should be administered only once, maintaining its validity across various denominations. Furthermore, it advocates for the mutual recognition of baptisms among differing churches.

With respect to the Eucharist, the document defines it as an act of thanksgiving, a memorial, and an invocation. It emphasises the real presence of Christ in the Eucharist while recognising that this perspective does not resolve all existing doctrinal disagreements. The document encourages a shared comprehension of the Eucharist as a sacrament of unity and highlights the communal and eschatological dimensions of the celebration.

Concerning ministry, the document articulates that it is grounded in the ministry of Christ and is perpetuated through the Church. It acknowledges a 3-fold ministry model comprising bishops, presbyters, and deacons. The document supports the mutual recognition and reconciliation of ministries and stresses the pastoral, missionary, and teaching obligations inherent to ordained ministers.

The concept of unity in the World Council of Churches (WCC) evolved significantly with the merger of Life and Work and Faith and Order in 1948, which highlighted the importance of both shared service and doctrinal agreement. The WCC adopted a comprehensive understanding of unity, encompassing spiritual and outward solidarity, a common mission and witness, as well as mutual recognition and theological dialogue. A notable aspect of this approach is the recognition of unity as both a visible structure and a spiritual communion, which requires ongoing theological discussions and cooperation. Additionally, the acknowledgement of plurality plays a crucial role, demonstrating that unity can coexist with diversity. Today, the promotion of unity continues to depend heavily on sustained dialogue among different faith traditions.

5.2.4. International Missionary Conference at Crans in 1920

In June 1920, before the establishment of the International Missionary Council (IMC) in 1921, a temporary International Missionary Conference took place in Crans, Switzerland. This event was relatively small in scale, with Mott serving as the leader of the Business Committee and Oldham acting as its secretary. The organisers ensured that the relevant national authorities were informed about the conference's plans.[149] The participants in Crans worked to dispel any misconceptions surrounding the ongoing challenges in missionary work. They reached a consensus on the necessity of forming a committee within the National Christian Councils dedicated to

[149] Kenneth Scott Latourette, "Ecumenical Bearings of the Missionary Movement and the International Missionary Council: A History of the Ecumenical Movement 1517-1948," edited by Ruth Rouse and Stephen Charles Neil (London: SPCK, 1954), 366.

international missionary efforts and securing funding for it.[150] The success of this initiative ultimately led to the creation of the International Missionary Council (IMC).

5.3. International Missionary Council (IMC) 1921-1961

In the fall of 1921, an important gathering took place in Lake Mohonk, New York, where 61 individuals from various countries convened to establish the International Missionary Council (IMC). The idea for this international council was initially proposed by visionary leaders in Edinburgh, who had advocated for a cooperative model based on national missionary organisations eleven years earlier. Despite initial apprehensions about embarking on such a bold initiative, the movement gained momentum over time, especially after overcoming significant challenges during World War I. By 1921, nearly all the countries represented at the meeting had established national missionary cooperation organisations, which sent representatives to Lake Mohonk to form the IMC.[151] The assembly included delegates from diverse regions, such as Finland, Norway, Sweden, Switzerland, France, the Netherlands, Great Britain, Canada, the United States, Australia, and South Africa. Notably, Dr. S. K. Datta from the National Missionary Council of India, along with Dr. Ma Saw Sa from Burma, also participated, highlighting the global reach of this initiative. However, it is worth mentioning that there was no representation from Germany[152] at this event.

Among the 17 national organisations that joined the IMC, 4 were from newer churches or previously mission-focused areas. Functioning as a confederation of national Christian councils, the IMC also published the *International Review of Missions*, which became a key platform for ecumenical discussions worldwide.[153] Following its establishment, the focus of the council shifted from being solely missionary-oriented to encompassing broader gatherings of church leaders.

The IMC held its 2nd conference in 1928 in Jerusalem, with representation from 50 countries and over 250 members attending. The conference took place at a sanatorium located on the Mount of Olives, which had been constructed by German Protestants before World War I and was made available to the IMC.[154] Theological discussions at the Jerusalem Conference often centred on topics such as salvation, evangelism, the role of other faiths, the dynamics of younger churches, and various social and

---

[150] See Snaitang, A History, 107.

[151] See Hogg, Ecumenical, 202.

[152] See Hogg, Ecumenical, 203.

[153] See Snaitang, A History, 107.

[154] See Hogg, Ecumenical, 203.

global challenges. The conference aimed to address these concerns through a cooperative and ecumenical lens.

The text summarises key discussions and events from various IMC over the years, highlighting their focus on the relationship between the Christian message and non-Christian beliefs, the dynamics between younger and older churches, and the challenges faced in religious education, missions, and social issues. Key topics addressed at these conferences included:

1) The impact of non-Christian systems of thought on the Christian message.
2) The evolving roles of younger and older churches.
3) Issues related to religious education.
4) The intersection of missions with rural challenges.
5) The influence of industrialism on missions.
6) Challenges posed by race conflicts.
7) The importance of international cooperation among missionaries.

Notable attendees at these conferences included Erasmo Braga, Cheng Ching-Yi, T. C. Chao, Francis C. M. Wei, David Z. T. Yui, Dr. Jaswant Chitambar, K. T. Paul, S. K. Datta, P. Ooman Philip, Michio Kozaki, Bishop Kogoro Uzaki, Miss Helen Kim, Davidson Jabavu, Sirwano Kulubia, Augustine Ralla Ram and other prominent leaders.[155] A significant milestone was achieved when the IMC established strong relationships with Eastern churches, facilitated by access to the Galilee Church on the Mount of Olives and the Jerusalem residence of the Greek Orthodox Church, which included an inspiring performance by the Russian archbishop's cathedral choir. Russian nuns welcomed female participants to their convent.[156]

The 3rd IMC conference took place in Tambaram, Madras, in 1938, attracting 471 delegates from 69 nations. This conference showcased a strong representation from younger churches, with Bishop Azariah leading sessions on several critical topics.[157] The topics during the Conference included:[158]

- The essence of faith for the church's living.
- The relationship between Christian witness and non-Christian religions.
- The mission of evangelism.
- The life and functions of the Church.
- The Church's environment, cooperation, and unity.

---

[155] See Hogg, Ecumenical, 245.

[156] See Hogg, Ecumenical, 246.

[157] See Hogg, Ecumenical, 291.

[158] See Snaitang, A History, 109.

The conference highlighted a renewed focus on the Church as central to missionary efforts, reshaping perceptions about its role in evangelisation. The discussions in Madras reflected a novel understanding of the Church at a time when it was often viewed as an outdated element of Christianity. While some debated the emphasis placed on the Church, Madras acknowledged its imperfections and the need for divine judgment.[159] Moreover, the conference called for a balanced respect for various faiths while maintaining the Church's mission at its core. This was articulated through the publication of "Rethinking Christianity," which voiced the concerns of Indian leaders about Western methodologies.[160]

The Madras conference also stressed the importance of the biblical basis of revelation, drawing upon insights from Karl Barth's theology, as presented by keynote speaker Hendrick Kraemer.[161] Furthermore, the first actual assembly of churches convened in Madras, merging representatives from both Western missionary groups and younger churches from around 50 countries. This assembly proposed that the Church, seen as a holistic community of believers, should take on a central role in evangelism, thus framing mission as a collective responsibility of all Christians[162] rather than a segmented church activity.

The representation of younger churches at the conference signified their growing influence and capability in discussions, which was appreciated alongside the contributions of older churches. The younger churches were given equal status in Jerusalem, but Madras was appreciative of their contribution.[163]

In 1947, the fourth IMC Conference was held in Whitby, Ontario, Canada, featuring 120 delegates from 40 countries. With a focus on "The Christian Witness in a Revolutionary World," this conference was particularly significant as it occurred in the aftermath of World War II.[164] Unlike previous gatherings in Jerusalem and Madras, which were council meetings, Whitby represented a broader meeting of the Committee of the Council.[165] This conference shifted the focus towards a collaborative theology in mission, emphasising the critical need for evangelism and hope amid the backdrop of global turmoil and uncertainty.

---

[159] See Hogg, Ecumenical, 298.

[160] See Snaitang, A History, 110.

[161] See Snaitang, A History, 110.

[162] See Hogg, Ecumenical, 298.

[163] See Hogg, Ecumenical, 298.

[164] Snaitang, A History, 110, 111.

[165] See Hogg, Ecumenical, 335.

The theology of collaboration in mission emerged at the Whitby Conference, contrasting with the Church-centric approach emphasised at the Tambaram Conference. Participants recognised that evangelism was vital for the world's needs and expressed hope in God despite human tragedies and shortcomings. This perspective highlighted the importance of both older and younger churches in achieving shared mission objectives. Western missionaries aligned with younger congregations as part of a new mission policy, empowering these younger churches to initiate missionary work, determine the necessity of missionary presence, and define specific areas of engagement.[166]

The 1952 Conference, themed "Mission in Unity," took place in Willingen, Germany, where 40 out of 190 delegates from 50 countries represented younger churches. This conference reframed the theological understanding of mission, shifting focus from the Church to the triune God. It also advocated for the establishment of regional study centres to facilitate the sharing of information and ideas, emphasising the role of laypeople[167] in mission efforts.

The 2nd Assembly of the World Council of Churches (WCC) was held in Evanston, Illinois, before the IMC's 6th conference in Accra, Ghana, from 28th December 1957 to 8th January 1958. The highlight of this conference was the impending merger with the WCC. A total of 215 representatives participated, reinforcing the necessity for lay involvement in mission and revisiting key points from previous gatherings. The constitutional clause facilitating the merger between the IMC and the WCC was officially accepted.[168] Following the approval of the merger documents by the IMC's authorised administrative committee in 1959, the IMC became one of the departments of the WCC at the third WCC Assembly in New Delhi on 19th November 1961. This led to the establishment of the Commission of World Mission and Evangelism, which was later renamed the Division of World Mission and Evangelism within the World Council of Churches.[169]

---

[166] See Snaitang, A History, 111.

[167] See Snaitang, A History, 111.

[168] See Snaitang, A History, 111, 112.

[169] See Snaitang, A History, 112.

Chapter 6

World Council of Churches

The World Council of Churches (WCC) assumes a crucial role in embodying the ecumenical vision within contemporary Christianity. This organisation emerged from the aspiration to unify diverse Christian traditions for a shared mission and service, evolving from a rich history of ecumenical endeavours, notably the Faith and Order and Life and Work movements of the early 20th century. The establishment of the WCC was not the result of a singular event but rather the culmination of extensive inter-church dialogues, theological contemplation, and collaborative initiatives to achieve visible unity in Christ. This section expounds on the origins, structural framework, theological underpinnings, and global impact of the WCC, emphasising its progressive role in promoting Christian unity while honouring the integrity and diversity of its member churches.

6.1. Beginning and Development of WCC

The WCC originated from the aspirations of various ecumenical leaders rather than being a mere historical coincidence. In 1937, representatives from the Faith and Order and Life and Work movements convened in London before participating in separate meetings in Oxford and Edinburgh. During this gathering, they agreed to merge these two movements to form a global representative ecumenical body. The primary aim was to gain the trust and respect of the diverse churches involved, emphasising that the new organisation would not have the authority to enact laws or bind churches to actions without their consent. The establishment of the WCC was intended to include prominent laypeople and was formally proposed during the meetings in Edinburgh and Oxford, where both organisations approved the idea. In May 1938, a newly formed committee convened in Utrecht, led by General Secretary W. A. Vissert Hooft and chaired by Archbishop William Temple,[170] to oversee the development of the WCC.

The term "World Council of Churches" was proposed by Samuel McCrea Cavert, the General Secretary of the Federal Council of Churches in the United States. Initially, the Provisional Committee aimed to hold the first General Assembly of the WCC in August 1941, but plans were significantly disrupted by the outbreak of World War II in 1939. During 1940 and 1946, in various informal meetings held in England, Switzerland, and the United States, members worked to sustain interest in the initiative and maintain stable leadership amidst the turmoil of war. Following the war, there was renewed vigour among committee members who believed that the challenging experiences of the conflict had reinforced the movement's resolve to bridge divides, heal wounds, and foster Christian unity and peace.[171]

Despite the historical conflicts, organisations like Life and Work and Faith and Order demonstrated the sense of unity among Christians that transcended national boundaries.[172] By early 1948, the WCC had garnered support from up to 90 churches expressing an interest in joining. The leadership aimed for a membership that was diverse both geographically and confessionally, inviting various international ecumenical organisations, national churches, and national councils of churches[173] to participate.

The WCC was officially established in Amsterdam in 1948. The Roman Catholic Church, however, does not participate in the WCC for practical and ecclesiological reasons. According to Catholic ecclesiology, the unity envisioned by Christ exists within the framework headed by the Pope and collaborating bishops. Thus, the Catholic Church refrains from joining the WCC due to the potential for its authority to dominate the organisation, given its extensive global presence and resources. While the Catholic Church does not hold formal membership in the WCC, it engages in many of the organisation's initiatives. Authority remains a critical concern for the Catholic Church in the context of global ecumenism, with the role of the Bishop of Rome posing a significant barrier.[174] Nevertheless, there is a prevailing sentiment that collaboration and commitment to shared goals are preferable to formal membership.

---

[170] See Snaitang, A History, 128.

[171] See Snaitang, A History, 128.

[172] See Goodall, *The Ecumenical Movement,* 2nd ed., Oxford, New York, 1964, p. 200.

[173] See Snaitang, A History, 128.

[174] See Couto, May They All be One., 128, 129.

The Assembly convened on 22nd August 1948,[175] under the honourable presidency of John R. Mott. The inaugural Secretary General was W. A. Vissert Hooft, a Dutch Reformed Pastor. This foundational meeting saw the participation of 147 churches from 44 countries, representing a diverse array of denominations. Among the newer groups were the Presbyterian Church in Korea and various Anglicans, Lutherans, Calvinists/Reformed, Baptists, and Methodists. Notably, the Assembly also included some of the oldest churches, such as the Church of Ethiopia and the Orthodox Syrian Church of Malabar. The representation of younger churches, particularly from Asia, was significant, with 22 delegates participating, highlighting an increase in involvement compared to previous gatherings in Oxford and Edinburgh. However, many young African and Latin American congregations were not yet ready[176] to join the Council.

Other denominations, including Old Catholics, Congregationalists, Quakers, and members of the Salvation Army, were among the willing participants.[177] The Assembly also saw representation from the Russian Exarchate in Western Europe, the Church of Greece, and the Orthodox Church in the United States, along with the Orthodox churches from the historic Patriarchates of Alexandria, Antioch, Constantinople, and Jerusalem.[178] Key figures like John R. Mott, who chaired the 1910 Edinburgh Conference, and J. H. Oldham, who had prophesied the establishment of such a council in 1920, represented the pioneering generation. Additionally, Prof. Hamilcar Alivisatos recalled his presentation of the concept for a world council in Geneva in 1920, while Archbishop Germanos reflected on the realisation of his 1919 vision.[179]

With input from the interim committee, the Utrecht constitution was ratified with ease. The Assembly determined that the constitution provided a sufficient framework for the Council's current objectives, and churches wishing to propose modifications were invited to submit their suggestions to the Central Committee. This committee was tasked with ongoing research into potential amendments to the Christological concept[180] detailed in the Basis.

---

[175] See Hooft, The Genesis, 63.

[176] See Hooft, The Genesis, 64.

[177] See Couto, May They All Be One, 128, 129

[178] See Hooft, The Genesis, 64.

[179] See Hooft, The Genesis, 64.

[180] See Hooft, The Genesis, 64.

6.2. The Basis

The constitution of the WCC delineates a fundamental requirement for membership, which mandates that churches must concur with the foundational basis established during its inaugural assembly in Amsterdam in 1948. This foundational principle articulates, "The World Council of Churches is a fellowship of churches which accept our Lord Jesus Christ as God and Saviour." The phrase "fellowship of churches" originated from discussions at a 1938 meeting in Utrecht, initiated by a committee of 14 members representing both the Life and Work (L&W) and Faith and Order (F&O) conferences.

By the time of the WCC's establishment in 1948, the concept of "fellowship" had become a well-understood term in ecumenical dialogue. This notion is rooted in ecclesiological ideas such as "koinonia," or communal fellowship, as articulated in an ecumenical encyclical from the Ecumenical Patriarchate of Constantinople in 1920. While the English term "fellowship" may not fully encapsulate the richness of the Greek original, it underscores a divinely ordained sense of unity rather than one that is solely a product of human constructs. This understanding also serves to refute any perception of the WCC as a "super-church."[181]

The phrase "Which accepts our Lord Jesus Christ as God and Saviour" draws from concepts introduced in 1855, the basis of the Young Men's Christian Associations and later adapted by the World Young Women's Christian Association in 1894 and the World Student Christian Federation. The invitations extended to the inaugural world conference of Faith and Order were directed towards churches endorsing this Christological affirmation. Reactions to this phrase have varied, with individuals from liberal and conservative backgrounds expressing reservations. For example, Unitarians and members of the Society of Friends preferred to eschew rigid doctrinal statements, while more orthodox Christians contended that it did not sufficiently represent the humanity of Christ.[182] Critics, including theologian William Adams Brown, have observed that this wording could carry implications perceived as heretical in the early ecumenical councils.

In a memorandum regarding the WCC constitution from 1938, William Temple, who chaired the Utrecht meeting, highlighted 2 significant implications of the established basis. Firstly, it underscored that the WCC is a fellowship rather than a federation, indicating that it cannot exercise constitutional authority over its member churches. Secondly, it confirmed

---

[181] See T. K. Thomas, "WCC, Basis of," in *Dictionary of the Ecumenical Movement,* 2nd ed., edited by Nicholas Lossky et.al. (Geneva: WCC Publications and Grand Rapids: Eerdmans, 2002), 1238–39. Hereafter cited as Thomas, "WCC."

[182] See Thomas, "WCC," 1238-1239.

that the foundation of the Council is rooted in the faith in Jesus Christ as God and Saviour, which encapsulates essential doctrines of the incarnation and atonement; however, it is intended not to serve as a doctrinal test for assessing churches or individuals. Rather, member churches retain the autonomy to interpret this faith within their contexts.[183] The accepted basis serves as a reference point for members of the WCC and provides a foundation for coherence among its member churches. It is important to note that the WCC, as a collective of churches, does not possess legislative, judicial, or executive authority over its member organisations. In other words, Christian churches may participate in the WCC as long as they align with its principles[184] and do not have any fundamental disagreements with its tenets.

Since the Utrecht meeting, there have been debates regarding the necessity of a formal basis, as some individuals fear that such a basis could foster a culture of ecclesiastical judgment that might undermine the *koinonia*. Others have proposed that foundational documents such as the Nicene or Apostles' Creed could serve as viable alternative bases. Although the Amsterdam Assembly deemed the original basis adequate for the WCC's objectives, it recognised the necessity to clarify or expand upon the Christian faith referenced, particularly within a Christological framework. A subsequent study by the central committee concluded that while modifications to the basis were unnecessary, it was crucial to elucidate its implications, especially concerning the incarnation and the Trinity.[185]

6.3. Assemblies of WCC

6.3.1. First Assembly: Amsterdam, Holland, 1948

Theme: Man's Disorder and God's Design.

On Sunday, 22nd August, 1948, the WCC held its opening service in the Nieuwe Kerk in Amsterdam. The formal establishment of the WCC occurred on the morning of Monday, August 23, 1948, when Dr. Marc Boegner, one of the Presidents of the Provisional Committee and the Chairman of its Administrative Committee, introduced the motion to declare the formation of the World Council of Churches as complete.[186] The assembly included 4 key segments that explored a major theme. The topic "The Universal Church in God's Design" was addressed under the Faith and Order section, while "The Church and the Disorder of Society" was the focus of Life and Work discussions. Additionally, the segment titled "The Church and the

---

[183] See Thomas, "WCC," 1238-1239.

[184] See Snaitang, A History, 131.

[185] See Thomas, "WCC," 1238-1239.

[186] See Rouse, A History, 719, 720.

International Disorder"[187] highlighted the work of the newly established Commission of the Churches on International Affairs.

The discussions also considered the perspectives of the Secretariat for Evangelism, which the World Council intended to establish, alongside the International Missionary Council, in addressing "The Church's Witness to God's Design."[188] The successful preparation of preliminary materials benefited from a decentralised approach. It was unanimously decided by the Joint Committee of the World Council and the International Missionary Council that their titles should reflect their interconnectedness.

Furthermore, it was agreed that one of the World Council's key roles would involve supporting churches in their evangelistic efforts.[189] Importantly, it was emphasised in 1948 that the World Council was not intended to function as a church that presides over others. Instead, its purpose was to gather churches in alignment with their mission to embody the Church of Jesus Christ. However, questions remained about how this understanding of the Council's spiritual nature aligned with the self-awareness of member churches.[190]

6.3.2. Second Assembly: Evanston, 1954

Theme: Jesus Christ, the Hope of the World.

The Second Assembly held in Evanston in 1954 explored a central theme divided into 6 sections. These sections addressed various aspects pertinent to the church and society:

1) Faith and Order – Discussed the oneness in Christ and the existing disunity among churches. 2) Evangelism – Focused on the church's mission towards individuals outside its community. 3) Social Questions – Examined the concept of a responsible society from a global perspective. 4) International Affairs – Addressed the role of Christians in the quest for a unified world community.
5) Intergroup Tensions – Delved into the church's position amid racial and ethnic tensions.
6) The Laity – Highlighted the Christian's role within their vocation.[191]

Evanston's slogan emphasised the idea of flourishing together, contrasting with Amsterdam's commitment to staying together. The Assembly provided

[187] See Hooft, The Genesis, 63.

[188] See Hooft, The Genesis, 63.

[189] See Hooft, The Genesis, 64.

[190] See Hooft, The Genesis, 69.

[191] See Brown, The Ecumenical, 40.

a clearer definition of a "responsible society," calling on governments to avoid aggression and denounce all weapons of mass destruction. Furthermore, it reaffirmed the church's responsibility for promoting peace and justice,[192] underscoring the necessity of racial equality through statements on intergroup interactions and religious liberty.

6.3.3. Third Assembly: New Delhi, 1961

Theme: Jesus Christ the Light of the World.

The New Delhi Assembly in 1961 was structured around 3 key sections: witness, service, and unity, all centred on a Christocentric theme. The 1st section tackled the theological challenge of understanding diverse religions in the light of Jesus Christ. The 2nd section offered an in-depth examination of the political, economic, and social challenges faced by developing nations. Importantly, the 3rd section presented a vision of unification[193] for the ecumenical movement, marking a significant milestone in its history.

To maintain autonomy from the global ecumenical organisation, the International Missionary Council aligned with the WCC to create the Division on World Mission and Evangelism. This period also saw the introduction of a biblical foundation emphasising "according to the scriptures" and a Trinitarian formula[194] to the WCC's Christocentric approach.

6.3.4. Fourth Assembly: Uppsala, Sweden, 1968

Theme: Behold I Make All Things New.

The 4th Assembly convened in Uppsala in 1968 and engaged in discussions across 6 sections:

1) Holy Spirit and the Catholicity of the Church.
2) Renewal in Mission.
3) World Economic and Social Development.
4) Towards Justice and Peace in International Affairs.
5) Worship.
6) Approaches to New Styles of Living.

A notable event during this Assembly was the appointment of Dr. M. M. Thomas, a lay Indian theologian, as the Central Committee Moderator, which was significant for Asian and Indian Christians. W. A. Vissert Hooft and Joseph Oldham held honorary president positions. The Uppsala Assembly made historic decisions, leading to the establishment of new

---

[192] See Couto, May They All be One, 114.

[193] See Couto, May They All be One, 114.

[194] See Snaitang, A History, 137, 138.

WCC programs, including the Commission on the Churches' Participation in Development, the Christian Medical Commission, dialogue initiatives with individuals of various faiths, an educational sub-unit, and the program aimed at combating racism. These developments were essential, given the complexities churches faced amid changing global circumstances[195] and the imperative responsibility of the Church.

6.3.5. Fifth Assembly: Nairobi, Kenya, 1975

Theme: Jesus Christ Frees and Unites.

A total of 676 delegates from 285 member churches took part in the Assembly. Edward W. Scott acted as the Moderator of the Central Committee, while W. A. Visser't Hooft remained in the position of Honorary President.[196] The Assembly extensively discussed the issue: "What does unity truly demand?" Additionally, it was determined that the following 2 conditions are essential:[197]

1) a commonly accepted goal, that is goal of visible unity, and
2) a fuller understanding of the context:
    a) Handicap and wholeness of the family of God.
    b) Community of women and men and wholeness of the Body of Christ.
    c) Organisation and personal community in the unity of the Church.
    d) Political struggle and the unity of the Church.
    e) Search for cultural identity and oneness of the Universal Church.

6.3.6. Sixth Assembly: Vancouver, 1983

Theme: Jesus Christ, the Life of the World.

847 delegates from 301 member churches attended the Assembly.[198] It had 8 groups to discuss issues: witnessing in a divided world; taking steps towards unity; moving towards participation; healing and sharing life in community; confronting threats to peace and survival; struggling for justice and human dignity; learning in community; communicating credibly.[199]

---

[195] See Snaitang, A History, 138.

[196] See Snaitang, A History, 139.

[197] See Couto, May They All be One, 114.

[198] See Snaitang, A History, 139.

[199] See Couto, May They All be One, 117.

6.3.7. Seventh Assembly: Canberra, 1991

Theme: Holy Spirit, Renew the Whole of Creation.

It had 842 delegates from 842 member churches. There were as many as 10 guests from other faiths in addition to 1,300 visitors and 200 observers from non-member churches.[200] The 4 sub-themes were giver of life – sustain your creation; spirit of truth – set us free; spirit of unity – reconcile your people, Holy Spirit – transform and sanctify us.[201]

6.3.8. Eighth Assembly: Harare, Zimbabwe, 1998

Theme: Turn to God – Rejoice in Hope.

The Assembly was held in honour of the 50th anniversary of the World Council of Churches. There were 339 member churches in attendance. A half-century after the official founding of the WCC, its member churches reaffirmed their dedication to unity, and the delegates expressed their commitment to stand in solidarity with their African hosts. The Assembly emphasised 2 interconnected aspects. First, it reflected on its history and activities over the last 50 years and called for a spirit of repentance. This was a call for transformation.[202] The second focus was on a shared commitment to progress with optimism, renewed vigour, and joy.

6.3.9. Ninth Assembly: Porto Alegre, Brazil, 2006

Theme: God, Transform World in Grace.

The recent Assembly saw participation from over 4,000 individuals representing 348 member churches, alongside observers and visitors. The central theme of the Assembly was Christian unity, culminating in the adoption of a new document titled "Called to be the One Church." This document emphasises the importance of unity, inclusiveness, baptism, and prayer among the World Council of Churches (WCC) and its member churches. In addition to this, delegates approved a significantly revised Constitution and Rules, which shifted the WCC to a consensus-based decision-making framework and updated its membership criteria. There were also initiatives introduced to promote the active engagement of youth[203] in the Council's activities and initiatives.

---

[200] See Snaitang, A History, 140.

[201] See Couto, May They All be One, 118.

[202] See Snaitang, A History, 140, 141.

[203] See Couto, May They All be One, 120.

6.3.10. Tenth Assembly: Busan, South Korea, 2013

Theme: God of Life, Lead Us to Justice and Peace.

345 member churches were represented. There were 20 official delegates of the Indian churches.[204] The public statements issued after the Assembly delineate the primary commitment areas of the World Council of Churches along with its member organisations and partners, emphasising the necessity for enhanced efforts toward justice and peace. These focus areas encompass the Middle East, where Christians frequently encounter restrictions on religious freedom; the conflict-impacted region of Congo; and Korea, which continues to be affected by the consequences of division and conflict. One resolution advocated for the prohibition of all weapons of mass destruction, while another highlighted the imperative to safeguard the rights of stateless individuals. Furthermore, delegates urged a thoughtful reflection on the forthcoming centennial of the Armenian genocide, which will be commemorated in 2 years.

6.3.11. Eleventh Assembly: Karlsruhe, Germany, 2022

Theme: Christ's Love Moves the World to Reconciliation and Unity.

Originally planned for 2021, the event was postponed by 1 year because of the gravity and uncertainties related to the COVID-19 pandemic. In Germany, the participants were acutely aware of the various crises impacting our global society. Representatives from the Orthodox Churches of both Ukraine and Russia were present, and the Assembly's statement concerning the War in Ukraine, as well as concepts of Peace and Justice in the European Region, explicitly "[condemned] this illegal and unjustifiable war" and "[reiterated] the call for an immediate ceasefire to prevent further loss of life and destruction, as well as for dialogue and negotiations to achieve enduring peace."[205]

The process of developing a joint statement regarding the tensions and violence in Israel and Palestine underscored the diversity of perspectives; however, all delegates expressed a unified commitment to transforming these declarations into tangible actions aimed at reconciliation, as emphasised by the statement's title, "Seeking Justice and Peace for All in the Middle East." The public issues committee's focus extended beyond these prominent

---

[204] See James Massey, "Whither Ecumenical Movement? 10th WCC Assembly," in History of Ecumenical Movement: Issues, Challenges and Perspectives, edited by Watimongla Jamir (Kolkata: SCEPTRE, 2014), 350.

[205] See "Report on the Eleventh General Assembly of the World Council of Churches Karlsruhe, Germany: 31 August – 8 September 2022," https://churchinwales.contentfiles.net/media/documents/WCC_General_Assembly_-_Karlsruhe_2022_-_Report.pdf (13 May 2025), Hereafter cited as "Report on the Eleventh."

conflicts, with calls for reconciliation resonating concerning West Papua, Nagorno-Karabakh, the divided Korean peninsula, and the commemoration of the approximately half a million Syriac-Aramaic Christians who tragically perished in 1915 as victims of genocide. Resolutions addressing racism, casteism, xenophobia, gender-based violence, and discrimination were denoted as offences against divine principles, alongside the imperative to seek reconciliation with indigenous populations,[206] several of whom participated in the Assembly or engaged in preliminary meetings.

The statement entitled "The Things that Make for Peace: Moving the World to Reconciliation and Unity" reaffirmed the global Christian community's dedication to peace-building through dialogue and interreligious collaboration. The Pilgrimage of Justice and Peace, initiated during the 10th Assembly in Busan (2013), was further enhanced in Karlsruhe, evolving into a Pilgrimage of Peace, Reconciliation, and Unity. Additionally, renewed calls for the inclusion of all individuals and the cessation of gender-based violence were represented by the well-known Thursdays in Black campaign.[207]

6.4. Postcolonial Reading of the WCC

6.4.1. Colonial Heritage and Eurocentrism

The establishment of the WCC in the mid-20th century was profoundly influenced by the missionary and theological frameworks of Western churches, particularly those originating from Europe and North America. While these churches aimed to promote unity and address pressing global issues such as the devastation of the World Wars and widespread economic inequality, their perspectives frequently mirrored the underlying assumptions of imperial power and Eurocentric theological paradigms.[208]

From a postcolonial perspective, the voices of indigenous and colonised groups were largely marginalised in the WCC's initial framework. The early theological dialogues and decision-making processes predominantly favoured Western ideologies, which inadvertently reinforced a civilizational hierarchy. This hierarchy positioned churches in the Global South as mere recipients of ecumenical theology and policies, rather than equal collaborators in the theological discourse and creation of ecclesial practices.

6.4.2. Mission and Empire's Legacy

Within the discourse of the WCC, Christian mission is viewed as one of the most contentious issues when examined through a postcolonial lens. The

---

206 "Report on the Eleventh," 2.

207 "Report on the Eleventh," 2.

208 Cf. Gladson, *Decolonising*, 12.

1910 Edinburgh Missionary Conference, often regarded as the precursor to the WCC, encapsulated a predominantly colonial interpretation of mission, where Western churches actively dispatched missionaries to evangelise non-Western populations,[209] frequently correlating this activity with colonial expansion.

Postcolonial critics contend that this approach conflates the processes of evangelisation with colonisation, leading to the imposition of Western Christianity at the expense of indigenous cultures and spiritual practices. Although the WCC has made strides to reformulate its understanding of mission - most notably in seminal documents such as "Mission and Evangelism: An Ecumenical Affirmation" (1982) and "Together Towards Life" (2013) - it continues to wrestle with the challenge of dismantling the vestiges of colonialism entrenched within its mission theology.

The Commission on World Mission and Evangelism further advanced this discourse with "Together Towards Life: Mission and Evangelism in Changing Landscapes" in 2012. This document introduced significant themes including "Spirit of Mission: Breath of Life," "Spirit of Liberation: Mission from the Margins," "Spirit of Community: Church on the Move," and "Spirit of Pentecost: Good News for All," emphasising the integral role of the Holy Spirit in the mission of the Triune God. Core concepts emerging from Together towards Life include an affirmation of life, justice, transformation, and mission from the margins,[210] suggesting that mission is a reflection of Trinitarian love active in the world, one that transcends geographical boundaries and does not discriminate based on location.

6.4.3. Global South Involvement and Participation

A significant achievement in the postcolonial context within the WCC has been the increasing engagement and participation of churches from the Global South. This includes a notable resurgence of voices from regions such as Africa, Asia, Latin America, and Oceania. These churches have brought forth rich and distinct theological insights that reflect their diverse cultural and social realities. For instance, feminist and womanist perspectives offer critical reflections on gender inequality and social justice, while tribal and indigenous spiritualities emphasise the importance of ancestral traditions and ecological stewardship.

Additionally, the emergence of Dalit theology provides a voice to marginalised communities in India, addressing caste-based discrimination, while postcolonial theology critiques dominant Western narratives and

---

[209] Cf. Gladson, *Decolonising*, 13.

[210] See Ida Heikkilä, "The World Council of Churches' Mission Statement 'Together Towards Life': Mission, Evangelism and Missio Dei," 82, 83. Academia.edu. (15 June 2025).

highlights the importance of local contexts. Liberation theology, rooted in the struggles against oppression, resonates deeply in many Global South contexts, emphasising the need for social and economic justice. Despite these advancements, critical questions persist regarding the WCC's commitment to genuine empowerment of these diverse voices. Does the WCC truly uplift and integrate these perspectives, or does it merely offer a framework that is predominantly shaped by Western institutional norms and theological constructs?

Furthermore, are the WCC's operational structures inadvertently reinforcing enduring power imbalances that stem from historical colonial systems, or do they represent a truly egalitarian approach that values and prioritises the contributions of all member churches equally? These inquiries challenge the WCC to reflect on its role in fostering an inclusive and equitable theological dialogue that respects and celebrates the richness of global Christian diversity.

The rigorous postcolonial scrutiny emerging from the Global South has prompted a comprehensive re-evaluation of the concept of unity, necessitating a re-narration of the collective witness of churches, along with a contextual understanding of ecumenism that resonates politically. Through this re-evaluation process, the ambition has been to broaden and enrich ecumenical perspectives by inviting local experiences of diversity and distinction into the dialogue.[211] These concerns are notably apparent in areas such as agenda-setting, funding dynamics, and theological discourse, where Western interpretations may continue to prevail, potentially overshadowing the voices and interpretations from the Global South.

6.4.4. Philosophy of Emancipation and Equity

The WCC has increasingly engaged in discussions surrounding justice through initiatives such as its Programme to Combat Racism, launched in 1969, as well as campaigns focusing on economic and environmental justice. These efforts aim to address the systemic inequalities that arise from global capitalism and colonialism, viewed through a postcolonial lens. The WCC held several significant assemblies in its early years, including the Amsterdam Assembly in 1948, the Evanston Assembly in 1954, and the New Delhi Assembly in 1961, culminating in the Uppsala Assembly. However, establishing a solid foundation for a comprehensive programme concerning racism proved to be a challenge, as actionable elements were limited despite the strong rhetoric employed. The 1969 Canterbury declaration reflected

[211] See Gladson, *Decolonising*, 33.

on these past efforts as "irrelevant and timid," suggesting they were insufficient[212] and late in addressing race relations.

At the Uppsala Assembly, the decision to take decisive action against racism emerged not from a strategic plan but rather as a response to the demands of the participants. In addition to recognising these movements, postcolonial analysis encourages the WCC to acknowledge the ongoing subtle manifestations of colonialism.[213] These include the marginalisation of oral, indigenous, or grassroots theological perspectives, tokenism in leadership roles, and epistemic injustices that favour Western modes of understanding.

6.4.5. Ecumenical and Intercultural Cooperation

Postcolonial thought emphasises that colonialism has not only disrupted Christianity but also created a sense of superiority among Christian traditions over other faiths.[214] As a result, the WCC is encouraged to broaden its understanding of Christian unity to include interfaith and intercultural collaboration. This approach recognises the value and wisdom found in diverse religious traditions, especially those that have historically faced marginalisation due to Christian colonial activities. By fostering ecumenism within this broader framework, the WCC can contribute to a more inclusive dialogue that respects and uplifts various cultural and faith perspectives.

Conclusion

Since its formal inception in 1948, the WCC has emerged as a significant representation of the ecumenical commitment toward unity, service, and collective witness among Christian denominations. Its primary focus on fellowship rather than federation, and faith in Christ rather than stringent doctrinal conformity, continues to define its inclusive character. Although the Catholic Church is not an official member, its involvement in various collaborative efforts illustrates the WCC's capacity to transcend ecclesiastical divisions. Through numerous assemblies and a robust theological foundation, the WCC has established a platform for global dialogue and joint action, affirming that irrespective of the differences in

---

[212] See E. Claude Welch, "Mobilizing Morality: The World Council of Churches and Its Program to Combat Racism, 1969-1994." *Human Rights Quarterly*, 23/4, (2001), 863–910. JSTOR, http://www.jstor.org/stable/4489365 (15 June 2025). Hereafter cited as Welch, "Mobilizing Morality."

[213] See Welch, "Mobilizing Morality."

[214] Cf. Pynhunlang N. M. Shullai, "Colonialism, Christianity and Mission Activities In India: A Postcolonial Perspectives," in International Journal of Humanities & Social Science Studies, 3/5, (March, 2017), 324-334.

tradition and practice, the Christian imperative to pursue unity remains a critical and ongoing mission within the life of the global Church.

The WCC faces a significant challenge from a postcolonial perspective, necessitating a transformation that is both decolonial in its content and ecumenical in its organisational structure. This represents a multifaceted issue that involves prioritising the spiritual and theological voices of underrepresented communities. It requires a re-evaluation of the power dynamics in decision-making and leadership roles, and a redefinition of the mission to emphasise unity and mutual witness rather than conversion. Furthermore, the WCC must commit to reparative justice while acknowledging its historical involvement in colonialism. Embracing a postcolonial viewpoint entails accepting diversity without hierarchical structures, fostering cohesion without demanding homogeneity, and promoting mission efforts devoid of dominance. Only by undertaking these transformative steps can the WCC aspire to achieve a truly just and global Christian fellowship.

Chapter 7

Continental Ecumenical Movements

The ecumenical movement, frequently situated within the global framework of church unity and mission, has also evolved in distinct manners across various continents, shaped by local histories, cultures, and socio-political contexts. In the postcolonial era, Christian communities in Asia, Africa, and Latin America have begun to assert their roles in defining the meanings of unity, mission, and theology according to their specific circumstances. Regional forms of ecumenism, particularly in Asia, demonstrate a dynamic interaction between established missionary structures and local initiatives that emphasise contextual relevance and theological authenticity.

This chapter investigates the development and importance of 3 prominent continental ecumenical organisations and movements in Asia: the Christian Conference of Asia (CCA), the Ecumenical Association of Third World Theologians (EATWOT), and the Church's Auxiliary for Social Action (CASA). Each of these entities has significantly contributed to articulating contextual theological insights, advocating for social justice, and fostering Christian unity amidst diversity and division. From the emergence of Asian ecumenical consciousness at Tambaram and Bangkok to the theological radicalism exemplified by EATWOT and the grassroots activism of CASA, these movements have not only challenged Eurocentric perspectives but have also enriched the global ecumenical dialogue. By prioritising liberation, inclusion, and contextual engagement, these continental initiatives illustrate the necessity for a more diverse and participatory approach to ecumenism.

7.1. Christian Conference of Asia

The participation of Asian Christians in the ecumenical movement has deep historical roots, originating from the vital Edinburgh Conference in 1910. This significant gathering saw the involvement of 17 representatives from Asia's emerging churches, among whom V. S. Azariah and Cheng Ching Yi emerged as influential voices in the unfolding dialogue. Azariah passionately advocated for the position that Asian churches should have the autonomy to define the nature of their ecumenical relationships, marking a crucial shift in perspective. In the wake of John R. Mott's influential visits to the region, a network of national councils began to take shape across various Asian countries, providing a platform for local churches to express their unique contexts and aspirations.

The establishment of the International Missionary Council (IMC) in 1921 further empowered these national councils to articulate their desire for a distinct regional ecumenical organisation. The IMC played a vital role in recognising both the distinct identity of Asian Christianity and its equal standing within the broader ecumenical movement. The 1938 Tambaram Conference became a stage for Asian leaders to voice their vision for the future. They asserted the urgent need for East Asia Conferences, with influential national leaders from China and Japan even proposing that the IMC Far East Office be headquartered in Tambaram. Unfortunately, the outbreak of World War II thwarted these ambitious plans,[215] casting a shadow over the progress made.

At the inaugural Assembly of the World Council of Churches (WCC) in 1948, many Asian leaders felt that the discussions were overly focused on matters concerning the older churches, sidelining the distinct issues faced by Asian congregations. Out of the 26 Asian delegates present in Amsterdam, a strong appeal emerged for the convening of an Asian Conference. This request was taken seriously by the Joint Committee of the IMC and WCC, leading to concerted efforts to organise an Asian Conference in Bangkok in 1949. The conference featured 36 delegates from 12 Asian countries and included 5 official representatives from both the IMC and WCC.[216]

The primary goal of the Bangkok gathering was to foster deeper fellowship among the churches of Asia, enhance their active participation in the global ecumenical body, confront the pressing challenges facing Asia, and promote a vision of world peace. As a result of the conference, a proposal was put forth to appoint a Secretary for the East Asia Conference, culminating in the selection of Rajah B. Manickam from India for this

[215] See Snaitang, A History, 190, 191.

[216] See Snaitang, A History, 191.

crucial role in 1950.[217] The inaugural meeting of the East Asia Christian Conference (EACC) took place in 1957 in the serene setting of Prapat, Indonesia,[218] marking the genesis of the CCA.

This gathering was a defining moment for Niles, who embarked on what would become the primary focus of his last decade. At Prapat, a landmark decision was made to establish an East Asia conference of churches, with Niles stepping in as its first general secretary.[219] The meeting brought together 44 representatives from 21 national councils in Asia, focusing on "The Common Evangelistic Task of the Churches in Asia." The Conference underscored the interconnectedness of Christian unity and mission, highlighting the socio-economic and political issues that permeated the region. M. M. Thomas profoundly stated that at Prapat, the churches and NCCs of Asia decided to establish a regional fellowship to express their dedication to ecumenism and common mission, encapsulating the spirit and intent of that formative gathering.

The Asian ecumenical movement is gaining momentum as a thoughtful response to the historical overshadowing of traditional missionary paternalism and Western denominationalism. Asian leaders have actively voiced their concerns and aspirations to global ecumenical organisations, willingly accepting their guidance and support in organising meetings and conferences. Since the inception of the East Asia Christian Conference (EACC), a fundamental conversation has revolved around the identity and role of the Christian Conference of Asia concerning the World Council of Churches. Notably, D. T. Niles once remarked that at the genesis of the EACC in Prapat, a significant decision was reached:[220] the conference would not operate as a mere regional arm of the WCC. This resolution emphasised the necessity for the World Council to remain a direct, unmediated association of churches, while allowing the EACC the flexibility to maintain open membership for those congregations that chose not to, or could not, align with the WCC. This rationale led to the intentional use of the term "Conference" instead of "council," underscoring a commitment to view the EACC as more than a bureaucratic entity - it aims to foster a vibrant and participatory community.

---

[217] See Snaitang, A History, 191.

[218] See Mathews George Chunakara, *Ecumenism in Asia: Prospects and Challenges* (Tiruvalla: Christava Sahitya Samithi, 2014), 47.

[219] See J. E. Lesslie Newbigin, "Niles, Daniel Thambyrajah," in Dictionary of the Ecumenical Movement, ed. by Nicholas Lossky, José Míguez Bonino, et.al. (Geneva: WCC Publications, 1991): 729-31.

[220] D.T. Niles, "Ideas and Services," Report to the EACC General Assembly, 1968.

The enduring vision and mandates of CCA was declared:[221]

> Believing that the purpose of God for the churches in East Asia is life together in a common obedience to Him for the doing of His will in the world, the EACC is hereby constituted as an organ of continuing cooperation among the churches and National Christian Councils in East Asia within the frame work of the wider ecumenical movement.

However, challenges persist. The discussions often focus narrowly on the CCA and National Christian Council (NCC) constituencies in Asia, thereby neglecting the considerable diversity of Christian communities across the continent. This limited perspective excludes significant groups such as the Roman Catholic Church, Evangelicals, Pentecostals, and, not to mention, Christians in China, Vietnam, and Mongolia. This exclusion raises urgent questions about how to genuinely revitalise a more inclusive Asian ecumenical movement. For instance, the China Christian Council (CCC), currently the sole member church representing China in the WCC, claims millions of adherents. Yet, due to their disconnection from the CCA, Chinese Christians often remain unrecognised as part of the broader Asian ecumenical narrative. As Mathews George Chunakara insightfully pointed out,[222] actively seeking ways to engage the Church in China is essential for their meaningful integration into the mainstream movement. Asian Christians must guard against the divisive effects of missionary colonialism,[223] which can further fragment local churches and undermine the collective ecumenical mission across the continent.

The modern ecumenical movement initially emerged as a grassroots initiative led by passionate youth. Regrettably, contemporary youth participation has waned drastically compared to those early, vibrant days. While Asian youth are engaged within their local congregations, they frequently lack exposure to broader ecumenical platforms that could equip them to emerge as future leaders within this movement. Moreover, many young Christians are increasingly drawn to digital ministries or independent non-ecumenical movements, which adds another layer of complexity.

Another pressing challenge confronting the Asian ecumenical movement is the reality of religious pluralism. Many churches across the

---

[221] D. T. Niles, "A Church and Its Selfhood," in *A Decisive Hour for the Christian Mission* (London: SCM Press Limited, 1960), 72.

[222] See Mathews George Chunakara, *Ecumenism in Asia: Prospects and Challenges* (Tiruvalla: Christava Sahitya Samithi, 2014), 38, 39.

[223] Ninan Koshi, *A History of the Ecumenical Movement in Asia*, Vol. I (Hongkong: CCA, 2004), 19. Hereafter cited as Koshi, A History of the Ecumenical.

region grapple with the acknowledgement of diverse faiths present in their midst. Early leaders of the Asian ecumenical movement were acutely aware of their theological and missional imperatives, often striving to navigate the unique challenges of their context. They encouraged churches to contribute to the broader ecumenical landscape while reflecting the distinct qualities of Asia. Today, we continue to wrestle with the repercussions of traditional missiological interpretations inherited from the colonial missionary era. As Ninan Koshy aptly observed, "part of the missionary failure was in not understanding the dynamics of Asian reaction and its religious dimension."[224] Asian churches must avoid repeating these past mistakes in the contemporary context.

Additionally, the CCA faces the ongoing challenge of financial instability. A heavy dependence on external funding sources, particularly from Western ecumenical partners, leaves the CCA vulnerable to the shifting priorities of donors. Economic disparities among member churches further complicate their capacity to contribute.

Theological and political divisions also exacerbate the CCA's struggles. Tensions between liberal and conservative theological perspectives, particularly regarding critical social issues like LGBTQ+ rights and interfaith dialogue, create friction that hampers unity. Geopolitical tensions, particularly in regions like Myanmar, Korea, or India-Pakistan, add layers of complexity to the pursuit of harmonious relationships.

The rising competition from other Christian organisations poses an additional challenge; Evangelical and Pentecostal networks are expanding rapidly, often perceiving the CCA as overly liberal or politically aligned. Furthermore, the emergence of non-denominational megachurches diminishes reliance on traditional ecumenical structures.

Looking towards the future, there is significant promise in fostering South-South cooperation. There is potential to strengthen ties with ecumenical movements in Africa and Latin America, promoting collaborative advocacy efforts that could enrich the Asian ecumenical movement.

7.2. Ecumenical Association of Third World Theologians (EATWOT)

The Ecumenical Association of Third World Theologians (EATWOT) is a dynamic and diverse collective of theologians predominantly hailing from Africa, Asia, and Latin America. This organisation is dedicated to the development of theology that is deeply rooted in the specific cultural, social, and economic contexts of these regions. EATWOT actively critiques conventional Christian theology, asserting that it is often too Eurocentric

---

[224] Koshi, *A History of the Ecumenical*, 19.

and fails to adequately address the pressing issues of poverty, injustice, and oppression faced by many communities.

Founded in August 1976 during a historic gathering in Dar es Salaam, Tanzania,[225] EATWOT emerged after nearly 2 years of dedicated preparation. The meeting brought together theologians from 3 major Christian traditions - Catholic, Protestant, and Orthodox - who convened to discern the "signs of the times." Their collective goal was to foster the creation of "new models of theology" that not only interpret the Gospel but also resonate profoundly with the lived experiences of the peoples in the Third World, supporting their arduous quest for liberation.

Among the ground-breaking theological frameworks developed during this period were the Latin American Theology of Liberation, which emphasises social justice, the Black Theology of Liberation advocating for the dignity of African descent communities, Minjung Theology from Korea highlighting the plight of marginalised groups, Dalit Theology in India addressing caste discrimination, and the Theology of Struggle emerging from the Philippines in response to political oppression.

The inaugural gathering featured a diverse group of 22 theologians: 7 from Africa, 7 from Asia, 7 from Latin America and the Caribbean, and 1 representing the black minority in the United States. These pioneering scholars were inspired by numerous prominent liberation theologians, such as Gustavo Gutierrez, who championed the cause of the poor, Enrique Dussel, known for his critique of Western thought, Sergio Torres, Hugo Assman, Tissa Balassuriya, Virginia Fabella, Mercy Amba Oduyoye, and James Cone, each of whom contributed significantly to the theological discourse on liberation and social justice.[226] EATWOT continues to be a crucial platform for those seeking to articulate a theology that speaks to the struggles and hopes of marginalised communities worldwide.

Liberation theologies emerged in Latin America, Asia and Africa - almost in the same time – in the early 1970s. As Gustavo Gutierrez (Peruvian and Dominican priest), one of the pioneers in Latin America, describes it:[227]

> Theology of liberation offers us not so much a new theme for reflection, as a new way to do theology. Theology as critical reflection on historical praxis is a liberating theology, a theology

[225] See David J. Bosch, *Transforming Mission: Paradigm Shifts in Theology of Mission* (Bangalore: Omega Book World, 2021), 473. Hereafter cited as Bosch, Transforming Mission.

[226] See Luiza E. Tomita, "Eatwot Global History," www.eatwotglobal.com/history.html (14 May 2025). Hereafter cited as Tomita, "Eatwot Global History."

[227] Gustavo Gutierrez, *A Theology of Liberation: History, Politics and Salvation* (Maryknoll, New York: Orbis Books, 1973), 15.

> of the liberating transformation of the history of mankind (sic) and therefore that part of mankind (sic) – gathered into ecclesia – which openly confesses Christ. This is a theology which does not stop with reflecting on the world, but rather tries to be part of the process through which the world is transformed.

From the very beginning, EATWOT has embarked on a transformative journey, embracing a contextual, liberating, and inclusive approach that consciously steers clear of any monopolistic claims on methodology. Its mission has been to support the collective endeavour of reimagining theology in ways that resonate deeply with the authentic aspirations and struggles of marginalised populations in the Third World. This important shift in theological thought, moving from the 'centre' to the 'periphery,' transcends mere geographic or cultural considerations; it is fundamentally rooted in a profound epistemological transition. This shift emphasises the critical role of praxis - active engagement in the world - and advocates for a thorough and reflective examination of reality as it unfolds. As a result, it calls for a radical rethinking of theological methodologies, effectively dismantling the traditional academic frameworks that have been dominated by Western-centric perspectives.[228]

In its formative years, the EATWOT theologians encountered a myriad of challenges, one of the most pressing being the unwavering demand from women to have their voices and experiences recognised, valued, and fully integrated within the organisation. For feminist theologians, this represented what they termed an "irruption within the irruption," a significant event that unfolded during the New Delhi conference in August 1981. This gathering symbolised a burgeoning awareness for some participants and an awakening consciousness for others, marking an important shift toward acknowledging and embracing women's contributions in both the church and the broader realm of theological discourse.

As a result of this crucial conference, feminist liberation theology emerged as the most thoroughly articulated iteration of liberation theology to date. It made a profound impact by directly challenging Third World male liberation theologians to reflect on their use of sexist language and patriarchal perspectives. This confrontation not only questioned existing norms but also heralded a new era of inclusivity and justice within theological discussions. Since that transformative moment, feminist theologians within EATWOT have enriched the academic landscape with numerous influential publications, exploring various dimensions of faith and gender.

---

[228] See Aruna Gnanadason, "A Kairos Moment for Renewing and Revitalizing Eatwot," Academia.edu.file:///C:/Users/Downloads/ A_Kairos_Moment_for_Reviewing_and_Revital. pdf) (14 May 2025).

EATWOT operates under a carefully drafted constitution and is guided by an executive committee. The organisation convenes a general assembly every 5 years, fostering collaboration and strategic planning, yet it does not maintain a permanent secretariat - a testament to its dynamic, grassroots ethos. The coordination of EATWOT is thoughtfully divided into 4 distinct regions: Africa, Asia, Latin America, and a dedicated region for "minority groups" - referred to as the "diaspora" in the original constitution - representing those situated outside the more traditional territories. This structure reflects EATWOT's commitment to inclusivity and diversity, ensuring a broad spectrum of voices contributes to the ongoing theological dialogue.[229]

7.2.1. Aims and Objectives of Eatwot

1) To promote contextual theology that responds to the lived experiences of the poor and marginalised.
2) To challenge Eurocentric and colonial theological paradigms.
3) To facilitate dialogue among theologians from different oppressed contexts.
4) To promote justice, liberation, inculturation, and interfaith dialogue.

7.2.2. Key Themes in EATWOT Theology

1) Liberation Theology

This fundamental aspect of EATWOT theology focuses on addressing deep-rooted issues of economic, political, and social inequality. It advocates for the marginalised and oppressed, emphasising the need for justice and liberation from systemic injustices that have long plagued society.

2) Postcolonial and Decolonial Thought

EATWOT theology critically engages with postcolonial and decolonial frameworks, actively questioning the pervasive influence of theological imperialism. It seeks to dismantle narratives that perpetuate colonial mindsets, fostering a more equitable understanding of faith that respects diverse cultural contexts.

3) Feminist and Womanist Theologies

Central to EATWOT is the amplification of women's voices, particularly those from the Global South. By integrating feminist and womanist perspectives, this theological approach highlights the unique experiences,

[229] See Tomita, "Eatwot Global History," 2.

struggles, and insights of women, thereby enriching the broader discourse on spirituality and justice.

4) Indigenous Theologies

EATWOT theology plays a vital role in revitalising indigenous spiritual practices, advocating against cultural erasure that often accompanies globalisation. It honours and respects native traditions, promoting a return to ancestral wisdom while fostering resilience in the face of modern challenges.

5) Interreligious Dialogue

In our increasingly diverse societies, such as India and Southeast Asia, interreligious dialogue emerges as a crucial theme within EATWOT theology. This approach encourages mutual understanding, respect, and collaboration among different faiths, recognising the richness that diverse religious perspectives bring to the communal and spiritual landscape.

7.2.3. Notable Theologians in EATWOT

1) Latin America

Widely recognised as the architect of Liberation Theology, Gustavo Gutiérrez (Peru) emphasises the "preferential option for the poor," which advocates for the marginalised and oppressed in society. His seminal work, "A Theology of Liberation," challenges traditional theological perspectives by intertwining faith with social justice, calling for active engagement in alleviating poverty and injustice.

Leonardo Boff, Brazil, is a prominent figure in the development of eco-theology, integrating concepts from Liberation Theology with ecological concerns. His writings explore the interconnections between environmental stewardship and social justice, arguing that the degradation of the earth is linked to the oppression of the poor. Boff's influential works promote a holistic understanding of salvation that includes ecological awareness.

2) Africa

An important figure in the struggle against apartheid, Desmond Tutu's theological insights intertwine faith with activism. As the first black Archbishop of Cape Town, he championed nonviolent resistance and reconciliation. His commitment to justice and human rights is encapsulated in the concept of *Ubuntu*,[230] emphasising the interconnectedness of humanity and the moral imperative to stand against oppression.

[230] In South Africa, the term "Ubuntu" refers to the moral principles, sense of community, and capacity for cooperation of the nation. "A quality that includes the essential

Jesse Mugambi (Kenya) is known for advocating Reconstruction Theology, particularly in the context of post-conflict societies. His work critically addresses the need for rebuilding communities and restoring dignity after violence. By emphasising the importance of engaging with indigenous traditions alongside Christianity, he seeks to create a theology that resonates with the realities of African life.

3) Asia

Aloysius Pieris (Sri Lanka) is a prominent theologian who fosters meaningful dialogue between Buddhism and Christianity, keenly addressing the socio-economic challenges faced by the poor. His approach, known as "interreligious dialogue," emphasises mutual understanding and respect. Pieris's contributions highlight how Christian theology can be contextualised within Asian realities while promoting social justice.

An influential Indian Christian thinker, M. M. Thomas, engaged deeply with secularism, nation-building, and the complex dynamics of interfaith dialogue in a diverse society. Thomas advocated for a contextual theology that speaks to the realities of Indian culture, promoting harmony and coexistence among various religious traditions. Vidyajyoti Scholars, a group of Indian Jesuits, including scholars like Michael Amaladoss, focuses on inculturation and contextual theology, seeking to integrate the richness of Indian culture and spirituality with Christian doctrine. Their work emphasises the importance of understanding and expressing faith within the local cultural contexts, providing insights into how the Christian message can be meaningfully communicated in India.

These theologians collectively illustrate the vibrant landscape of theological thought emerging from EATWOT, emphasising social justice, ecological awareness, and intercultural dialogue in their pursuits of faith and advocacy.

7.2.4. EATWOT and Indian Contextual Theology

India has played a profound and transformative role in the evolving landscape of EATWOT (Ecumenical Theology of the World's Oppressed). One of the critical contributions is the development of Dalit theology, a vibrant and dynamic discourse that confronts and elucidates the struggles faced by the marginalised and oppressed castes within Indian society. This theological framework not only seeks to illuminate their experiences but also champions their fight for justice and dignity.

---

human virtues of compassion and humanity" is a concise word from the Nguni languages of Zulu and Xhosa that has a rather broad English definition.

Additionally, the voices of Tribal or Indigenous theology have emerged prominently, particularly drawing insights from the unique cultural and spiritual heritage of the regions of Northeast India and central India. This theology seeks to honour and integrate indigenous perspectives, celebrating the rich traditions and experiences of these communities.

Moreover, women's theology has surfaced as a crucial area of focus, addressing complex issues intertwined with caste, patriarchy, and the rich tapestry of religious diversity in India. This approach critically examines the intersections of gender and caste, advocating for equitable treatment and representation for women.

Among the prominent Indian theologians who have significantly contributed to EATWOT are James Massey, recognized as a trailblazer in Dalit theology, whose work has inspired many to engage with the socio-political realities of the oppressed. V. Devasahayam stands out for his relentless emphasis on social justice and the urgent need to address the systematic oppression faced by marginalized castes. Furthermore, R. P. Ekka, Wati Longchar, K. Thanzauva and Lalrinawmi Ralte represent powerful voices within Tribal Theology, advocating for the rights and recognition of indigenous peoples and their spiritual heritage.

The Evangelical and Ecumenical voices in India have harnessed EATWOT as an essential platform to challenge colonial legacies in theology and to weave in local narratives and cultural contexts. Through this engagement, they strive to create a more inclusive, just, and contextually relevant theological discourse that resonates with the lived experiences of all oppressed communities in India.

7.2.5. EATWOT and Northeast Indian Theology

EATWOT embodies a profound alignment with the theological emphases prevalent within the churches of Northeast India, particularly highlighting several pivotal areas of focus. Firstly, it seeks to reclaim and celebrate indigenous identities and spiritual practices that are often overshadowed or forgotten. This reclamation emerges as a vital act of resistance against dominant Indian theological perspectives that frequently neglect or misunderstand the diverse tribal and ethnic worldviews that enrich the region's spiritual landscape.

Furthermore, EATWOT engages in the critical reconstruction of mission history and cultural narratives from a postcolonial lens. This approach allows for a deeper understanding of the historical injustices faced by these communities, fostering a more inclusive theological discourse. It courageously addresses the pressing issues of violence, displacement, and marginalization that many tribal communities endure, advocating for their recognition and justice within a broader societal context.

Among the key theological themes that resonate deeply with EATWOT's mission in Northeast India are the celebration of Community Harmony and Identity, underscoring the rich tapestry of relationships that define tribal life. The sacredness of Land and Creation is emphasised, reflecting a profound reverence for the environment as integral to spiritual existence. Additionally, the importance of oral traditions and narrative theology is acknowledged, serving as vital channels for conveying faith and wisdom across generations. Lastly, the themes of Peace and Reconciliation are woven throughout, highlighting the essential work of healing and unity in the face of historical and ongoing challenges.

7.2.6. EATWOT's Legacy and Ongoing Relevance

The Ecumenical Association of Third World Theologians (EATWOT) is passionately committed to fostering grassroots theological reflection that prioritises the lived experiences and voices of marginalised communities, including the economically disadvantaged, indigenous peoples, and women. This vibrant association serves as a dynamic global platform that empowers theologians from India and Northeast India to actively participate in and influence theological discourse on a broader scale.

EATWOT champions a diverse array of theological frameworks, such as postcolonial, feminist, ecological, and interreligious theologies, which are experiencing a rich blossoming in South Asia today. Through its initiatives, EATWOT not only addresses the urgent social issues facing these communities but also amplifies their unique perspectives, thereby cultivating a deeper and more inclusive understanding of faith and spirituality.

7.3. Church Auxiliary for Social Action (CASA)

After decades of British colonial rule, India triumphantly declared its hard-won independence at midnight on 15th August 1947, becoming an independent nation. However, this newfound freedom came at a steep price, as the partition of India and Pakistan plunged the subcontinent into turmoil, resulting in heartbreaking tragedies marked by significant loss of lives and the devastation of property. Millions were forced to migrate across newly drawn borders, confronting alien environments and enduring inhumane conditions that left indelible scars on humanity.

In the wake of this monumental upheaval, the fledgling government, under the visionary leadership of Prime Minister Jawaharlal Nehru, urgently called upon various organisations to mobilise and provide relief to the suffering populace. In response, the National Council of Churches in India, under Bishop J. Waskom Pickett's guidance, initiated the establishment of the 'NCC Relief Committee.' This vital organisation, born out of compassion and necessity, eventually evolved into the Church's Auxiliary for Social Action (CASA), an example of hope that transformed into one of India's leading relief and development entities.[231] Initially focused on delivering immediate aid to victims of both natural calamities and man-made disasters, CASA gradually broadened its horizon to embrace a holistic approach aimed at empowering marginalised communities and fostering sustainable development strategies.

The Relief Committee had several names over the years:

1947: Central Relief Committee or Refugee and Famine Relief Committee;[232]

1955: Committee on Relief and Gift Supplies (CORAGS);[233]

The Church's Auxiliary for Social Action is currently in place,[234] as is the Christian Agency for Social Action.

Operating without discrimination based on religion, caste, creed, gender, or ethnicity, CASA's mission reflects a commitment to inclusivity and social equity. Headquartered in the bustling capital of New Delhi, CASA extends its reach across the nation through 3 strategically located zonal offices in Mumbai, Kolkata, and Chennai, supplemented by 31 sector offices that span 22 states. This extensive network ensures the effective implementation and monitoring of its vast array of programs, supported by a dedicated workforce of over 300 employees. Resource centres have been established in nearly every region, enabling CASA to function independently in around 5,000 villages across 26 states, reinforcing its commitment to localised, impactful interventions.[235]

Funding for CASA's initiatives is procured from a combination of national and international sources, solidifying its financial sustainability and allowing for the continuation of its vital work. In its journey, CASA has demonstrated remarkable resilience and adaptability, reflecting its profound acceptance and relevance within society. Its ability to assess and respond to the complex, evolving socio-economic landscape has been invaluable in the pursuit of empowering marginalised and underprivileged communities. By the mid-1970s, CASA adopted a broader perspective on the intricate relationship between relief and development,[236] straddling the

---

[231] See "About Casa India," https://casa-india.org/about-us (15 May 2025), 1. Hereafter cited as "About Casa India."

[232] See The National Christian Council Review, Volume 97, (Wesley Press, 1977), 139.

[233] See H. Dwight Swartzendruber, Forty Years of Service Beyond Our Borders (Morgantown: Masthof Press), 2012.

[234] See Harold C. Fey, ed. *A History of the Ecumenical Movement,* Volume 2 (Eugene: Wipf and Stock, 2004), 228.

[235] See "About Casa India," 1.

[236] See "About Casa India," 2.

line between immediate response to crises and the implementation of long-term developmental initiatives across the nation.

The organisation's focus increasingly shifted towards the empowerment of marginalised populations, viewing development through the prism of sustainability. This involved emphasising the crucial role of community participation and ownership in every developmental endeavour. CASA's strategy hinges on nurturing robust and self-sufficient indigenous organisations, which are at the heart of its development activities. These community-based organisations genuinely represent the voices of the people, identifying pressing issues within their communities and villages. The apex bodies play a pivotal role in determining beneficiaries for all economic initiatives.[237] Thus, CASA's approach is firmly rooted in the principles of community ownership, participatory engagement, and sustainable development, ensuring that the process is centred around the people it aims to serve.

Conclusion

Movements such as the CCA, EATWOT, and CASA exemplify the intricate and multifaceted nature of Christian unity and theological expression in the Global South. Their histories reflect an ongoing struggle for autonomy, recognition, and relevance amid the legacies of colonialism, theological marginalisation, and socio-political unrest. These movements do not merely replicate Western ecclesiastical models; rather, they innovatively reinterpret ecumenism in light of local contexts and global injustices. The Christian Conference of Asia offers an inspiring model of regional fellowship grounded in shared missions and common struggles, despite navigating internal diversity and external challenges. EATWOT emerges as a prophetic voice that critiques theological imperialism, advocating for a theology that emanates from the lived experiences of the poor, the colonised, and the marginalised. CASA, through its action-oriented approach, exemplifies how ecumenism can be tangibly realised through acts of compassion, development, and justice.

Collectively, these movements encourage the global church to reconceptualise ecumenism not as a mere institutional connection but as a vibrant, contextual, and justice-oriented fellowship. They remind us that authentic unity must be established on mutual respect, careful listening to local contexts, and a commitment to progressing together in solidarity with the marginalised and overlooked. Through their witness, the continental ecumenical movements not only provide critique but also outline constructive pathways toward a more inclusive, comprehensive, and transformative vision of the church in the contemporary world.

---

[237] See "About Casa India," 2.

Chapter 8

Key Concepts in Ecumenism (Exploring Terms that Shape Christian Unity and Dialogue)

The ecumenical movement, which seeks unity among Christians, has developed a complex and varied vocabulary that encompasses its theological, historical, and practical dimensions. To grasp the full extent of its significance, it is essential to understand the key concepts that underpin this movement. This chapter offers a critical analysis of fundamental terms such as comity, wider ecumenism, orthodoxy, conciliarism, and reconciliation - concepts that not only delineate the internal logic of ecumenism but also function as tools for promoting dialogue, resolving conflicts, and envisioning a unified Christian testimony. By contextualising these terms within their historical and theological frameworks, this chapter aims to equip readers with the conceptual knowledge required for meaningful engagement in ecumenical discussions.

8.1. Comity

8.1.1. Meaning

In the secular context, "comity" signifies a harmonious community atmosphere, social peace, and the voluntary and unofficial acceptance of another jurisdiction's laws and rulings by its courts.[238] Within the religious domain, this term is adopted by mission agencies to prevent overlapping efforts, as there are numerous regions to evangelise and limited resources

[238] See "Comity," https://www.merriam-webster.com>dictionary>comity (20 Jan. 2025).

available. The entire field must be allocated to avoid waste due to multiple societies operating within the same area or overlapping in identical fields, thereby ensuring economic efficiency, and maintaining harmony among different missionary organisations.[239] In essence, it involves refraining from encroaching on another religious group's followers. In comity agreements, mission organisations or churches were allocated different areas to work to avoid unnecessary competitions.

The term "comity" was coined in the 1880s[240] and was frequently used in the presentations and debates at the 1888 Centenary Conference on the Protestant Missions of the World in London. Up to 1,600 members showed up for this ecumenical event.[241] Protestant overseas missionary organisations have continued to use the word in their mission fields ever since.

8.1.2. Cooperation and Unity in Mission Fields

At the beginning of the 19th century, comity was already a feature of missionary discourse and practice. The increased enthusiasm for international missions among Protestant churches led to a new concern for cooperation. The desire to share the Gospel with everyone sparked new efforts at unity and cooperation. At the Liverpool Conference on Missions (1860), which took place in Liverpool, this newly discovered worry was voiced.[242] Across the 19th and 20th centuries, numerous missionary conferences expressed this concern for mission and unity.

It was, on the one hand, the sharing of territory into areas of occupation and, on the other, the refraining from meddling in each other's business. Its goal was to avoid unnecessary repetition, rivalry, and display of different religious and political practices[243] that could mislead people of other faiths and impede the spread of the Gospel.

8.1.3. Benefits and Challenges of Comity

There has been significant discussion about the benefits and drawbacks of comity. Naturally, the benefits that are outlined in terms of the advantages

---

[239] See N. G. Clark, *True and False Economy in Missions* (Boston: American Board of Commissioners for Foreign Missions, 1891), 3.

[240] See R. Pierce Beaver, *Ecumenical Beginnings in Protestant World: A History of Comity* (New York: Thomas Nelson & Sons, 1962).

[241] See *Report of the Centenary Conference on the Protestant Missions of the World,* Held in Exeter Hall (June 9th - 19th), London, 1888, Vol. I, edited by James Johnston (London: James Nisbet & Co., 1888), xiii.

[242] See Michael W. Goheen, "Mission and Unity: The Theological Dynamic of Comity," 3, in https://missionworldview.com›wp-content›uploads (12 Jan. 2025).

[243] Beaver, "Comity," Concise Dictionary of the Christian World Mission, edited by Stephen Neill, Gerald Anderson, and John Goodwin (New York: Abingdon Press, 1971), 123.

for Western missionary organisations are the main topic of discussion. The process of draughting comity agreements leads to communication and respect between parties; resources are distributed over a larger region; and missionary societies avoid competition[244] and overlap.

8.1.4. Benefits

8.1.4.1. Newbegin's Articulation

However, what are the benefits of harmony amongst the native churches? Newbigin has an answer to that question. The South Indian church has profited from Newbigin's articulation of the religious dynamic of comity. It is this dynamic that sheds light on the first mission-driven drive for unification. According to him, the Indian church was influenced by the comity principle in certain ways. It promoted a feeling of missionary accountability. "There usually exists but one Christian community, and upon this community lies the obligation for the evangelisation of the geographical region allotted..." [245] was the definition of comity in practice. When a church was the only one in a community, evangelisation of the surrounding area became the top priority.

Comity, in part, was the reason that the younger churches were forced to embrace this feeling of duty and their missionary orientation from the very beginning. It influenced the churches' personalities, beliefs, and organisational designs. They realised that "evangelism was their lifeblood" and that "the idea of mission dominated their life."[246] The church cannot tolerate division if it has a missionary vision: "When Christians are working on the missionary obedience task, they are in the situation where the Church is truly the Church."[247] They truly participate in the apostolate of Christ. In that case, the division between churches that are not involved in missionary work, which is sometimes taken for granted, becomes unbearable.

8.1.4.2. Comity Fosters Solidarity among Christians

The ecumenical goal of "visible unity" aligns with the principle of comity, as it promotes cooperation and respect among various denominations, prioritising shared values over differences.

---

[244] Dyck, Cornelius J. and Dennis D. Martin, eds. *Mennonite Encyclopaedia*, Volume 5. (Scottsdale, PA: Herald Press, 1990), 169.

[245] Newbigin, Lesslie. *The Reunion of the Church: A Defence of the South India Scheme* (London: SCM Press, 1948), 12.

[246] See Michael W. Goheen, "Mission and Unity: The Theological Dynamic of Comity," 6, in https://missionworldview.com›wp-content›uploads (12 Jan 2025). Hereafter cited as Goheen, "Mission and Unity."

[247] See Goheen, "Mission and Unity," 6.

8.1.4.3. It Minimises Resource Duplication

Comity effectively reduces redundancy and optimises resource utilisation by coordinating efforts related to social services, mission work, and communal worship.

8.1.4.4. It Encourages Collaborative Engagement

Enhanced understanding of religious and cultural variances emerges from cooperation and dialogue, which mitigates prejudice and fosters a sense of peace.

8.1.4.5. It Strengthens the Global Witness

In a fragmented world, the credibility of the Church's witness is heightened when social, ethical, and spiritual challenges are confronted with unity.

8.1.4.6. It Improves Resource Sharing

Churches can more effectively support communities by pooling resources - whether material, human, or financial - for joint initiatives, including healthcare, education, and disaster relief.

8.1.4.7. It Promotes Harmonious Coexistence

By delineating areas of influence and encouraging collaborative relationships, comity can prevent disputes in regions plagued by sectarian tensions.

8.1.5. Challenges of Comity in the Ecumenical Movement

8.1.5.1. Negotiations on Theological Authenticity

Churches may experience pressure from comity to downplay significant theological differences, potentially leading to a perceived or actual dilution of theological integrity.

8.1.5.2. Opposition from Denominations

Certain churches may exhibit reluctance or opposition to comity initiatives, viewing them as threats to their autonomy or mission objectives.

8.1.5.3. Concerns Regarding Justice

Comity arrangements that favour larger or more influential churches might render smaller or minority denominations feeling marginalised or undermined.

8.1.5.4. Restrictions on Missionary Efforts

Agreements that inhibit competing efforts in specific areas may constrain evangelism and missionary work, leaving some communities underserved.

8.1.5.5. Risk of Superficial Harmony

The pursuit of comity may result in fragile unity if agreements emphasise external collaboration over addressing deeper theological or relational issues.

8.1.5.6. Cultural and Contextual Challenges

Despite established comity agreements, actual collaboration may be hindered by differing cultural backgrounds and attitudes toward ministry.

8.2. Wider Ecumenism

Wider ecumenism represents a significant evolution in the understanding of Christian unity, extending beyond traditional denominational confines. This approach aims not only for harmony among Protestant, Catholic, and Orthodox churches but also seeks to include a diverse array of Christian groups, such as Evangelicals, Pentecostals, and various independent movements. In certain contexts, wider ecumenism even fosters interreligious dialogue, embracing exchanges between Christianity and other faith systems, including Judaism, Islam, Buddhism, and Hinduism. The ultimate goal is to cultivate a more inclusive and understanding global Christian fellowship, one that emphasises shared values, collaborative efforts on pressing social issues, and a united witness in an increasingly pluralistic and interconnected world.

Moreover, wider ecumenism broadens its focus to engage in comprehensive interfaith dialogue, aspiring to build understanding and collaboration across all religious traditions. This approach involves active partnerships with representatives from diverse faiths to tackle critical global challenges, such as peacebuilding, social justice, environmental stewardship, and the promotion of human rights. By doing so, wider ecumenism aims to create a vision of spiritual unity and ethical cooperation that benefits humanity as a whole.

Theological perspectives and interpretations are inherently dynamic; they evolve and adapt over time in response to changing cultural contexts and societal needs. Consequently, the notion of ecumenism has expanded from its original aim of church unity to encompass a broader vision that includes the welfare of the entire human community across the globe. To thoroughly grasp the concept of *oikoumene*, it is essential to consider both its spiritual dimensions and its missionary-social components in tandem. *Oikoumene*, derived from Greek, refers to the concept of "inhabited earth" and signifies a relational, dynamic understanding of the human community as part of the entire creation, transcending mere fellowship among Christians and churches. The mission of the ecumenical movement is fundamentally about transforming the *oikoumene* into God's envisioned household (oikos), recognising that the earth is shared by people of diverse races, languages, religions, and cultures, all of whom are integral to one human family. This perspective marks a crucial advancement toward the ideals of wider ecumenism.

Isaac Devadoss, in his work "A Historical Survey of Ecumenism in India,"[248] highlights a growing concern that the term 'ecumenical' has been narrowly applied in recent years, often relegated to discussions focused on internal church developments. He argues compellingly that if the term 'ecumenical' is to truly reflect a commitment to the "whole inhabited earth," it must encompass the world's rich plurality, including its myriad religious traditions. A rising number of individuals and communities resonate with his perspective, advocating that the ecumenical movement should embody an effort to unite the world's diverse religious traditions in a collective pursuit of peace, harmony, and the overall well-being of the human family. To ensure that the deeper essence of Christian ecumenism is recognised, this broader pursuit has come to be referred to as 'Wider Ecumenism.' Some proponents also label it 'New Ecumenism,' 'Mega Ecumenism,' or the 'Ecumenism of Religious Traditions.'[249] Regardless of the terminology employed, the core message remains clear: a thoughtful re-examination of Christian ecumenism is necessary, positioning it within a larger and more inclusive quest for the unity and solidarity of all humankind.

Some Christians perceive the modern ecumenical movement as a significant threat, often resisting the use of the term "ecumenical" to characterise interfaith initiatives. Wesley Ariarajah identifies 3 principal concerns that underpin this perspective.[250] The first concern revolves around the belief that an emphasis on broader ecumenism might dilute and ultimately overshadow the need for genuine Christian unity. Those who hold this view argue that Christian ecumenism itself requires fresh energy, renewal, and a revitalised impetus for progress. They fear that expanding the ecumenical focus at this point in history could detract from the vital efforts aimed at achieving unity within the Christian tradition. Indeed, it is evident that Christian ecumenism has languished in its pursuit of innovative developments,[251] in part due to insufficient progress toward meaningful unity among various denominations.

---

[248] Isaac Devadoss, "A Historical Survey of Ecumenism in India," in *History of Ecumenical Movement: Issues, Challenges, and Perspectives,* edited by Watimongla Jamir (Kolkata: Sceptre, 1014), 188 (177-197).

[249] See S. Wesley Ariarajah, "Wider Ecumenism," in *Current Dialogue,* Issue 47, (June, 2006), 1. Hereafter cited as Ariarajah, "Wider Ecumenism."

[250] See Ariarajah, "Wider Ecumenism," 2.

[251] See Ariarajah, "Wider Ecumenism," 2.

The Faith and Order movement has been diligently striving for church unity since the 1920s.[252] While it is true that the ecumenical movement and the efforts of Faith and Order have facilitated reconciliatory steps past historical enmities, severe rivalries, and mutual excommunications, profound divisions among churches, rooted in large confessional families and deep-seated doctrinal differences, persist even after more than 70 years. Given the numerous agreements that remain unimplemented, scepticism about the authenticity of the church's pursuit of unity has emerged, prompting some to view these enduring divisions as more "cultural" than "doctrinal." Nonetheless, the quest for Christian unity is crucial for both the vitality of the church [253] and the well-being of the society it serves.

Furthermore, it has become increasingly clear that other religious traditions, including Judaism, Islam, Hinduism, and Buddhism, also require impactful forms of inner ecumenism to safeguard against internal divisions that could lead to conflict. Thus, the call for wider ecumenism should not be perceived as an alternative to the internal dynamics of ecumenism within each faith tradition. Rather, these 2 levels of ecumenical engagement can be viewed as concentric circles, both orbiting around the theme of unity and serving overlapping communities. In other words, wider ecumenism does not supplant Christian ecumenism; instead, it offers a new and invigorating context for it. Many Christians can actively participate in ecumenism at both levels[254] without feeling that commitment to one entails a betrayal of the other.

The second apprehension arises from the perception that wider ecumenism promotes the idea that "all religions are the same," suggesting that distinctions between diverse faiths hold little significance. Many people interpret the push for broader ecumenism as an implicit form of Universalism that overlooks the unique identities of different religions. Similar concerns emerged when interfaith dialogue was integrated into the ecumenical movement as a means of engaging with individuals from other faith traditions. Participants in these dialogues were tasked with clarifying that fostering mutual respect, building relationships, and nurturing a nuanced understanding does not equate to endorsing the notion that all religions are identical. Rather, the essence of dialogue lies in recognising and embracing the distinct visions of reality that each tradition offers. In these conversations, religions participate in an "encounter of commitments"

---

[252] See Lukas Vischer, "Faith and Order Reports: their Nature and Significance," in *A Documentary History of the Faith & Order Movement 1927-1963,* ed. by Lukas Vischer (USA: WCC, 1963), 8.

[253] See Ariarajah, "Wider Ecumenism," 2.

[254] See Ariarajah, "Wider Ecumenism," 2.

to create a "community of communities." Wider ecumenism aspires not to establish a universal religion or diminish the uniqueness of various faiths, but to advocate for unity in diversity, promote collaboration amid differences, and foster togetherness in a world often marred by discord.

Metropolitan Mor Coorilos, the moderator of the CWME, emphasises that the Holy Spirit operates not solely within the confines of the Church but also in the broader world.[255] He asserts that "God's Spirit can be encountered in all cultures and faith traditions where life in its fullness is affirmed."[256] This perspective highlights the belief that divine presence and inspiration extend beyond traditional religious boundaries, promoting an inclusive view of spirituality and mission in various contexts.

The 3rd concern arises from apprehensions about the future of the church's mission. A traditional understanding of Christian mission frequently bifurcates the world into the "saved" and those "in need of salvation," implying that other faiths do not present valid pathways to salvation and that all individuals must hear the Gospel and be urged to join the ranks of the "saved" community. Consequently, for those who embrace this worldview, wider ecumenism may be perceived as a threat to this missionary imperative. Fortunately, most churches are increasingly distancing themselves from this restrictive understanding of mission. Dissenting voices within the ecumenical movement first emerged at the World Missionary Conference held in Edinburgh, Scotland, in 1910 and were later reaffirmed at the 2nd conference in Jerusalem in 1928.[257]

The discussions that began during these conferences ultimately contributed to the development of the concept of the "Mission of God" (Missio Dei) at the World Mission Conference in Mexico City in 1968. This concept shifted the focus away from a binary view of the world divided into "saved" and "unsaved," fostering a more inclusive[258] and compassionate understanding of mission.

In exploring the expansive theme of wider ecumenism, Johnson Thomaskutty[259] invites us to delve into the richness of the Gospel of John as a valuable resource. He draws our attention particularly to John 17:10,

---

[255] See Mor Coorilos, Geewarghese, "Mission Towards Fullness of Life," in *International Review of Mission* 103/1, (2014): 41. Hereafter cited as Coorilos, "Mission."

Coorilos, "Mission," 45.

[256] Coorilos, "Mission," 45.

[257] See Snaitang, A History, 108.

[258] See Ariarajah, "Wider Ecumenism," 2, 3.

[259] See Johnson Thomaskutty, "Oneness in John 17:1–26 as a Paradigm for Wider Ecumenism and Dialogue," HTS Teologiese Studies/ Theological Studies 78/3, (Oct, 2022), a7838. https://doi.org/10.4102/hts.v78i3.7838 (16 May 2025). Hereafter cited as Thomaskutty, "Oneness in John 17:1–26."

where we witness a profound and dynamic unity between God the Father and the Son. This intimate relationship comes to the forefront in John 17:11, where Jesus expresses the desire that 'they may be one, as we are one.' This poignant phrase illustrates the exemplary nature of the bond between God and Jesus, the Son, serving as a powerful model for human relationships. The term "one" signifies unity and fosters an essential group identity, linking the Johannine disciples with the singular and divine God of Israel. This concept of shared identity and interconnectedness forms the bedrock of Thomaskutty's discussion[260] within the Johannine text.

John 17:23 reinforces this idea with the compelling phrase *hōsin teteleiōmenoi eis hen*, which translates to 'they may become completely one.' This repetition in Jesus' prayer underscores that the pursuit of oneness is not merely an aspiration but a central and urgent concern of the storyteller. As God and the Son (the two persons in the Trinity) exist in a harmonious relationship, this ideal of unity is meant to extend to believers[261] in both their personal and communal interactions.

Furthermore, this collective oneness among believers invites a broader community engagement, allowing the fellowship of the persons in the Trinity and believers to expand into a greater universal cohesion. In a heartfelt moment, Jesus prays that believers will bask in the fullest measure of divine joy within their communities. By embracing the word of God and steadfastly maintaining their faith in Jesus, they form a consecrated group, distinctly set apart from the rest of society. Through this sacred unity, they are called to reflect the divine nature of their relationship with God while fostering a spirit of belonging and love among themselves and the world at large.

A profound layer of unity in prayer emerges from the intricate relationship among the persons in the Trinity, believers, and the broader external world. This oneness transcends a mere closed and exclusive entity; instead, it is characterised by its open-ended and inclusive nature, extending a warm and welcoming invitation to the non-believing world. With this inclusive purpose, God bestows authority upon the Son over all humanity, although the gift of eternal life is reserved exclusively for those who believe.[262]

The expansive unity expressed in Jesus' prayer becomes even clearer when considered in connection with the *Paraklētos*.[263] In the Greco-Roman

---

[260] See Thomaskutty, "Oneness in John 17:1–26," 1.

[261] See Thomaskutty, "Oneness in John 17:1–26," 3.

[262] See Thomaskutty, "Oneness in John 17:1–26," 4.

[263] Paraklétos: Advocate, Helper, Comforter, Counsellor. Original Word: παράκλητος. Part of Speech: Noun, Masculine.

context, the *Paraklētos* was seen as a 'helper in court,' or 'one who is summoned' within the judicial realm. In John's writings, the 'indwelling' nature of the *Paraklētos* and their profound oneness with the persons in the Godhead and believers is prominently emphasised. As Jesus departs from the world, he implores the disciples not to drown in sorrow, for the *Paraklētos* will empower them to recognise Christ's enduring presence. The term 'another' should not imply a difference in essence but rather indicate one of the same kind. The Holy Spirit, therefore, does not proceed as a separate entity but as a person within the Trinity,[264] sharing the same divine essence.

The 'another *Paraklētos*' is described as Jesus' Alter Ego, destined to remain with the disciples permanently, perpetuating the mission of Christ on earth. The *Paraklētos* acts as a guiding light, reflecting Jesus' earthly mission by steering the disciples towards the path of truth amidst a challenging and often tumultuous environment. The unity cultivated by the persons in the Godhead, *Paraklētos*, and believers serves as a model of oneness, one that is receptive to the broader realities of the world, inviting dialogue and conversation. Christianity's inclusive mission encompasses 2 essential aspects: first, witnessing to Christ and, second, bearing witness to the struggles faced in the world.[265]

The Johannine community has developed a rich concept of unity that bridges the ideologies from 'above' and 'below,' extending an invitation to the larger world to embrace the harmonious unity shared by the two persons in the Godhead, *Paraklētos*, and believers. The open-ended unity experienced within the Johannine community can serve as an inspiring model for contemporary Christian churches, fostering greater integration and cross-pollination of ideas and practices. In a multifaceted and pluralistic global context, a broader ecumenical understanding must be cultivated, considering: first, the integration of Catholic, Orthodox, Protestant, Pentecostal, and Charismatic perspectives; and second, fostering meaningful dialogue[266] among Christian traditions and other religious beliefs.

The Christian theological curriculum holds significant potential to advance internal unity efforts and promote open-ended approaches to celebrating oneness in the broader context. The Johannine practice of internal unity and inclusivity can manifest as a tangible reality when the Christian church and inter-religious organisations engage in ecumenical endeavours. This collaborative approach will enhance a broader, ecumenical, and open-ended mission for the church. In India, numerous established

---

[264] See Thomaskutty, "Oneness in John 17:1–26," 5.

[265] See Thomaskutty, "Oneness in John 17:1–26," 5.

[266] See Thomaskutty, "Oneness in John 17:1–26," 5, 6.

theological institutions and universities operate within inter-denominational and ecumenical frameworks. The Senate of Serampore College (SSC) and the Asia Theological Association (ATA) offer exclusive theological degree programs, while a variety of Catholic institutions across India provide programs in diverse disciplines and levels,[267] while also welcoming non-Catholic students.

Recently, secular universities, such as the University of Madras, University of Mysore, Madurai Kamaraj University, and University of Calicut, have begun introducing theological degree programs through their Christian Studies Departments, promoting deeper interactions between Christian theology and various religious or secular fields. This establishment of Christian Studies Departments within secular universities represents a pioneering shift towards organising theological discussions with a broader ecumenical perspective and provides newfound opportunities for public awareness.[268] Today, Christian theology becomes part of a wider academic dialogue, encapsulating an array of perspectives from Catholic and Protestant traditions alongside inter-religious and interdisciplinary viewpoints, finely reflecting a rich tapestry of ideas in these crucial discussions.

Marina Ngursangzeli[269] articulates a critical perspective on the teaching of ecumenism as a worldwide phenomenon, emphasising the necessity for caution in the process of contextualisation. She warns that this practice, while essential for making theology relevant, could inadvertently foster a separation of one context from others. This separation may lead to a troubling form of theological self-isolation, which could significantly impede the mission of theological education for ecumenism. Rather than uniting Christians, this fragmentation occurs not through differences in doctrine but through the distinct, often divergent, contextual theologies unique to various communities. Ngursangzeli underscores the importance of ensuring that these theologies remain relevant to the circumstances in which they are created and lived. Yet, ecumenism challenges us to transcend localised perspectives[270] and engage with a broader, global context.

To navigate this complexity, she draws upon the insights of Catholic theologian Robert Schreiter. His innovative method seeks to promote

---

[267] See Thomaskutty, "Oneness in John 17:1–26," 5, 6.

[268] See Johnson Thomaskutty, "Faith and Theology in the Johannine Community and in the Reformation: A Paradigm in the Indian Context," in W. Kinzig & J. Winnebeck (eds.), Glaube und Theologie: Reformatorische Grundeinsichten in der ökumenischen Diskussion, Evangelische Verlagsanstalt, Leipzig 2019, 75-96.

[269] See Marina Ngursangzeli Behera, "Ecumenism in Theological Education," in *Bangalore Theological Forum,* LIV/1 (June, 2022), 21. Hereafter cited as Marina Ngursangzeli, "Ecumenism in Theological Education."

[270] See Marina Ngursangzeli, "Ecumenism in Theological Education," 21.

interaction among the rich diversity of theological viewpoints, ensuring they engage with and reflect on influences beyond their specific contexts. Ultimately, Ngursangzeli posits that the teaching of ecumenism must thoughtfully incorporate the interplay between local theologies and global influences,[271] fostering a more cohesive and inclusive understanding of faith that transcends borders and cultural barriers.

Conclusion

The examination of the core concepts of ecumenism reveals the intellectual and spiritual depth of a movement devoted to achieving Christian unity. Terms such as comity and reconciliation underscore the practical and relational dimensions of unity, while orthodoxy and conciliarism highlight the theological and structural challenges faced. Wider ecumenism extends the discourse beyond traditional Christian boundaries, advocating for a more inclusive and comprehensive vision of unity. Collectively, these concepts establish a crucial framework that continues to guide ecumenical efforts toward mutual understanding, collaborative testimony, and the reconciliation of divisions within the body of Christ.

[271] See Marina Ngursangzeli, "Ecumenism in Theological Education."

Chapter 9

Different Models of Church Unity

Concepts and frameworks for church unity serve as reflections of the inherent nature and intricate structure of the church's complete visible oneness, which represents the ultimate aspiration of the ecumenical movement. This term is typically associated with the traditional visions of church unity, closely tied to either the formation of united churches or the multilateral dialogues facilitated by the Faith and Order commission within Christian World Communications. Unlike the precision of mathematical or scientific frameworks, these models have succeeded in fostering meaningful dialogue among diverse church communities,[272] illuminating the complex issues, possible options, and critical decisions they face on their journey toward achieving visible unity.

Rather than viewing these various frameworks as competing ideologies, it is essential to understand their collective importance. They support the ecumenical movement in identifying a form of unity that allows all Christians, in their rightful diversity, to feel an authentic sense of belonging to one Body of Christ. This unity empowers them to collectively voice and act on matters of shared faith and life.

---

[272] See Thomas F. Best, "Union, Organic," in Nicholas Lossky, *Dictionary of the Ecumenical Movement,* 2nd ed., edited by Nicholas Lossky, Jose Miquez Bonino, John Poboe, and Tom F. Stransky1 (Geneva: WCC, 2002), 1173-1175. Hereafter cited as Best, "Union, Organic."

9.1. Cooperative Action

The Faith and Order report from the Second World Conference held in Edinburgh from 3 - 18th August 1937 articulates a vision of unity as a confederation or alliance of churches dedicated to collaborative efforts. In realms where shared objectives and tasks align, such cooperation is largely achievable without the need to compromise individual conscience. Church "federations" are recognised as significant manifestations of unity and are regarded as one of the most promising avenues toward understanding and kinship among differing denominations. However, the report underscores that such federations, established for collaborative engagement, should not be misconstrued as embodiments of "federal union."[273]

Some participants expressed a conviction that the aspiration for "federal union" is not merely the ultimate goal they can pursue, but indeed the highest threshold they should aim for. They acknowledged that while cooperation among churches that are unable to attain intercommunion or seek collaborative union is valuable, allowing them to honour their diverse consciences and maintain separate loyalties, this effort does not encompass their ultimate vision. Mere cooperation, they argued, cannot fully convey to the world the authentic essence of the Church[274] as a unified community committed to faith, worship, and service.

9.2. Organic Union

The concept of organic union presents a visionary model that aspires to foster a deep fellowship, allowing historic divisions to fade into the background. In this ideal, transcending barriers becomes not just feasible but essential for a shared witness and collaborative service. Exemplifying this model are the Church of South India and the Church of North India, both of which were established by individuals dedicated to the principles of organic union. This approach involves a comprehensive merger of the participating churches, where distinct structural identities and names yield to a unified structure and identity. The result is an official single church entity, yet within this oneness, diverse expressions of thought and practice flourish[275] in harmony with collectively embraced doctrines, practices, and governance.

---

[273] See Lukas Vischer, *A Documentary History of the Faith and Order Movement,* 1927-63, (USA: WCC, 1963), 61. Hereafter cited as Vischer, A Documentary History.

[274] Vischer, *A Documentary History,* 61, 62.

[275] See V. V. Thomas, "Historical Models of Church Unity," in *History of Ecumenical Movement: Issues,* Challenges and Perspectives, edited by Watimongla Jamir (Kolkata: SCEPRE, 2014), 209.

William Adams Brown[276] characterises organic union, as recognised within the Faith and Order movement, as a formation in which 2 or more previously sovereign bodies unite to create a singular corporate entity endowed with the authority to communicate and act on behalf of the entire body within defined parameters.

The Faith and Order report from the Edinburgh Assembly in 1937 elaborates on this vision, stating that:[277]

> Its members would move freely from one part to another and find every privilege of membership open to them. The sacraments would be the sacraments of the whole body. The ministry would be accepted by all as a ministry of the whole body...In particular, and with immediate reference to the existing world situation, we do not believe that a Church, corporately united, could be an effective international community without some permanent organ of conference and counsel, whatever might be the authority and powers of that organ.

Historically, the Faith and Order movement envisions a church so profoundly united that every member's ultimate allegiance would rest with the whole rather than any individual segment. This envisioned unity resembles that of a vibrant organism, showcasing the diversity integral to the members of a healthy body, as articulated in the Edinburgh 1937 document. The 3rd assembly of the World Council of Churches in New Delhi highlighted the profound institutional transformation required for such unity, indicating it would necessitate "nothing less than a death or rebirth of many forms of church life as we have known them."[278]

This path ultimately leads to the dissolution of denominational identities, making room for new local churches that collectively embody the fullness of Christ's presence in their specific locales. Although no single local union has yet managed to encompass all churches in a given area, this aspirational vision has been partially realised in over 60 united churches established across the globe in the past 2 centuries.[279] As the Body of Christ, the church is aptly described as an organism intricately "joined and knit together by every ligament with which it is equipped as each part is working properly" (Ephesians 4:6).

---

[276] See William Adams Brown, *Toward A United Church: Three Decades of Ecumenical Christianity* (New York: Charles Scribner's Sons, 1946), 51, 52.

[277] Vischer, A Documentary History, 63, 64.

[278] Thomas F. Best, "Unity, Models of," 1173-1175.

[279] See Thomas F. Best, "Unity, Models of," 1173-1175.

Therefore, its unity is accurately characterised as organic. The discussion surrounding organic union often arises when churches striving for closer unity hold differing perspectives on the relationship between unity and diversity within the Body of Christ. Churches that share similar policies have generally navigated the terrain of organic union with greater ease, as demonstrated by numerous intraconfessional unions that occurred throughout the 20th century. The World Missionary Conference in Edinburgh in 1910 engaged in a thorough examination of the merits and drawbacks of both organic and federal forms of church union. Delegates, including the notable Charles Brent, Episcopal Bishop of the Philippines, argued passionately that mere practical cooperation was insufficient; only a united church could extend a credible invitation to followers of the major religions of the East.[280] His advocacy sparked the inaugural call for a world conference on Faith and Order. During the initial gathering of the responding churches in New York in 1913, it was collectively agreed that while organic unity ought to be the ideal for all Christians to hold in their thoughts and prayers, the immediate priority was to patiently explore the underlying reasons for existing disunity.

Dating back to 1870, W. R. Huntington, an American Episcopalian, proposed a bold plan for organic union among American churches, based on what later became known as the Chicago-Lambeth Quadrilateral:[281] scripture, the ancient creeds, the sacraments of baptism and Eucharist, and the historic episcopate. Although this vision would later be overshadowed by federal ideas that led to the establishment of a council of churches in its home country, it nonetheless laid a foundational appeal presented to all Christian people during the Lambeth Conference of 1920. This call envisioned "an outward, visible, and united society, holding one faith, possessing recognised officers, utilising divinely instituted means of grace, and inspiring all members toward the worldwide service of God's kingdom."[282]

This appeal, along with the Anglican initiatives that emerged from it, played a crucial role in ecumenical unity discussions throughout the subsequent 4 decades. The proposal to regard the historic episcopate as the visible focal point for restoring unity was particularly significant and

[280] See Thomas F. Best, "Unity, Models of," 1173-1175.

[281] The Chicago–Lambeth Quadrilateral, frequently referred to as the Lambeth Quadrilateral or the Lambeth–Chicago Quadrilateral, is a four-point articulation of Anglican identity, often cited as encapsulating the fundamentals of the Anglican Communion's doctrine and as a reference point for ecumenical discussion with other Christian denominations.

[282] The sixth Lambeth Conference was held in 1920, delayed by two years on account of the Great War (World War I). 252 Bishops gathered from all over the world, almost all deeply impacted by the long conflict of the preceding years.

became a cornerstone of these dialogues. The World Council of Churches (WCC) establishment in 1948 introduced a new framework within which it was imperative to reassure member churches that their participation in the Council did not obligate them to adhere to any specific interpretation of church union.

This reassurance was articulated in the Toronto statement issued by the WCC's central committee in 1950. This statement emphasised that the Council served as a forum for exploring the concept of unity without predetermining its outcomes, fostering an open discussion environment. The following decade witnessed heightened and earnest discussions concerning the nature and theological implications of the unity being pursued, culminating in the emergence of the New Delhi statement in 1961.[283] Although it stopped short of explicitly using the term "organic union," this statement reflected what is generally understood as an aspiration towards such a union - a profound interconnectedness of churches.

Before this declaration and since, the WCC had never so comprehensively committed to the objective of achieving organic unity among its member churches. However, during the time the New Delhi statement was being formulated, significant developments were reshaping the landscape of ecumenical discourse. Notably, the Eastern Orthodox churches from the Eastern alliance, previously excluded from the Council, became full members and began to exert a considerable influence on its discussions and perspectives. Importantly, none of these Orthodox churches had previously engaged in any conversations about organic union with non-Orthodox communities,[284] which significantly shifted the dynamics at play.

At the same time, the Second Vatican Council (1962-1965) marked a transformative period for the Roman Catholic Church, leading to its complete involvement in Faith and Order discussions for the first time. This active participation brought forth a tremendous wave of influence, catalysing a shift in focus from localised initiatives for organic union to broader relational dynamics among the World Confessional Families, the Catholic Church, and other ecclesiastical bodies. During this period, the idea proposed by Cardinal Willebrands gained traction, suggesting that the objective should evolve from seeking organic unity to fostering coexistence among diverse "types" of church life, a paradigm shift that reflected the changing realities of the Christian landscape. In the ensuing years, while organic intraconfessional unions continued to occur - indicative of a desire

[283] See "Lesslie Newbigin, "Union, Organic," in *The Ecumenical Movement: An Anthology of Key Texts and Voices,* 2nd ed., edited by Michael Kinnamon (Geneva: WCC, 2016), 1160, 1161. Hereafter cited as Newbigin, "Union, Organic."

[284] See Newbigin, "Union, Organic," 1160, 1161.

for deeper collaboration among churches sharing similar convictions - the sole instance in which the Lambeth appeal directly resulted in an organic union between episcopal and non-episcopal churches took place in the Indian subcontinent.[285]

Many other initiatives aimed at fostering organic unity in different regions around the globe encountered significant challenges and ultimately did not succeed. Compounding these difficulties, the Anglican Communion began to lose the influential role it had historically played in spearheading union movements, a stark contrast to its earlier prominence. Additionally, developments in biblical scholarship began to challenge the presuppositions underlying the Lambeth appeal, specifically the belief that the mission of reunion was to restore a previously existing organic unity that had been fragmented over time. A considerable body of New Testament scholarship has contended that such an idealised unity may not have existed even in the earliest church communities.[286] Moreover, the emergence and proliferation of para-church organisations and church-based communities across various regions of the globe have reinforced a growing tendency to transcend the doctrinal divisions that separate major confessions.

These entities often prioritise practical matters of peace, justice, and collaborative social action over traditional ecclesiastical unity discussions. Consequently, the urgency for organic union appears to be diminishing. Nevertheless, as long as churches continue to uphold and cherish the scriptural discourse surrounding the Body of Christ, the topic of organic union will remain a relevant and significant concern. Periodic gatherings of united and uniting churches demonstrate the tangible benefits of consolidations between churches with differing ecclesial structures and traditions.[287] In light of these ongoing endeavours, it remains challenging to envision any ultimate goal other than the profound and enduring aspiration for the organic unity of one body in Christ.

9.3. Conciliar Fellowship

Established during the landmark 5th assembly of the World Council of Churches (WCC) in Nairobi in 1975, the concept of conciliar fellowship emerges not merely as a structural model but as a profound vision aimed at cultivating organic unity among diverse local united churches. These congregations, although separated by various geographical, cultural, or temporal factors, come together periodically to showcase their unity through councils that include representatives from all local churches at different

---

[285] See Newbigin, "Union, Organic," 1160, 1161.

[286] See Newbigin, "Union, Organic," 1160, 1161.

[287] See Newbigin, "Union, Organic," 1160, 1161.

geographical tiers. In this context, the richness of authentic Christian diversity is not viewed through the lens of historical disunity stemming from confessional or denominational divisions. Instead, it reflects the vibrant cultural and geographical diversity of God's people,[288] cultivated through the indigenisation of the Gospel across the myriad regions and cultures of the world.

The term "conciliarity" is derived from "council," signifying both the importance of representation and the significant gathering of the unified church. The English term "council" encompasses a dual meaning: it represents a) a representative assembly of the one, united Church, and b) the provisional fellowship of still-divided churches. Other languages, however, offer more clarity; for instance, in French, "concile" refers specifically to the formal gathering of the unified Church, whereas "conseil" pertains to the fellowship among divided entities.[289]

Defining conciliarity theologically proves to be a complex endeavour, as interpretations vary significantly among the myriad confessional families, churches, and theologians. The initial attempt to elucidate this term was presented at the 1968 Bristol meeting of the Faith and Order Commission, which described conciliarity as an inherent necessity for assemblies that truly represent the Church throughout its history.[290] Conciliarity is viewed as a timeless structure that embodies an essential dimension of the Church's very nature.

The concept of Conciliar Union presents a distinctive form of unity founded on the principle of council, emphasising that all actions within this realm must receive the approval of such councils. Although ecumenists began exploring this theme as early as the 3rd WCC Assembly in New Delhi in 1961, it was the Nairobi Assembly in 1975 that truly crystallised the vision of the Conciliar model of church unity. Conciliar unity is recognised as a fundamentally local phenomenon.

First, the definition underscores the paramount importance of the local church, positioning it as the grassroots origin from which the idea of union springs forth. Second, it envisions a unity that transcends local, national, ethnic, and linguistic divides, advocating for an inclusive and

---

[288] See Thomas F. Best, "Unity, Models of," 1173-1175.

[289] See Aram Keshishian, "Conciliar Fellowship: A Model of Church Unity: the Emergence and Development of Conciliarity in the World Council of Churches," A dissertation submitted in partial fulfilment of the requirements for the degree of doctor of philosophy in the Department of Theology at Fordham University, New York, 1989 11, 12. Hereafter cited as Keshishian, "Conciliar Fellowship."

[290] See "The Importance of the Conciliar Process in the Ancient Church for the Ecumenical Movement," in Councils and the Ecumenical Movement (Geneva: World Council Studies, 1968), 10.

holistic fellowship among local churches. Third, it urges each local church to cultivate a deep sense of belonging within the broader family of local churches, contributing to the collective testimony of all congregations while upholding the bonds of unity among themselves.

Furthermore, local churches united under a conciliar union must establish robust and well-structured frameworks that are capable of nurturing cohesion and addressing the diverse challenges they face.[291] Ultimately, the call is for churches to relinquish previously entrenched animosities, abandon irrelevant condemnations and anathemas, and learn the vital principles of coexistence in love, unity, truth, and hope, all while actively supporting one another in this sacred journey.

The Louvain meeting of the Faith and Order Commission in 1970 offered an expansive interpretation of the term "conciliarity." It defined conciliarity as the gathering of all Christians, whether on local, regional, or global scales, for shared prayer, counsel, and decision-making. This gathering is grounded in the faith that the Holy Spirit can work through such assemblies to achieve the Church's mission of reconciling, renewing, and reforming itself, ultimately guiding it toward the fullness of truth and love.[292] The same meeting identified conciliarity as "an essential feature" of church life, characterising it as the communion that unites diverse local churches.

Meanwhile, the Salamanca consultation of 1974 aimed to refine the concept of conciliarity, asserting that it transcends the gatherings of divided churches, instead highlighting the reciprocal relationships that exist among local churches within the one, undivided Church.[293]

This understanding was wholeheartedly embraced by the Nairobi Assembly, which affirmed that conciliarity is intended to express an aspect of the life of the unified Church at every level. At the Bangalore meeting of the Faith and Order Commission in 1978, the meaning of conciliarity and its variations was interpreted in two distinct, yet interconnected, ways. Firstly, the term may refer to gatherings or assemblies of official representatives from local churches that share a fully united sacramental fellowship. Secondly, it can denote the associations of churches at local, national, regional, and universal levels that have emerged from the ecumenical movement, despite lacking full sacramental communion. The Conference

---

[291] See Paominlen Kipgen, "Church Union Movement – Changing approaches and types of union," https://www.academia.edu/31041030/Church_Union_Movement_Changing_approaches_and_types_of_union (20 May 2025).

[292] See Lukas Vischer, *Faith and Order, Louvain, 1971: Study Reports and Documents* (Geneva: WCC, 1971), p. 226.

[293] See "The Unity of the Church-Next Steps: The Report of Salamanca Consultation of Faith and Order, September 1973," in The Ecumenical Review, 26/2, (April 1974), 293.

of European Churches succinctly described conciliarity as "an attitude in which the Churches express their desire not to live and exist as Christians without others who also call upon the name of Jesus Christ."[294] This notion underscores the church as an eucharistic assembly rooted in a specific location.

Through the celebration of the Eucharist, the church not only exhibits its unity and universality but also relies on the bishop to establish communion with other local churches. The Eucharist is at the heart of conciliar fellowship, with sacramental fellowship serving as its essential foundation. Conciliar fellowship should not be perceived as a stagnant state; rather, it is a dynamic journey. It represents "a way forward," "a goal," and a "vision" that the churches are called to pursue collectively. The current state of ecumenical fellowship is often regarded as a "pre-conciliar fellowship" due to its lack of eucharistic communion and unified faith. Nonetheless, it can be perceived as a framework and instrument guiding the journey toward complete conciliar fellowship.[295] Despite the many ecclesiological challenges that exist, the attainment of conciliar fellowship remains possible.

As the ecumenical landscape evolves, increasing unity and collaborative initiatives, especially at the grassroots level, should eventually pave the way for churches to reach consensus on essential matters such as baptism, the Eucharist, and ministry, as well as to converge in their apostolic faith as the foundation of conciliar fellowship. Although the widely accepted idea that unity must precede conciliar fellowship holds ecclesiological validity, it is often not practically sustainable. The processes of consensus-building, convergence, and the development of common decision-making structures are interdependent and complementary, and thus should progress together.[296] Conciliar fellowship invites churches to remain true to the essence of the Church as a *koinonia*,[297] reflecting the fundamental nature of unity as the communion of local churches.

Initially articulated by the Roman Catholic Church, conciliarity is described as "a complete and substantial communion of local churches among themselves and with the Church of Rome, which oversees the entire assembly of charity." It extends to "Councils of churches and

---

[294] Sharing in *One Hope: Commission on Faith and Order,* Bangalore 1978, Reports and Documents (Geneva: WCC, 1979), 240.

[295] See Keshishian, "Conciliar Fellowship," 13.

[296] See Keshishian, "Conciliar Fellowship," 13.

[297] Koinonia is a Greek term "κοινωνία" that translates to concepts such as fellowship, mutual participation, and collective contributions. This word holds significance in theological contexts, although it is not frequently referenced in discussions. Its implications extend beyond mere social interactions, emphasizing the importance of community and shared experiences.

Christian councils (conseils) ... partnerships of churches and other Christian organisations striving to collaborate, engage in dialogue, and resolve existing divisions and misunderstandings." Among notable theologians, Geoffrey Wainwright, an Anglican scholar, has explored conciliarity from both spatial and temporal dimensions. He delineated a spatial approach into 3 levels: the first level encompasses foundational structures, referring to the interconnectedness of churches based on the salvific work of the Triune God; the second level involves daily practices, which include communication, exchange, mutual assistance, and joint ventures; the third level is represented by the council itself, acting as the culmination or embodiment of the preceding two levels.[298]

9.4. Intercommunion

An important aspect of church unity is encapsulated in the concept of "intercommunion," which embodies the deepest form of mutual recognition among two or more churches. This profound acknowledgement is manifested through shared membership and cooperative ministry, symbolising a commitment to collective faith. The report from 1937[299] underscores the belief that sacramental intercommunion is a fundamental element necessary for achieving genuine church unity.

In its most comprehensive sense, intercommunion signifies a relationship among churches wherein the communion of each is readily accessible to all members of the others at all times. This stands in stark contrast to instances where one church's communion is granted to members of other churches without a full reciprocal acknowledgement of identity and belief.[300] Moreover, it is markedly different from occasional situations where a church permits members from other churches to partake without typically including them in its communion practices.

For a thorough understanding of intercommunion, it is essential to emphasise the importance of regularity and mutual acknowledgement. When addressing church unity through the lens of intercommunion, it is crucial to clearly articulate its definition to avoid misunderstandings. Additionally, we must acknowledge instances where, during collaborative gatherings of Christians striving toward a shared objective, a church extends an invitation to all who hold full standing in their respective congregations to partake in the Holy Communion per the customs of the host church. Such instances occurred notably during the Conferences held in Oxford and

---

[298] See Keshishian, "Conciliar Fellowship," 13.

[299] See Lukas Vischer, *A Documentary History of the Faith and Order Movement, 1927-63,* (USA: WCC, 1963), 61, 62. Hereafter cited as Vischer, A Documentary History.

[300] See Vischer, A Documentary History, 61, 62.

Edinburgh in 1937.[301] It is important to distinguish this practice from the broader perception of intercommunion, as well as from the joint celebration that took place in Jerusalem in 1928, ensuring clarity in the understanding of these significant events.

9.5. Spiritual Model

The concept of spiritual unity represents a profound, yet often abstract, ideal that lacks formalised structures or institutional frameworks. Unlike traditional models of unity that derive authority from creed, governance, or signed agreements, this spiritual model emerges organically from the heart of the faith community. It is an instinctive response to the overarching love for one another, rooted deeply in the teachings of Jesus Christ. In the Gospels, Jesus articulates a vision for spiritual unity that is fundamentally anchored in renewal, faithful commitment, and divine love. He reaches out to individuals who have undergone transformative spiritual experiences, inviting them to accept Him as their Lord and Saviour. In John 10:14-16, He poignantly remarks about having "other sheep" not currently part of His fold, indicating His intention to bring them into a singular community, thus reinforcing His role as the shepherd. This metaphor illustrates that spiritual kinship is not confined by human-made barriers but is bound by a divine call to belong to a larger spiritual family,[302] transcending denominational distinctions and human congregational boundaries.

Unlike formal organisational integrations often characterised by bureaucratic structures, the spiritual model of church union represents a fresh approach to ecumenism, emphasising spiritual fellowship, a shared faith, and a holistic Christian identity. Even as distinct denominations maintain their unique characteristics, this model asserts that genuine unity can be experienced through a collective belief in Jesus Christ, the practice of baptism, and the abiding presence of the Holy Spirit. In John 17:21, Jesus fervently prays, "that they may all be one... so that the world may believe," establishing this unity as essential not only for believers but as a testament to the world of God's love and mission. Integral to this model is the recognition of one another's ministries, sacraments, and Christian legitimacy, which allows for vibrant collaborative efforts without necessitating a merger of governance structures or liturgical traditions. It encourages joint prayer initiatives, worship services, and ecumenical dialogue, thus fostering a spirit of collaboration while cherishing the rich diversity inherent within the body of Christ.

---

[301] See Vischer, A Documentary History, 61, 62.

[302] See Snaitang, A History, 79, 80.

This approach underscores the importance of prayer, worship practices, and spiritual conversations as foundational elements that nurture unity among diverse Christian communities. A significant aspect of this model is spiritual ecumenism, as articulated by documents like the Roman Catholic Church's *Unitatis Redintegratio*.[303] Rather than advocating for a top-down institutional unification, this approach manifests through grassroots initiatives such as interdenominational Bible study, local prayer groups, community service projects, and partnerships aimed at addressing current social issues collectively.

A prime example of the spiritual model in action is the Taizé Community, founded by Brother Roger Schütz in the 1940s. This ecumenical monastic community in rural France embodies the desire for Christians from various backgrounds and traditions to gather in prayer, symbolising the potential for harmony not only within the church but also in the broader world context.[304] This spiritual framework is particularly valuable in contexts where visible unity is sought, yet structural unity remains unattainable due to ongoing theological or ecclesiological divergences. Furthermore, this model can be traced back to movements such as the Pietistic movement, the Evangelical Awakening, and various Student Movements, where individuals from diverse denominational backgrounds united under the shared experiences of regeneration through faith, personal transformation, and a commitment to a lifestyle of prayer and scriptural engagement.

Motivated by the desire to witness and share their faith journeys, these individuals often cultivate deeper connections that bridge doctrinal divides.[305] In essence, the spiritual model of unity invites us to celebrate and engage in a holistic Christian fellowship, recognising that, amid our diversity, our shared faith in Christ forms an unbreakable bond that transcends individual beliefs and practices, illuminating a path toward a more unified expression of the Church.

---

[303] *Unitatis Redintegratio* is the Second Vatican Council's Decree on ecumenism, promulagated by Pope Paul VI in 1964. It affirmed that the Church includes all Christians and is not limited exclusively to the Catholic Church.

[304] See Stephanie Saldana, "Taizé: A Musical Monastic Community, Formed in Response to a Global Crisis, Faces New Ones," https://crss.edu/taize-a-musical-monastic-community-formed-in-response-to-a-global-crisis-faces-new-ones (20 May 2025).

[305] See Snaitang, A History, 79, 80.

Chapter 10

Ecumenism in Northeast India (Tribal Ecumenism) Trials and Emerging Ecumenical Trajectories

10.1. The Emergence of Christianity in Northeast India

10.1.1. Mizoram

In the verdant hills of Mizoram, a remarkable vision emerged when an individual named Darphawka experienced an inspiring dream of transformation. In this vision, he foresaw missionaries arriving to disseminate their faith within his homeland. Upon recognising the significance of this dream, he encouraged his family to embrace the new religion. When the missionaries ultimately arrived, his family became one of the first to convert to Christianity, marking a crucial point in the region's religious evolution.

Historically, Christianity's arrival in Mizoram was aligned with the year 1894, marked by the dedication of Rev. J. H. Lorrain and F. W. Savidge. However, contemporary historians have conducted further research, revealing an alternate narrative. They propose that the foundations of Christianity were laid 3 years earlier, in 1891, when the Welsh Presbyterian missionary Rev. William Williams journeyed to Mizoram from Meghalaya, accompanied by several Khasi associates. This perspective has gained recognition, leading the Mizoram Presbyterian Church to acknowledge Rev. Williams as the first missionary to enter Mizoram.

Following these initial efforts, Rev. J. H. Lorrain and F. W. Savidge established a permanent presence in Aizawl on 11th January 1894, where they diligently ministered until 1900.[306] Their mission in Mizoram significantly advanced when Rev. D. E. Jones joined them on 31st August 1897, also dispatched by the Welsh Presbyterian Mission.[307] Collectively, they laid the groundwork for the Presbyterian Church in Mizoram, originally titled the Welsh Calvinistic Methodist Church.

A significant moment in the religious history of the region occurred on 25th June 1899, with the first baptism of a Mizo convert.[308] Although initially directed by his benefactor, Robert Arthington, to expand into Arunachal Pradesh, Rev. Lorrain's enduring desire for Mizoram prompted his return in 1903.[309] With the backing of the London Baptist Missionary Society, he ventured into the southern areas of the region, specifically Lunglei, where he and his colleagues established the Baptist Church of Mizoram in 1903.[310] Consequently, Mizoram developed into a tapestry of faith characterised by the Presbyterian missions in the north and the Baptist initiatives in the south. Presently, the religious landscape features approximately 80 denominations, with prominent groups including the Presbyterian Church, Baptist Church, Salvation Army, United Pentecostal Church, Roman Catholic Church, Lairam Isua Krista Baptist Kohhran, Evangelical Church of Maraland, and Seventh Day Adventist Church, among various indigenous beliefs.

10.1.2. Arunachal Pradesh

The narrative of Christianity's introduction to Arunachal Pradesh illustrates a fusion of missionary zeal and official endorsement. In the initial phases, foreign missionaries, supported by British officials, embarked on endeavours to propagate the faith. The first attempt was led by the Baptist Missionary Society (BMS) under the direction of political agent David Scott, culminating in the establishment of a crucial mission station in Guwahati. This initiative aimed to engage both the plains and the mountainous communities, including the Adi tribe of Arunachal Pradesh.

In 1836, at the behest of Chief Commissioner Francis Jenkins, American Baptists dispatched Nathan and Eliza Brown to Sadiya, thereby

---

[306] See Lalfakawma Ralte, "Revival in Mizoram as Resistance Movement from 1987 to the Present," D.Th. Dissertation, Senate of Serampore College, 2023, 97. Hereafter cited as Lalfakawma Ralte, "Revival as Resistance."

[307] Lalfakawma Ralte, "Revival as Resistance," 101.

[308] See John Hughes Morris, *The Story of our Foreign Mission* (Liverpool: Hugh Evans & Sons Ltd, 1930), 80.

[309] See Lalfakawma Ralte, *Ni leh Thla Betute Zinga Pathian Hnathawh Ropui* (Wondrous Works of God in Arunachal Pradesh), reprinted (Aizawl: Lalchamliana, 2013), 50. Hereafter cited as Lalfakawma Ralte, Ni leh Thla.

[310] See Lalfakawma Ralte, "Revival as Resistance," 105.

enhancing their missionary activities in the region.[311] Over the years, numerous missionaries - including Father Nicholas Michel Krick, Dr. N. E. Grass, John Firth, Rev. J. H. Lorrain, F.W. Savidge, L. W. B. Jackman, and Reverend John Selender - dedicated their lives to this challenging work.

Approaching the 1960s, missionaries from Northeast India, particularly from Mizoram and Nagaland, began exploring deeper into the region. Pioneers such as L. Dothuama, H. Lalzinga, Reverend Rokhuma, C. Zathuama, and Zakamlova played essential roles as initial missionaries, paving the way for a new spiritual awakening.[312] Research on "The Impact of Christianity among the Adi Tribe of Arunachal Pradesh"[313] reveals that indigenous communities welcomed Christianity with enthusiasm, especially after local missionaries from Mizoram and Nagaland took the initiative during the postcolonial era. While the initial advocates were indeed foreign missionaries, it was ultimately the faithful individuals from Northeast India who emerged as the true forerunners in facilitating transformative change within their communities.

10.1.3. Meghalaya

The history of Christianity in Meghalaya commences with the conversion of 2 significant figures, U Dawan and U Anna, who were baptised in 1813 CE. As the first recorded converts among the indigenous population of Northeast India, their baptism marks the beginning of a new spiritual epoch in the region. Krishna Chandra Pal, following an 8-month tenure in Pandua, successfully baptized seven individuals - comprising 4 sepoys, 2 Khasi natives, and 1 from Assam.[314] Although Pal's missionary efforts among the Khasis were relatively brief, they were significant in that they contributed to the inclusion of the Khasi language in the broader initiative undertaken by Serampore to translate the Scriptures[315] into various languages.

Alexander B. Lish was appointed to the Khasi Hills by the Serampore Mission following the tenure of Krishna Pal. Upon his arrival, he established 3 schools in the regions of Mawmluh, Mawsmai, and Cherrapunji, which collectively hosted 36 pupils. Lish quickly forged strong friendships with the local Khasi community, demonstrating a deep respect for their culture and traditions. Unfortunately, his time in Khasi Hills was cut short when

---

[311] See Lalfakawma Ralte, *Ni leh Thla,* 47.

[312] See Lalfakawma Ralte, *Ni leh Thla,* 56-65.

[313] Lalfakawma Ralte, "The Impact of Christianity among the Adi Tribe of Arunachal Pradesh," M.Th. dissertation, Senate of Serampore College, 2004.

[314] See Frederick S. Downs, *History of Christianity in India, Volume V, Part 5 – Northeast India in the Nineteenth and Twentieth Centuries,* reprint (Bangalore: CHAI, 2003), 66. Hereafter cited as Downs, History of Christianity.

[315] See Downs, History of Christianity, 66.

he fell seriously ill with lung inflammation in November 1838. Following medical advice, he left the Khasi Hills[316] to seek treatment in Calcutta.

The history of Christianity's introduction and establishment in the Khasi and Jaintia Hills gained momentum with the arrival of the Welsh Calvinistic Methodist Mission. Thomas Jones, a pioneering missionary, was the first to reach the Khasi Hills, landing in Cherrapunji on 22nd June 1841. He not only focused on evangelism but also placed a strong emphasis on education; he introduced primary schooling and laid the foundation for a more structured educational framework. Jones took innovative measures to prepare local young men for teaching positions, ensuring that they were equipped to educate their peers in various villages. His quest extended beyond the Khasi Hills into the Jaintia Hills and the Ri-War region as he diligently searched for suitable villages to establish mission fields[317] and set up additional schools, aiming to spread both literacy and the Christian faith throughout the area.

In 1847, Francis Jenkins, succeeding David Scott as the commissioner of Assam, took a significant step towards education and cultural exchange by establishing a school in Goalpara, strategically located near the Assam-Garo Hills border. This institution admitted several Garo boys, marking a pivotal moment in the interaction between British colonial education and indigenous cultures. Among the students, two notable individuals, Omed Watre Momin and Ramkhe Watre Momin, excelled in their studies and eventually converted to Christianity, a transformation that was likely influenced by a pamphlet produced by the Serampore Mission, which aimed to spread Christian teachings in the region.[318] In 1863, after their baptism in Guwahati - an important religious and cultural centre - they were inspired to contribute to their community's spiritual life.

However, when the American Baptist Mission encountered challenges in finding missionaries to serve in the Garo Hills, Omed and Ramkhe made the courageous decision to leave their secular jobs. They dedicated themselves to missionary work within their own community, addressing the spiritual needs of their people despite facing considerable opposition from traditionalists who resisted the encroachment of foreign religions. Their commitment bore fruit when American Baptist missionary Miles

---

[316] See A. Jayakumar, *History of Christianity in India: Major Themes* (Kolkata: Sceptre, 3013), 231, 232. Hereafter cited as Jayakumar, History of Christianity.

[317] See Jayakumar, *History of Christianity.*

[318] See Lalsangkima Pachuau, "Church-Mission Dynamics in Northeast India," in International *Bulletin of Missionary Research*, *27*(4), (2003), 154-161. https://doi.org/10.1177/239693930302700402 (21 May 2025). Hereafter cited as Pachuau, "Church-Mission Dynamics."

Bronson visited the Garo Hills in April 1867.[319] During his visit, he found that 37 Garos were ready for baptism, a testament to the Momin brothers' successful outreach efforts. Bronson baptised these individuals, marking the establishment of the first Garo church. In recognition of Omed's leadership and dedication, he was ordained as the minister of this fledgling congregation, laying the foundation for future Christian communities in the region. This moment not only solidified the presence of Christianity among the Garo people but also initiated a profound transformation[320] within their cultural landscape.

10.1.4. Manipur

The introduction of Christian missionaries in Manipur can be traced back to the aftermath of the Anglo-Manipur War in 1891.[321] Before the 19th century, Christianity was relatively unknown in the princely state of Manipur.[322] The American Baptist Mission in Myanmar was the first entity to attempt the establishment of a mission station in Manipur as early as 1836.[323] The arrival of Christianity in Manipur can be summarised in 2 distinct phases:

10.1.4.1. The Establishment of the Arthington Aborigines Mission

In 1885, Robert Arthington of Leeds, England, communicated his intent to the Assam Baptist Mission (ABM) to initiate missionary work among the Singphos, proposing a station at Mankum or Ledo in Upper Assam.[324] However, this initiative did not come to fruition at that time. The Arthington Aborigines Mission (AAM), a private endeavour founded by Robert Arthington, primarily aimed to preach the Gospel of Jesus Christ to non-believers, rather than to focus on literature or translation efforts.[325] Christianity was firmly established in Manipur following the extensive network of missionary activities that had already been undertaken in the

---

[319] See Pachuau, "Church-Mission Dynamics," 2.

[320] See Pachuau, "Church-Mission Dynamics," 2.

[321] See Adakho Poji K, "Advent of Christianity in Manipur and its Impact on the Mao Naga Tribe," *Indian Church History Review,* 44/1 (June, 2010): 67.

[322] See Lazar Jayaseelan, "Christianity in Manipur," in *A Concise Encyclopaedia of Christianity in India*, edited by Errol D' Lima (Pune: Jnana-Deepa Vidyapeeth, 2014), 232. Hereafter cited as Jayaseelan, "Christianity in Manipur."

[323] See Lal Dena, *Christian Missions and Colonialism: A Study of Missionary Movement in North East India with Particular Reference to Manipur and Lushai Hills 1894-1947* (Shillong: Vendrame Institute, 1988), 31.

[324] See Milton S. Sangma, *History of the American Baptist Mission in North-East India (1836-1950): Vol.I* (New Delhi: Mittal Publications, 1987), 273.

[325] See Lawmsanga, *Theology of Mission: Postcolonial Perspective* (Aizawl: Lalmuanpuii, 2016), 76.

remote areas of Assam by various Mission Societies, including CBCNEI, the Presbyterian Church, and the Roman Catholic Church.[326]

The first missionary to enter Manipur with the endorsement of British officials, specifically A. Porteous, the acting Political Agent, was Pettigrew from the AAM Society.[327] Pettigrew faced multiple rejections regarding entry into Manipur until the British authority had been fully established. Once this occurred, he received permission to proceed and arrived in Imphal, the state capital, on 6th February 1894.[328] Through the endeavours of the ABM, the initial baptism in Manipur was conducted by U. M. Fox in December 1914[329] while Pettigrew was on leave.[330] By 1917, Pettigrew had successfully established 335 church members and 5 churches.[331] The increasing number of local churches and the expansion of the missionary outreach led to the formation of the Manipur Christian Association (MCA) in November 1916, whose inaugural convention took place in Ukhrul in 1917. In 1928, the MCA was renamed the Manipur Baptist Convention (MBC).[332]

10.1.4.2. The Establishment of the Welsh Presbyterian Mission

The introduction of the Gospel to the Southwestern part of Manipur is closely associated with the contributions of Watkin Roberts. It was Roberts, in conjunction with Peter Fraser, who journeyed to the Lushai hills (present-day Mizoram) in December 1908, thereby facilitating the dissemination of the Gospel to the southern hills of Manipur in 1910.[333]

---

[326] K. M. Singh, *History of Christian Missions in Manipur and other Neighbouring States* (New Delhi: Mittal Publications, 1991), 53. Hereafter cited as Singh, History of Christian Mission,

[327] Frederick S. Downs, *The Mighty Works of God,* revised edition (Guwahati: Christian Literature Centre, 2014), 64. Hereafter cited as Downs, The Mighty Works of God.

[328] M. Thongkhosei Hoakip, *Ecumenism among the Kukis of North East India* (Secunderabad: The Author, 2016), 65. Hereafter cited as Hoakip, Ecumenism among.

[329] An American Baptist missionary who had served several years in Manipur. See, Kim Vaiphei, The Coming of Christianity in Manipur with Special Reference to the Kukis (Delhi: Joint Women's Programme, 1995), 12. Hereafter cited as Vaiphei, The Coming of Christianity.

[330] Vaiphei, *The Coming of Christianity*, 12.

[331] Milton S. Sangma, *History of American Baptist Mission in North East India: Vol.I* (Dibrugarh: NEIHA, 1981), 191.

[332] See Lal Dena, *Christian Missions and Colonialism: A Study of Missionary Movement in North East India with Particular Reference to Manipur and Lushai Hills 1894-1947.* Shillong: Vendrame Institute, 1988. Hereafter cited as Dena, Christian Missions.

[333] See Dena, Christian Missions, 49.

10.1.5. Tripura

Christianity came to Tripura originally without missionary efforts. Christians entered Tripura for the first time in 1683 when the Tripura Maharaja hired Portuguese Catholic mercenary artillerymen to repulse the Mughal. They began to reside in the then capital Udaipur and migrated along with the capital to Agartala to rent-free land allotted to them, becoming canoniers and farmers.[334]

They gave their settlement the name Mariamnagar, though they were hardly familiar with Christianity. Sambhu C. Mukherjee, a Tripura king's minister, who went to visit them in 1887, characterised them as proud, introverted, uneducated, and physically and morally deplorably degraded. While recognising their existence, the church in Tripura does not recognise them as the individuals who pioneered the Gospel to Tripura. With a Maharaja's invitation, Felix Carey, son of William Carey, came to Tripura,[335] but no missionaries accompanied him.

Rev. John Tackle, a New Zealand missionary, sought permission to labour in Tripura in 1899 but to no avail. Nevertheless, after 6 years, he was allowed to send 2 Bengali Christian workers, not, however, permitted to preach and limited to within the city of Agartala. Until the early part of the 20th century, efforts by missionaries to get into Tripura were unsuccessful, and no one could evangelise on account of the forbiddance by the palace. A band of Mizos from Mizoram settled in Tripura in 1911, among them some 45 Christians, including the family of their chief, Hrangvunga Sailo.[336] Due to the evangelistic work among the people by these Mizo Christians, Christianity gradually spread fast in north Tripura in the early 20th century as they evangelised among their own people and other tribal communities around them, such as the Darlong and Reang societies.

Around the same period, a considerable number of Garo Christian families and some Bengali Christians also moved into Tripura from present-day Bangladesh. But unlike the Portuguese Catholics and similar to the Miso Christians, they were shy and kept to themselves and soon became immersed in society following other religions[337] and lost their Christian identity and passion.

---

[334] See Samuel Lalduhsaka, *Striving for a Missional Mandate: Tripura Baptist Christian Union from Missional Church Perspective* (Agartala: Tripura Academy of Integrated Christian Studies, 2016), 6. Hereafter cited as Lalduhsaka, Striving.

[335] See Lalduhsaka, Striving, 7.

[336] See Sukhendu Debbarma, *Origin and Growth of Christianity in Tripura with Special Reference to the New Zealand Baptist Missionary Society 1938-1988* (New Delhi: Indus Publishing Company, 1996), 29.

[337] See Lalduhsaka, Striving, 9.

The New Zealand Baptist Missionary Society (NZBMS) came into Tripura following issues in another mission in another state, namely the Thadou-Kuki Pioneer Mission in Manipur. The Miso Christians in Jampui with their village of Phuldungsei were ministered to using pastoral care through the Welsh Presbyterian Mission in Mizoram. But in 1913, their contribution of Rs. 94.00/- was denied because it was not feasible for the mission to provide pastoral care to them[338] when they had settled in another region.

The new converts of Christians in Tripura sought the assistance of Watkin R. Roberts, who had begun the Thadou-Kuki Pioneer Mission (TKPM) in Senvawn, Manipur. Roberts sent them 3 evangelists in 1916, resulting in further Christians there as well as among the Darlong,[339] Reang, and Kuki tribes in Tripura. The TKPM was renamed Northeast India General Mission (NEIGM) in 1923, and in 1933, the Mizo mission work extended to Howaibari,[340] merely 20 miles east of Agartala.

The NEIGM withdrew its mission at Hawaibari in 1934; hence, Christians at Hawaibari called urgently to NZBMS through Rev. H. A. Jones at Brahmanbaria. In 1937, NZBMS sent Rev. M. J. Eade to work towards developing work in Tripura. Eade wrote an application to the Maharaja to enable them to work in Tripura. The Maharaja granted this permission while forbidding them from preaching to two tribes, the Halams and Reangs.[341] Following this, Christianity also gained ground in the state of Tripura.

In a vital moment for missionary work in the region, 1938 saw the New Zealand Baptist Mission, which was previously active in what is now Bangladesh, receive formal authorisation to extend its operations into Tripura. By December of that year, this mission successfully established the Tripura Baptist Christian Union (TBCU). This organisation united around 100 Christian converts, predominantly from the Garos and Kukis communities, who resided in Tripura, creating a foundation for Christian fellowship and worship. TBCU was managed by missionaries from the New Zealand Baptist Mission, who played a crucial role in nurturing the nascent Christian community until the early 1970s when the last missionary departed from Tripura. The Mizo Church, then known as the Jampui Presbytery, formally joined TBCU in 1940, further consolidating the Christian community in the state. The Darlong Church followed suit

---

338 See Lalduhsaka, Striving, 9.

339 See Pachuau, "Church-Mission Dynamics," 4, 5.

340 See Lalduhsaka, Striving, 9.

341 See M. J. Eade, "Beginnings," in *Towards the Sunrise: the Centenary History of the New Zealand Baptist Missionary Society,* edited by Angus H. MacLeod (Wellington: NZBHC, 1985), 152.

in 1944, marking a significant expansion in the Union's membership and influence,[342] ultimately contributing to the growth of Christianity within Tripura's diverse cultural tapestry.

10.1.6. Nagaland

The names Edward Winter Clark and his spouse, Mary Mead Clark, are closely associated with the pioneering missionary efforts directed towards the Ao-Nagas, an indigenous group in India. A significant figure in this initiative was Godhula, an Assamese convert frequently recognised as Clark's right-hand man. Upon receiving the Christian name Rufus Brown, Godhula undertook the important task of learning the fundamentals of the Ao language, which proved essential for effective communication with the local populace. In October 1871, he courageously entered the Ao territory without awaiting Clark's authorisation. Despite encountering hostility and threats to his life, including a brief period of incarceration, Godhula demonstrated remarkable resilience by successfully disseminating the message of peace and divine love among the Ao people. His persistent endeavours culminated in the formation of the first group of nine converts, who were later baptized by Clark in November 1872.[343]

Following these initial accomplishments, Clark relocated to Ao land in 1876 to advance his evangelistic mission. He adopted a multifaceted approach that encompassed preaching, the establishment of schools, and engagement in literary activities aimed at nurturing the burgeoning Christian community. Nevertheless, the early years of his mission experienced only limited conversions, as many local individuals found the Christian lifestyle challenging to adopt.[344] Subsequent missionaries often overlooked the original members of this nascent congregation, opting instead for a complete restructuring of the church.

Encouraged by Clark's efforts, additional mission stations were established among the Angami-Nagas and, briefly, among the Lotha-Nagas. Notably, C. D. King emerged as a pioneering missionary among the Angami-Nagas, commencing his influential work in 1879. Although he benefited from the protective support of the British administration, immediate visible results in terms of conversions remained scarce. During this period, evangelistic efforts led by Caleph, together with his Assamese associate Biney, involved extensive preaching tours that significantly contributed to the growth of the Ao communicant membership towards the late 19th century. As the first half of the 20th century progressed, an extraordinary

---

[342] See Pachuau, "Church-Mission Dynamics," 4, 5.

[343] See Pachuau, "Church-Mission Dynamics," 3.

[344] See Pachuau, "Church-Mission Dynamics," 3.

increase in conversions occurred among the Sema-Nagas, propelled by a wave of native evangelists who assumed responsibility for disseminating the Christian faith. This grassroots movement among the Semas is frequently characterised as a mass movement,[345] reflecting the profound and enduring impact of the early missionary endeavours in the region.

10.1.7. Assam

The early Christian engagement with Northeast India commenced in 1626, spearheaded by Jesuit missionaries, notably Reverend Stephen Cacell and J. Gabral, whose primary objective was to discover a passage to China and Tibet.[346] The inaugural Christian settlement in this region emerged at Rangamati, located in the Goalpara District of Assam. In 1696, Father Frey Sicardo, an Augustinian priest, documented the existence of two churches in Bencomatis' camp, which lies on the borders of Assam within the Mughal Empire.[347] These churches were dedicated to Our Lady of the Rosary and Our Lady of Guadalupe, respectively. Frederick S. Downs posits that the profiles of these early Christian communities laid the groundwork for what would become the Rangammati community. This viewpoint is reinforced by Fr. F. T. Laynez in January 1715, who held jurisdiction over S. Tome-Mylapore and suggested a historical continuity with Sicardo's observations.[348]

Downs theorises that these communities were not only situated in the same geographical area as modern Rangammati but also represent the historic Rangammati of Goalpara, referred to in some texts as Darrang Rangamatighat.[349] However, both Catholic churches mentioned ceased to function in 1765, concurrent with the Mughal cession of Bengal and Sylhet to the East India Company.[350] Documentation regarding early Roman Catholic endeavours is sparse due to the absence of established ecclesiastical structures. Downs further conjectures that the Christians in these locations

---

[345] See Joseph Puthenkurakal, *Baptist Missions in Nagaland: A Study in Historical and Ecumenical Perspective* (Shillong: Vendrame Missiological Institute, 1984), 72.

[346] See S. K., Bhuyan, *Early British Relations with Assam* (Shillong: the Department of Historical and Antiquarium Studies in Assam, 1949), 3.

[347] Quoted from H. Holsten, "The Earliest Recorded Episcopal Visitations of Bengal, 1712-1715," Bengal Past and Present VI (1910): 212 by Frederick S. Downs, "Rangammati: A Christian Community in North-East India During the Seventeenth and Eighteenth Centuries," ICHR, XII/2 (1972): 90.

[348] See Zadingluaia Chinzah, "History of Christianity in Assam: A Subaltern Perspective," a paper presented at M.Th. class seminar, Aizawl Theological College, 1 February, 2019.

[349] See Downs, "Rangammati," 91.

[350] C. Becker, *History of the Catholic Missions in North East India* (1890-1915), translated & edited by S. Stadler & S. Karotemprel (Shillong: Vedrame Missiological Institute, 1980), 99-103.

may have been part of the Mughal contingent - possibly numbering around 63,000 troops - that Aurangzeb dispatched against the Ahoms in 1669, or they could represent the initial repercussions of Jesuit missionary activities directed towards the Mughal court[351] during the sixteenth and seventeenth centuries.

The Serampore Mission commenced its missionary efforts in 1829 by founding a school in Guwahati, responding to a request from David Scott, the inaugural British commissioner of Assam. This initial educational establishment focused on providing quality instruction and promoting literacy among the local population. However, it faced challenges and ultimately closed its doors in 1836. Undeterred, the mission quickly established a new school in Cherrapunji, known for its abundant rainfall and stunning natural beauty, which became a hub for their educational initiatives.[352]

Simultaneously, in 1836, the American Baptist Mission had intended to extend its outreach to China but shifted its focus to the Northeastern region of Assam due to emerging travel constraints. As a result, the missionaries dedicated their efforts to evangelism and community development within Assam, engaging with local cultures, languages, and needs to foster a lasting impact in the region.[353] This pivot marked a significant turning point in the history of missionary work in Northeastern India, as it laid the groundwork for future educational and religious initiatives.

10.2. Attempts at the Formation of Church Union in Northeast India

The early 20th century marked significant developments regarding church unity in Northeast India, characterised by both promise and contention. In 1926, the Bengal Christian Council, an umbrella organisation that included churches from the Northeast region, expressed a willingness to join the proposed Church of North India (CNI). However, representatives from Northeast India, citing their unique geographical and cultural identities, ultimately chose not to join the CNI. This decision led to their withdrawal from the Bengal Christian Council, indicating an early divergence in the pursuit of unity.

By 1936, a crucial advancement in fostering unity occurred when eight mission representatives convened in Shillong. These missions included the American Baptist Mission, Santal Mission of the Northern Churches,

---

[351] See F. S. Downs, "Early Christian Contacts with North East India," in ICHR V/1, (June, 1971): 69, 70.

[352] See A. Jayakumar, *History of Christianity in India: Major Themes* (Kolkata: Sceptre, 3013), 230. Hereafter cited as Jayakumar, History of Christianity.

[353] See Jayakumar, History of Christianity, 230.

Gossner Evangelical Lutheran Mission, Cooperative Baptist Mission of North America, English Baptist Mission, Welsh Presbyterian Mission, the Church of God, and the Church of India. This gathering resulted in the establishment of the Assam Christian Council, which was subsequently rebranded as the Northeast India Christian Council (NEICC) in 1938,[354] reflecting a broader ambition for collaboration among diverse Christian communities.

The period from 1937 to 1977 witnessed a vigorous movement toward church union, with numerous consultations and meetings taking place in Shillong and Guwahati. In 1963, the NEICC convened in Kalimpong and urged the Church Union Committee to intensify efforts towards unification. This initiative culminated in the first North East Faith and Order Conference, held at Union Christian College (UCC) in Barapani from 7-10th January 1964. The conference featured 24 delegates representing twelve constituent bodies[355] and resolved to earnestly explore the potential for church union.

In 1965, the Church Union Committee, established by the NEICC, presented the inaugural draft for a basis of union, which garnered approval and momentum for future conferences, including:[356]

- The First Church Union Conference held in Shillong from 27-30th November 1965, which formally initiated discussions.
- The Second Church Union Conference, convened in Shillong during 19-20th September 1969, where a drafting committee was formed to develop the Plan of Union and the Draft Constitution for the Church of Northeast India.

By 1970, these documents were presented to the Council, which tentatively accepted the Draft but subsequently distributed it for feedback to affiliate bodies in July. Unfortunately, responses varied, with disagreements primarily centred around contentious issues such as baptism, episcopacy, and centralised organisational structures.

The Council of Baptist Churches in Northeast India (CBCNEI), representing a substantial segment of the region's Christian population, emerged as a significant barrier to unification. 1977 represented a crucial moment when the CBCNEI and the Cachar Hill Tribes Synod withdrew from the NEICC, effectively bringing the church union movement to a standstill. The main problems were on grounds of baptism, episcopacy,

[354] See Snaitang, A History, 161.

[355] See M. Thankhosei Haokip, *A History of Ecumenical Movement in Northeast India with Special Reference to the Northeast India Christian Council* (Delhi: ISPCK, 2015), 167, 168. Hereafter cited as Haokip, A History.

[356] See Haokip, A History, 168.

and centralised organisation.[357] Despite subsequent attempts in the new millennium to revive this vision of unity, such initiatives regrettably did not yield successful outcomes.

10.3. Challenges to Church Union Negotiations (A Period of Trials)

10.3.1. Doctrinal Factors

Deep-rooted doctrinal differences, particularly concerning the interpretation and significance of baptism, have significantly complicated efforts toward achieving unity among Christian denominations in Northeast India. While a multitude of doctrinal issues exists, the most pressing barrier to discussion about union is the divergent views on baptism. In this context, the differences are starkly pronounced between Baptist churches and denominations that practice infant baptism, such as Catholic and certain Protestant traditions. The ecclesiological understanding of baptism plays a crucial role in these differences, impacting not only the act of baptism itself but also the broader concept of church unity.

For Baptist churches, baptism is often viewed primarily as a symbol of personal faith and conversion - a public declaration of an individual's commitment to follow Christ, rather than a rite of initiation into the church community. This perspective emphasises the personal relationship between the believer and God, underscoring the importance of a conscious decision to accept Christ.[358] In contrast, denominations that baptise infants typically perceive baptism as a sacrament that initiates individuals into the faith community, fostering a sense of belonging to the church from an early age. This view is rooted in a belief in the covenantal nature of baptism, which includes the idea that the grace of God is bestowed upon the child, regardless of their understanding or decision.

Adding to this complexity, while there are Baptist churches around the world that have embraced a more inclusive approach due to ongoing ecumenical discussions - acknowledging the validity of baptisms performed in other traditions - Baptist churches within the Council of Baptist Churches in Northeast India (CBCNEI) remain hesitant.[359] These churches stand firm in their refusal to recognise any form of baptism outside their own tradition, which further entrenches the divide and hinders progress toward unity among the diverse Christian groups in the region.

---

[357] Haokip, A History, 169.

[358] See Dogmar Heller, "Baptism – the Basis of Church Unity? The Question of Baptism in Faith and Order," in *The Ecumenical Review*, 50/4, (October, 1998), 484-485.

[359] See Haokip, *A History*, 175.

10.3.2. Influence of Ultra-Conservative Theology

The influence of ultra-conservative theology, which engendered scepticism about church union, contributed to an atmosphere of uncertainty. Publications such as "A Red Paper" by C. Goldsmith, a member of the Jorhat Baptist Church, "A Picture of an Organic Church Union" by T. Likok from Nagaland, and "Now and Near Future" by Dan E. Staton further obfuscated dialogue among congregations.

10.3.3. Communalism

F. S. Downs articulated that the challenges of church union extended beyond mere denominational affiliations. He highlighted profound divisions between churches rooted in British and American traditions. Despite efforts to adapt, these churches often remain bound to their colonial legacies, complicating the establishment of a collective identity. The perspectives of varied tribes, each with distinct aspirations and identities, frequently overshadowed regional unity,[360] reinforcing a culture of tribalism.

10.3.4. Form of Worship

In Northeast India, worship styles demonstrate significant diversity, ranging from formal, liturgical practices that often incorporate structured prayers and hymns to more spontaneous and charismatic expressions characterised by emotional engagement and personal testimonies. This variety presents considerable challenges[361] in achieving a unified approach to worship among congregations.

10.3.5. Ecclesiastical Organisations

The religious landscape encompasses a mixture of Episcopal and non-Episcopal church structures, reflecting a broad spectrum of beliefs and governance styles. Notably, the Baptists have emerged as the most influential denomination within the non-Episcopal category, establishing a substantial presence especially in Nagaland through their emphasis on believers' baptism[362] and congregational autonomy.

10.3.6. Ecclesiastical Rituals and Lifestyle

Members of Northeast India's religious communities frequently share a common reverence for scripture; however, the introduction of new theological interpretations, divergent views on lifestyle choices, including smoking, chewing betel nuts, and attending cinematic productions,

---

[360] See Downs, *History of Christianity,* 129.

[361] See Sohan K. Mallick, "The Northeast India Church Union Movement," Academia. Edu., 3. Hereafter cited as Mallick, "The Northeast India."

[362] See Mallick, "The Northeast India," 3.

influences considerations[363] related to church membership and clergy ordination.

10.3.7. Churches' Internal Problems and Splits

The religious community has experienced ongoing internal conflicts and fragmentation due to unresolved tensions surrounding doctrinal differences and social issues, which have contributed to factionalism. This fragmentation has given rise to numerous independent churches, each possessing its own interpretations and practices, thereby creating additional obstacles to unity in faith and fellowship within the broader religious landscape of New England.

10.3.8. Denominational Ecumenism

Throughout the region, various denominational churches were established by missionaries from different Christian traditions. Many of these churches maintained their distinct sectarian practices and beliefs, often hindering joint efforts to foster unity among the diverse congregations. This challenge is further complicated by deep-seated theological differences and a prevailing mindset that views one's own faith as the exclusive and true path to salvation,[364] while perceiving other beliefs as misguided or incorrect.

Moreover, there is a pervasive concern that a united church might dilute the unique character and identity that each denomination holds dear. Many church leaders and congregants alike argue that their particular denomination is better equipped to meet the specific needs of the community, addressing local issues more effectively through tailored programs and outreach initiatives. This belief in the superiority of their own practices often leads to reluctance in exploring collaborative worship or joint community service projects,[365] ultimately perpetuating divisions within the broader Christian community.

10.4. The North East India Christian Council (NEICC)

The churches in North East India, formerly known as Assam, were initially affiliated with the Bengal Christian Council. However, this connection did not yield significant outcomes in terms of collaborative efforts or impactful initiatives. In 1936, responding to a need for greater unity and support among churches in the region, the Welsh Presbyterians took a proactive step by convening in Shillong.[366] Their goal was to unite various Christian

---

[363] See Mallick, "The Northeast India."

[364] See Haokip, A History, 180.

[365] See Haokip, A History, 175.

[366] See Mallick, "The Northeast India," 2, 3.

denominations to collaboratively address pressing issues and enhance mutual assistance.

As a result of these efforts, the Assam Christian Council (ACC) was formally established in 1937. The inaugural meeting of the ACC took place in December 1938 and was notable for the participation of representatives from 8 distinct denominations, demonstrating a commitment to interdenominational cooperation in the region. After several years of collaboration, the ACC decided to end its association with the Bengal Christian Council in 1945,[367] seeking a more independent and self-defined path for its member churches.

In 1962, reflecting an evolving mission and broader regional representation, the ACC was renamed the North East India Christian Council (NEICC). The records from the 8th session of the ACC, conducted in Shillong in 1945, contain a significant statement and resolution recommending the establishment of a committee focused on church union. During this session, the council urged its affiliated organisations to formally authorise the formation of this committee. In response to the growing desire for unity, the committee was subsequently established to explore the feasibility and implications of creating a unified church in Assam,[368] emphasising the ongoing commitment to collaboration and solidarity among Christian communities in the region.

The NEICC functions as the collective voice and unified expression of Protestant churches in Northeast India. Its mission is to promote Christian unity and foster a common witness among the diverse denominations in the region. With 35 affiliated bodies and 12 associate members representing the 8 states of Northeast India, the Council embodies a rich tapestry of faith communities. The affiliated organisations include significant bodies such as the Council of Baptist Churches in Northeast India (CBCNEI), the Presbyterian Church of India (PCI), and the ICI.

Meanwhile, the associate members primarily consist of essential para-church organisations, such as the YMCA, the Student Christian Movement (SCM) of Northeast India, CASA, NEICORD, and World Vision. The Council's headquarters is situated in the scenic city of Shillong. The NEICC operates through 7 foundational programmes that address various aspects of Christian life and community engagement, including Christian Home, Church Union, Theological Education, Civil Rights and Public Relations, Relief and Development, Mission and Evangelism, and Land and Property.

---

[367] See Mallick, "The Northeast India," 2, 3.

[368] See Mallick, "The Northeast India," 2, 3.

10.4.1. Common Project

In recognition of the necessity for a collaborative initiative, the Council embarked upon the ambitious project of establishing and maintaining the Union Christian College (UCC) at Barapani, a picturesque location near Shillong. This institution provides undergraduate and graduate programs in the fields of Arts, Science, and Commerce. Demonstrating communal cooperation, various member churches take turns fulfilling the vital role of Chaplaincy within the college community.

10.4.2. Strengths of NEICC

The Northeast India Christian Council functions as a vital bridge builder among various Christian communities, fostering unity amidst the rich tapestry of cultural and religious diversity found in the region. Strategically located in one of India's most vibrant areas, the Council leverages its modern facilities to host a range of activities that promote collaboration and mutual understanding.

Annual meetings, held each year in different locations, are complemented by thematic discussions that address pressing social and spiritual issues, encouraging participant engagement and collective problem-solving among the member churches and dedicated staff. With a strong and recognisable brand name, the Council has established a clear and impactful mission that resonates deeply within the communities it serves, strengthening relationships and reinforcing the shared values of faith, hope, and support across the fellowship.

10.4.3. Weaknesses of NEICC

Despite its notable strengths, the Northeast India Christian Council (NEICC) faces significant challenges largely stemming from the deep-rooted denominational identities connected to various tribal affiliations. For instance, the Presbyterian denomination prevalent among the Mizo and the Khasi and the Baptist denomination common among the Naga illustrate how these cultural ties can create barriers to establishing genuine unity and fostering effective cooperation among the diverse groups within the council.

In addition to these denominational challenges, the NEICC grapples with several other pressing issues. One major concern is the insufficient financial contributions from member churches and affiliated organisations, which undermines the council's ability to undertake meaningful projects and support initiatives within the community. The council also suffers from a shortage of capable leadership, resulting in a lack of direction and vision necessary for addressing its goals.

Furthermore, the representation of various tribes and denominations within the NEICC is often unequal, leading to feelings of marginalisation among smaller groups. Communication within the council can be ineffective, with information sometimes failing to reach all members and creating misunderstandings or a sense of disconnection. Lastly, there is a widespread perception of a lack of authority and accountability within the NEICC, which can erode trust and hinder collaborative efforts that are essential for fostering a cohesive Christian witness in the region.

10.5. Relationship between Roman Catholic and Protestant Churches

Historically, the relationship between the Roman Catholic and Protestant churches was characterised by tension until the 1960s. However, several factors, most notably the establishment of the Church History Association of India (CHAI), contributed to the emergence of a new common ground. This collaboration resulted in significant joint efforts, such as protests against the deportation of Western missionaries in the 1960s and a united front against the contentious Tyagi Bill, which aimed to restrict Freedom of Religion in Parliament in 1978. That year, Om Prakash Tyagi presented a private member's bill in the Rajya Sabha called the Freedom of Religion Bill[369] aimed at prohibiting conversions from one religion to another through coercion, inducement, or deceptive practices.

10.6. Emerging Ecumenical Trajectories

In the contemporary spiritual landscape, traditional church institutions frequently grapple with the complexities of addressing the deep spiritual longings of individuals in a rapidly changing society. In a postcolonial context, established religious systems and claims to absolute truths are increasingly interrogated as mechanisms of oppression wielded by those in power to maintain control and influence. This shift reflects a broader societal trend that embraces a multitude of meanings and interpretive frameworks, leading to a rich tapestry of spiritual expressions and making the pursuit of a singular truth not only elusive but often seen as restrictive.

In response, the ecumenical movement, which seeks to promote unity among diverse Christian denominations, along with the broader quest for visible unity among various faiths, must extend its reach beyond conventional doctrinal boundaries. This requires openness to inclusivity, dialogue, and the recognition of diverse spiritual paths, all while fostering a collective search for meaning that respects individual experiences and promotes communal understanding.

---

[369] See Subham Goyal, "When Parliamentarian OP Tyagi made efforts to stop illegal religious conversion," https://organiser.org/2023/01/14/104446/opinion/when-parliamentarian-op-tyagi-made-efforts-to-stop-illegal-religious-conversion/ (22 May 2025).

10.6.1. From the Institutional to the Mystical

While institutions, doctrines, and dogmas serve essential roles in shaping and guiding spiritual beliefs, there is a significant risk that, when rendered inflexible and unchangeable, they may stifle the original spiritual experience by confining it within rigid external structures. Such rigidity can lead to a spiritual landscape that rewards conformity over exploration, potentially diluting the richness and depth of genuine spiritual encounters that many seek.

In contemporary society, there exists a profound yearning for authentic spiritual experiences, which has prompted a noticeable shift among individuals toward exploring a wide array of faith expressions. This exploration often includes the vibrant and dynamic practices found within Pentecostal communities, where spontaneous worship, emotional expression, and a focus on direct, personal encounters with the divine characterise the spiritual experience.

Kuncheria Pathil[370] articulates that the core experience of Christianity is centred on the "Abba experience" of Christ, which underscores his deep sense of union with God, his complete transparency to the Divine, and his unwavering commitment to the well-being of humanity. He asserts that "the self-manifestation of the Divine in and through Jesus as the Christ is fundamentally the revelation of God as love." In this context, Jesus' announcement of the 'Kingdom of God' represents a profound declaration of salvation founded on God's unconditional love for all individuals. It signifies the emergence of a renewed humanity characterised by freedom, fellowship, and justice, extending these principles to every person, irrespective of their background.

Throughout history, diverse groups across various nations have engaged with the ultimate meaning of their existence through Jesus Christ, resulting in significant transformations that integrate them into a community of equals, united through love, freedom, and mutual sharing. This transformative experience of Christ has been articulated in numerous ways across different Christian traditions, cultures, and contexts, leading to a rich tapestry of Christological interpretations,[371] including those informed by Jewish, Hellenistic, Scholastic, Latin, and Syrian thought.

In the Indian context, there exists an urgent need to establish a distinct approach to Christological discourse that is Pneumatic, emphasising the role of the Spirit, while also being inclusive, cosmically expansive, liberative,

---

[370] See Kuncheria Pathil, "Theological Reflections on the Church from India," in Asian Horizons 6/4, (December, 2012): 677-706. Hereafter cited as Pathil, "Theological Reflections."

[371] See Pathil, "Theological Reflections," 677-706.

kenotic (self-emptying), and receptive to the insights of other religions. This new Christology should evolve from grassroots movements, termed "from below," embracing a narrative that is less centred on triumphalism and devoid of universalised or absolute claims. It should resonate with local beliefs, traditions, and cultural sensitivities, thus ensuring its authenticity and relevance to individuals living in contemporary India.[372] Such an approach not only honours the diverse expressions of Christianity but also promotes a spirit of dialogue and understanding among various faith traditions.

The Pentecostal movement, in particular, signifies a departure from institutional constraints, emphasising personal connection and experiential faith over adherence to traditional doctrines. Furthermore, mystical experiences - marked by a profound sense of unity with the Absolute or the divine - serve as a convergence point for various religions, illustrating the idea that the essence of spirituality transcends rigid dogmatic boundaries. These encounters, whether experienced in prayer, meditation, or communal worship, highlight a universal spiritual yearning that seeks to connect individuals to a greater reality beyond the confines of established religious structures.[373] Ultimately, this pursuit of genuine spirituality invites a re-examination of how faith is expressed and experienced across diverse traditions, reinforcing the notion that the quest for the divine is both deeply personal and profoundly shared.

10.6.2. From the Centre to the Margins

Traditionally, the ecumenical movement has been perceived as a journey toward a central truth, with Jesus Christ serving as its focal point and ultimate destination. This perspective raises profound questions for reflection: Is the presence of Christ limited exclusively to the structures and communities of historical Christian churches, or does it extend beyond them? Can we not argue that Christ's accessibility transcends cultural and religious boundaries, inviting all individuals, regardless of their faith traditions, to encounter God's presence?

Thinkers like Kuncheria Pathil serve to enrich this dialogue by suggesting that the dynamic presence of Christ is woven into the very fabric of the cosmos, thus implying that other religions and cultures are not devoid of His influence or grace. Pathil's assertion encourages a broader understanding of spirituality and faith, advocating for an appreciation of the Christ-like elements found in diverse belief systems. Moreover, the ongoing pursuit of doctrinal consensus and the aspiration for visible unity among

[372] See Pathil, "Theological Reflections," 677-706.

[373] See Kuncheria Pathil, *Future of the Ecumenical Movement* (Delhi: ISPCK, 2017).

various Christian denominations often prompt deeper contemplation on these crucial questions. As the ecumenical movement evolves, it challenges adherents to consider the implications of inclusivity and the shared pursuit of truth across the vast landscape of human belief. This ongoing discussion not only fosters unity among Christians but also invites a respectful engagement with the rich tapestry of global spirituality.

Chapter 11

National Ecumenical Movements

11.1. National Council of Churches in India (NCCI)

The National Council of Churches in India (NCCI) serves as a vital ecumenical body representing a diverse array of Protestant and Orthodox churches, alongside various ecumenical organisations, regional councils, and associated agencies throughout India. Established in 1914, it was originally founded as the National Missionary Council, primarily aimed at coordinating missionary efforts across the subcontinent. A significant development occurred in 1923 with the formation of the National Christian Council of India, Burma, and Ceylon, which sought to unify and amplify Christian witness in the region. Following the separation of the Councils of Burma and Sri Lanka, the body was officially renamed the National Council of Churches in India in 1979.[374]

As an autonomous and interconfessional organisation, the NCCI functions as a dynamic platform for ecumenical collaboration, actively initiating, promoting, and coordinating various ministries of service and outreach within both the Christian community and broader society. The Council is dedicated to uniting churches and Christian organisations for collective consultation, mutual support, and coordinated action on critical issues impacting the life and mission of the churches in India. Committed to promoting Gospel values such as peace, justice, and unity, the NCCI comprises 13 Regional Christian Councils, 18 All India Organisations, 32

[374] See "Introduction," https://ncci1914.com/introduction/#tab-id-1. (23 May 2025). Hereafter cited as "Introduction."

Member Churches, and 7 associated agencies. Together, these constituents represent an estimated 14 million individuals across India,[375] highlighting the extensive reach and influence of the Council.

Since its founding, the NCCI and its members have played a proactive role in various social reform movements, nation-building activities, and spiritual revitalisation efforts. The Council engages in numerous initiatives that advocate for responsible living, the preservation of human dignity, sustainable development, transparency, accountability, and social equity. Its work encompasses collaboration with civil society, non-governmental organisations (NGOs), grassroots movements, and supporters at local, national, and international levels. The governing structure of the NCCI is designed to ensure effective operation and strategy. The Assembly, which is the highest decision-making body, convenes every 4 years to set the overarching direction and priorities of the Council. In between Assembly meetings, the Executive Committee meets annually to oversee ongoing activities and initiatives. Furthermore, the Working Committee, which the Assembly appoints, gathers twice a year to provide guidance and management for the Council's operations,[376] ensuring that its mission and objectives are met with effectiveness and dedication.

At the commencement of the 20th century, various mission organisations collectively recognised the urgent nature of the evangelistic endeavour. The Ecumenical Conference held in New York in 1900 stated, "It is our duty to attempt now the speedy evangelisation of the whole world."[377] Two years thereafter, John R. Mott articulated a similar sentiment, emphasising the pressing need to evangelise globally.

During the All India Missionary Conference in Madras in 1900, a resolution was made mandating that each missionary society undertake concerted efforts to evangelise its respective field within that generation. Several factors contributed to the prevailing sense of urgency regarding evangelisation in India. Primarily, the rise of nationalism became notably pronounced following Japan's victory over Russia in 1905, suggesting that the British Empire's support of Christian missions might not be enduring. Concurrently, there was a marked increase in Hindu resistance to missionary work, exemplified by organisations such as the Ramakrishna Mission and the *Arya Samaj*. Nevertheless, the notion that this represented a pivotal moment for Christian missions was predominantly catalysed by the mass

---

375 See "Introduction," 1.

376 See "Introduction," 1.

377 As cited in K. Baago, *A History of the National Christian Council of India 1914-1964* (Madras: NCC, 1965), 3. Hereafter cited as Baago, A History.

movements among the disenfranchised classes,[378] which appeared to present extensive opportunities for the Church.

Noteworthy events included the conversions of sweepers in the United Provinces, the Mangs in the Marathi region, the mass movements in Telengana during the 1870s, and the group conversions among the Churhas in Punjab. Such inspiring developments underscored the need for Christian unity, indicating that the various missions and churches must collaborate effectively[379] to leverage these newfound opportunities.

The establishment of the South India Missionary Association in 1897 heralded the onset of formal ecumenical cooperation. The early 1900s also witnessed the formation of several ecumenical organisations, such as the National Missionary Council in 1914, the Student Christian Movement in India in 1912, the United Theological College in 1910, and the National Missionary Society in 1905.[380]

On 4-5th February 1914, 28 members of the YWCA convened at the YWCA building in Calcutta to review the Constitution and related amendments for the National Missionary Council, which subsequently ratified the Constitution with the proposed revisions. Transitioning from the National Missionary Council to the National Christian Council required re-evaluating the relationship between churches and missions in the context of the nationalist struggle for independence. J. H. Oldham articulated that international missionary activity aims to establish the Church of Christ as an agent of evangelisation across every region of the people of other faiths. During its conference in Ranchi in January 1923, the NMC was renamed the National Christian Council of India, Burma, and Ceylon.[381]

11.1.1. The Function of the National Christian Council

11.1.1.1. The National Movement and the NCC

The national struggle for independence had gained considerable momentum by the time the National Christian Council was established. The demand for *swaraj* became a central tenet of this nationalism, coinciding with the initiation of Mahatma Gandhi's *satyagraha* movement. The Council faced a dilemma regarding its response to the independence movement, opting neither to fully align itself with nor distance itself from the political struggle.

---

[378] See John Raleigh Mott, *The Decisive Hour of Christian Missions* (London: BMS, 1910), 146.

[379] See Baago, A History, 4.

[380] See Roger Gaikwad, "Churches Together in God's Mission," in *History of the Ecumenical Movement: Issues, Challenges and Perspectives*, edited by Watimongla Jamir (Kolkata: SCEPTRE, 2014), 214. Hereafter cited as Gaikwad, "Churches."

[381] See Baago, A History, 31.

11.1.1.2. NCC and Evangelism and Mission

Throughout various stages of evangelisation, a faction of missionaries and Indian church leaders raised concerns regarding the evangelical movement during the 1920s. Individuals such as Dr. L. P. Larsen articulated reservations about the movement's methodologies. The National Christian Council engaged in Industrial Mission Programs and Rural Reconstruction efforts within a country beset by communal strife, as well as severe economic and social challenges. The prioritisation of higher education in a transforming India emerged in the 1930s, particularly emphasising the study of Christian mass movements and the Christian identity of Christian universities. To support churches in their evangelistic initiatives, the National Christian Council began producing "Tracts for the Times" to provide relevant reports and ideas.

11.1.1.3. Church-Centric Focus within the Council

The 1930s saw a continual emphasis on the premise that evangelism constitutes the essence of the Church. Additionally, it was articulated that evangelism ought to centre around the Church itself. This strategic focus resulted in constitutional amendments for the Council in 1936, with the inclusion of a statement asserting, "The objects of the Council shall be to take all possible steps to give effect to the principle that in the Christian enterprise the Church is central and permanent."

11.1.2. Critique of the National Council of Churches in India

An important question emerged during the mid-1970s: "Did the Council effectively contribute to the vitality of the Churches and Indian society?" In response to this inquiry, the Council established an Evaluation Commission comprising its own members, which identified several underlying causes for the Council's challenges. Notably, despite the National Christian Council of India's prudent devolution of administrative responsibilities to various ecumenical organisations, the lack of a structured relationship that emphasised its spiritual commitment to the entirety of the Christian enterprise in India contributed to the Council's diminished impact.

11.2. The National Christian Council of Sri Lanka

The National Christian Council of Sri Lanka (NCCSL) is a significant ecumenical organisation representing the Christian community in Sri Lanka. Established in 1945, its mission is to promote ecumenical witness and to strive for the unity envisioned by our Lord Jesus Christ, to fully realise God's reign on earth. The roots of the NCCSL can be traced back to earlier formations, including the All Ceylon Conference in 1912, the Christian Council of India, Burma, and Ceylon in 1923, the Christian Council in

Ceylon in 1922, and the Ceylon Representative Council of Missions in 1920. The NCCSL aims to engage in ecumenical efforts to partner with God in establishing God's kingdom on earth.

The foundation of the Council's mission encompasses several core tenets: affirming faith in the Lord Jesus Christ as God and Saviour, following the Holy Scriptures; collaboratively fulfilling the shared calling in obedience to the Triune God – Parent, Son, and Holy Spirit; and encouraging one another toward visible unity in faith, Eucharistic fellowship, and collective witness and service.

The Comity Statement endorsed by member Churches and Ecumenical Organisations of the NCCSL articulates a commitment to a common faith in the Lord Jesus Christ, as defined by the Holy Scriptures. Collectively, member organisations strive to fulfil their shared calling in obedience to the Triune God, asserting that they constitute parts of the one body of Christ. A central objective is to diligently work towards the establishment of a visible Church, in alignment with the High Priestly Prayer of our Lord, "That they all may be one."[382]

The Church in Sri Lanka recognises its critical role in demonstrating the Reign of God through its life and mission, effectively disseminating the Gospel of Jesus Christ throughout the nation. Moreover, fostering healthy relationships among all Churches and Ecumenical Organisations, along with transparent mission methodologies, is essential for achieving this objective. Comity is characterised as a spirit of fellowship and fair dealings, rooted in Christian courtesy and common sense. The purpose of this statement is to delineate the principles of Comity and their application to Christian work and witness within the nation. The focus must be on promoting active cooperation among Christian bodies in Sri Lanka,[383] rather than allowing their operations to proceed in isolation.

There is a need to optimise the use of collective resources and to seek collaborative approaches to activities that do not necessitate separate engagements due to significant differences. This endeavour involves not merely organisations but also the active work of God; thus, it is imperative to plan in a manner that eliminates any obstacles to the divine collaboration intended. The NCCSL's primary mission is to advance ecumenical witness and relationships. Specific initiatives are in place to support ecumenical

---

[382] See "Comity Statement - National Christian Council of Sri Lanka," https://nccsl.org/comity-statemnt/ (25 May 2025). Hereafter cited as "Comity Statement."

[383] See "Comity Statement," 1.

witness and Christian unity, not only among constituent churches but also across all Christian denominations.[384]

Strategies for enhancing Christian unity and ecumenical witness include: inter-church dialogue and engagement, interfaith dialogue for the common good, common liturgy and worship, ethical guidelines for mission, joint retreats/worship, theological initiatives, and prayer and spiritual practices. The Commission for Justice and Peace was established by the NCCSL to safeguard human rights and promote equity for all individuals,[385] irrespective of gender, race, or ethnicity.

Its goal is to create a just and equitable society where each individual's dignity is honoured. Focus areas of the Commission include: human rights, social justice, peacebuilding and reconciliation, and environmental issues. Ongoing activities encompass: Muslim-Christian dialogue, a Young Professionals' Forum, interfaith initiatives, advocacy for migrant workers and asylum seekers, church-based awareness programmes, the *Awadhanayata* Bulletin, and advocacy on contemporary issues.[386]

Criticism of the NCCSL includes claims of insufficient representation, with some asserting that it primarily reflects the interests of mainline Protestant churches, such as Anglican, Methodist, and Baptist denominations, thereby marginalising a considerable number of Pentecostal, evangelical, and independent churches that have significant followings in Sri Lanka. Additionally, concerns about a lack of grassroots connection have been voiced, indicating that the NCCSL predominantly operates at leadership levels with minimal engagement with Christian communities on the ground, particularly in underserved or rural areas. Moreover, there are allegations of outside influence concerning the NCCSL's reliance on financial support and theological guidance from Western ecumenical bodies, including the World Council of Churches. Accusations of promoting liberal theology have also been directed at the Council from traditional or conservative factions within the Christian community.

11.3. Myanmar Council of Churches

11.3.1. An Overview

The Myanmar Council of Churches (MCC) was established as the Burma Christian Council in 1949, subsequently changing its name to the Burma Council of Churches in 1972, before adopting its current designation in 1989. This organisation evolved from the earlier Burma Regional Council,

[384] See "Commission for Ecumenical Relations," https://nccsl.org/ecumenical-relations/ (6 June 2025). Hereafter cited as "Commission for Ecumenical Relations."

[385] See "Commission for Ecumenical Relations," 1.

[386] See "Commission for Ecumenical Relations," 1.

which was a precursor to the National Christian Council of India, Burma, and Ceylon, founded in 1914. As a national ecumenical body representing a diverse array of denominational churches, the MCC is acknowledged as a religious organisation.

The Council collaborates primarily with over 45 local church councils throughout Myanmar. Notably, recent years have witnessed a significant deepening of collaboration with the Catholic Bishops' Conference of Myanmar (CBCM). Additionally, the MCC engages in cooperative efforts with various Myanmar-based International Non-Governmental Organisations (INGOs), local non-governmental organisations (NGOs), and United Nations entities.

11.3.2. Background Context

To promote collaborative efforts among Christian missions in Myanmar, the Burma Representative Council of Missions was established in 1913. In 1923, the organisation was rebranded as the Christian Council of Burma, shifting its emphasis from broader collaboration to the unification of missions. Following the political upheaval and the attainment of independence in 1948, the organisation adopted the name Burma Christian Council. On May 16, 1972, during the Annual General Meeting held in Mawlamyine, the Burma Christian Council was renamed the Burma Council of Churches.[387]

The Council's constitution was ratified during the Annual General Meeting in Pyin Oo Lwin on 14th May 1974. The Burma Council of Churches serves as a collective entity for Christian churches and organisations, facilitating discussions on faith, promoting mutual acceptance of doctrinal beliefs, and advocating for church unity. The Council underscores the importance of collaboration, mutual understanding, and recognition in the pursuit of upholding the name of the Lord, rather than fostering division. As such, the promotion of unity is regarded as an integral aspect of the Council's overarching mission.

11.3.3. Membership Criteria

To be eligible for membership, a church must affirm faith in the Triune God, as articulated in the Holy Scriptures, the Apostles' Creed, and the Nicene Creed, with the belief that the Bible offers the path to salvation for all humanity.

11.3.4. Mission & Ecumenism Department Purpose

The Mission and Ecumenism Department aims to encourage a spirit of ecumenism and fellowship through interactions and exchanges among

---

387 See "Myanmar Council of Churches," oikoumene.org/organization/myanmar-council-of-churches (30 May 2025).

both member and non-member churches, fostering understanding with other religious communities.[388] This department endeavours to promote the principles of dialogue and unity among denominational churches to seminary students within Myanmar, facilitating the concept of *koinonia.*[389] Furthermore, it aspires to inspire churches to learn from and support one another in their mission-oriented activities.

11.3.5. Strategic Plans

Organisation of a seminar on church unity and mission - Implementation of an Interfaith Dialogue Program - Hosting of the Dhamma Friends Fellowship Meeting[390] (Buddhist-Christian Fellowship).

11.3.6. Vision and Mission

The MCC envisions fostering unity among churches in Myanmar, advocating for solidarity among humanity, and promoting a life that is conducive to the Myanmar context. Established fundamentally by the churches within Myanmar, the MCC is committed to inclusive missions, peacemaking, justice, the enhancement of human dignity, gender equality, service, Christian witness, interfaith harmony, and collaboration. It strives for the unification of all churches in Myanmar through mutual recognition of faith and order, empowerment, capacity building, sharing local and global resources,[391] and fostering collaborative efforts.

11.3.7. Objectives

The primary objective of the Myanmar Council of Churches is to promote the unity of churches, foster the unity of all people, and enhance the quality of life in Myanmar through: (a) mutual fellowship and understanding; (b) mutual acceptance and acknowledgment of the diverse faiths and practices of various churches; (c) coordination and collaboration on shared concerns among churches; and (d) ongoing efforts toward the organic unity of the churches.

---

[388] See "Myanmar Ecumenical Institute (M.E.I)," https"//www.mccoikom.org/en/Myanmar-ecumenical-institute-m-e-e/ (1 June 2025). Hereafter cited as "Myanmar Ecumenical Institute (M.E.I)."

[389] A transliteration of the Greek word κοινωνία, koinonia alludes to ideas like camaraderie, shared participation, one's share in anything, a present given together, a collection, or a donation. Despite its rarity, it is a theologically significant term.

[390] See "Myanmar Ecumenical Institute (M.E.I)," 1.

[391] See "Myanmar Ecumenical Institute (M.E.I)," 1.

11.3.8. Myanmar Ecumenical Institute (M.E.I)

The Myanmar Ecumenical Institute serves as a platform to cultivate and advance an ecumenical spirit among church leaders, raise awareness of gender equality and peacebuilding for community benefit, and promote collaboration among ecumenical churches. Under the oversight of the board of management, the M.E.I. has implemented its programs in partnership with local church councils, member churches, and other church-related organisations.

11.3.9. Purpose

The purpose of the M.E.I. is to recognise the significance of fostering an ecumenical spirit among church leaders and members in the nation-building process. It seeks to disseminate this ecumenical ethos into society through the churches. Additionally, the institute aims to prepare Christian students, youth, and women to adopt an ecumenical mindset and develop as future leaders within society.

11.3.10. Plans

Lay Leadership Training Seminar on Current Issues - Shalom Related Seminar - Ecumenical Leadership Course - Ecumenical Education for All - Coordination and Promotion.

11.4. Criticism of the Myanmar Council of Churches

The MCC has frequently faced criticism regarding its perceived reluctance to confront the government, particularly concerning human rights and religious freedom for Christian minorities. Critics argue that the MCC emphasises its relationship with the government over its duty to advocate for marginalised groups.

11.4.1. Perceived Insufficient Advocacy

The MCC has been criticised for its inadequate vocalisation of opposition against government actions detrimental to Christians, including instances of discrimination and violence. Observers contend that the MCC's focus on maintaining government relations has resulted in a more restrained approach to addressing human rights violations.

11.4.2. Concerns Regarding Religious Freedom

The MCC has also been scrutinised for its insufficient confrontation of issues surrounding religious freedom, particularly regarding Christian minorities who experience discrimination and persecution. Critics assert that the MCC should adopt a more proactive position in defending the rights of Christians and other religious minorities.

11.4.3. Government Alignment

The MCC's strategy of sustaining amicable relations with the government has raised concerns among certain stakeholders, who perceive that it hinders the church's ability to speak truthfully to power. Detractors argue that the MCC's close ties to the government have led to hesitance in challenging governmental policies or actions with adverse impacts on the Christian community.

11.4.4. Internal Divisions and Unity Issues

The structure and composition of the MCC have also been criticised, with some asserting that it inadequately represents the diverse Christian communities in Myanmar. There are concerns that the MCC may struggle to address the varied needs and issues of all Christian groups, potentially leading to internal discord and a lack of cohesion.

11.4.5. Impact of Colonial History

Some scholars emphasise the historical association between Christianity and colonialism as a factor contributing to the marginalisation of Christian minorities in Myanmar. This historical context may impede Christians' acceptance and respect within the wider community, thereby complicating the MCC's advocacy efforts on behalf of their rights.

Chapter 12

Roman Catholics and Protestant Churches

The dynamics between the Roman Catholic Church and Protestant denominations have been historically influenced by a confluence of theological divergence, political conflicts, and cultural separations. The Protestant Reformation of the 16th century fundamentally transformed the landscape of Western Christianity, initiating a schism that would shape inter-church relations for centuries. The Catholic Church's initial responses, particularly via the Council of Trent, entrenched the divisions, leading to an extended period characterised by mutual antagonism and doctrinal censure. However, the Second Vatican Council (1962–1965) represented a critical juncture in Catholic-Protestant interactions. Through pivotal documents such as *Unitatis Redintegratio* and *Lumen Gentium*, the Catholic Church communicated a renewed willingness for ecumenical dialogue and a reassessment of its interactions with other Christian traditions.

This chapter delineates the trajectory of Catholic-Protestant relations from the pre-Vatican period of opposition to the post-Vatican ethos of reconciliation and mutual acknowledgement, scrutinising theological developments, shifts in ecclesial attitudes, and broader implications for the ecumenical movement.

12.1. Pre-Vatican Relationship

12.1.1. Historical Context

The European Reformation in the 16th century marked a pivotal moment in Western Christianity, resulting in a profound split between the Roman Catholic Church and the emerging Protestant Churches. This fracture was not merely a theological dispute but rather a complex interplay of political, social, and cultural factors. The Catholic Church, facing increasing dissent and questioning of papal authority, convened the Council of Trent (1545–1563) as a direct response to the Reformation. This Council sought to reaffirm Catholic doctrine and address the corruption within the Church that many Reformers criticised. Simultaneously, it worked to counter Protestant theology that was denounced as heretical, leading to an atmosphere rife with discord and mutual accusations of heresy.

12.1.2. Catholic Attitude toward Protestants

Within the historical framework of this schism, Roman Catholics viewed Protestants through a lens of suspicion and concern. Frequently described as "separated brethren" by official Church documents, Protestants nonetheless faced stark condemnation, labelled as "children of Satan," "heretics," and "schismatics."[392] This derogatory terminology reflected deep-seated views entangled in the Catholic tradition.

The Counter-Reformation emerged as a powerful movement aimed at the restoration and reinforcement of Catholic doctrine, spearheaded by the Jesuits and other religious orders. The term "mission," which initially referred to Jesuit efforts in regions like Northern Germany, took on anti-Protestant connotations, emphasising efforts to reconvert those who had strayed from Catholicism. The foundational mission of *Propaganda Fide*, established in 1622, was heavily focused on reclaiming Protestants for the Catholic fold, underscoring a strategy that persisted until approximately 1830 CE. Subsequent missionary encyclicals from the 20th century echoed this intent, advocating for the urgency of "tearing away non-Catholics from their errors" and calling upon "the separated brethren"[393] to return to what was viewed as the Mother Church.

The lack of formal recognition between the 2 churches translated into an absence of communication, collaboration, or shared sacraments. The prevailing sentiment among Catholic theologians was that Protestant sacraments, especially the Eucharist and ordination, were invalid, further entrenching division.

12.1.3. Protestant Views of the Catholic Church

In stark contrast, Protestants regarded the papacy as a symbol of corruption, viewing its authority as contrary to biblical teachings. They argued that the Roman Catholic Church had deviated from the principles of the Holy Spirit, believing it sought to control rather than submit to divine guidance. This

---

[392] See Bosch, *Transforming Mission*, 473.

[393] See Bosch, *Transforming Mission*, 473.

perspective was rooted in a belief that the doctrine of papal infallibility, asserting that the pope is incapable of error in matters of faith and morals when speaking *ex cathedra*,[394] was a dangerous theological error[395] that undermined the autonomy of individual believers.

Mariology, the theological study of Mary, emerged as one of the most contentious issues distinguishing Catholic and Protestant beliefs, second only to the authority of the papacy. Protestants voiced concerns that the increasing emphasis on Mary within Catholic devotion threatened to eclipse the centrality of Christ in faith and worship.[396] This tension over the role of Mary highlighted deeper disagreements over the nature of salvation and intercession.

Moreover, the relationship between Scripture and tradition was a critical point of departure. Protestants contended that reliance on ecclesiastical traditions from the medieval period had distorted the original messages within the Scriptures.[397] They promoted the doctrine of "sola scriptura," advocating that Scripture alone is the ultimate authority in matters of faith, which was a direct repudiation of the Catholic view that both Scripture and sacred tradition hold equal weight.

Further complicating relations, Protestants accused Catholics of idolatry, particularly in the reverence shown to saints and the use of religious icons, which they believed contradicted the commandment against graven images. Given this backdrop of theological divergence, many Protestant denominations fostered a strong anti-Catholic sentiment, fuelling an atmosphere of hostility, suspicion, and competition.[398] Such sentiments were widespread, leading to varying degrees of animosity across different regions and communities. The intense scrutiny and criticism that characterised Protestant thought towards Catholicism were reflective of a broader struggle for religious identity during this tumultuous period in history.

12.1.4. Vatican (1962–1965): A Turning Point

Pope John XXIII convened the Second Vatican Council, providing a significant shift in the Catholic Church's approach to modern challenges.

---

[394] The Latin expression ex cathedra translates to "from the chair." When the pope formally teaches a doctrine on a subject of faith or morals in his capacity as the global shepherd of the Church and addresses it to the entire world, he is referring to binding and infallible papal teachings.

[395] See Robert McAfee Brown, *The Ecumenical Revolution: A Interpretation of the Catholic-Protestant Dialogue* (London: Burns and Oates, 1967), 292, 293. Hereafter cited as Brown, *The Ecumenical Revolution*.

[396] See Brown, *The Ecumenical Revolution*, 298.

[397] See Brown, *The Ecumenical Revolution*, 300, 301.

[398] See Brown, *The Ecumenical Revolution*, 300, 301.

Unlike Vatican I, which focused primarily on the threats posed by modernity, and the Council of Trent, which was a response to the Protestant Reformation, Vatican II aimed at what Pope John XXIII termed "aggiornamento," meaning a process of updating and renewing the Church[399] to better engage with the contemporary world.

Following the Council, there was a notable transformation in the Catholic Church's perception of other Christian denominations. Formerly labelled as "children of Satan," Protestants began to be referred to as "dissenters" and "separated brethren." Eventually, this evolved into a more inclusive designation of "brothers and sisters in Christ,"[400] reflecting a growing acknowledgement of shared faith and values among Christians. A fresh and inclusive spirit infused all the dialogues and documents produced during the Council.

12.1.4.1. Key Documents

1) The Decree on Ecumenism, or *Unitatis Redintegratio*

This seminal document recognised the active role of the Holy Spirit in other Christian communities. It underscored the urgent need for improved relationships among Christians and the acceptance of one another's differences. The opening paragraph made a striking declaration that divisions among Christians "contradict the will of Christ, scandalise the world, and damage that most holy cause, the preaching of the Gospel to every creature." This decree identified the "restoration of unity among all Christians" as one of the Council's primary objectives,[401] that highlighted a shift from a previously insular approach to a more outward-looking, inviting stance regarding ecumenism.

This historic acknowledgement marked a radical departure from the Catholic Church's earlier self-sufficient perspective, embodied in the "return to the Catholic Church" theory, which posited that the Church of Christ was fully realised only within the Catholic Church. The shift was towards an understanding of the "restoration of Christian unity," positioning the Decree on Ecumenism as the Catholic Magisterium's foundational charter[402] for ecumenical dialogue and cooperation.

---

[399] See Edmund Kee-Fook Chia, "Asian Ecumenism from Roman Catholic Perspective," in *History of Ecumenical Movement: Issues, Challenges and Perspectives*, edited By Watimongla Jamir (Kolkata, SCEPTRE, 2014), 292. 291-299.

[400] See Bosch, *Transforming Mission*, 472.

[401] See Bosch, *Transforming Mission*, 473.

[402] See Couto, *May They All be One*, 142.

2) *Lumen Gentium*

Protestants were referred to as “separated brethren” rather than the previously held term “heretics.” This doctrinal constitution emphasised the significance of unity amidst diversity and balanced local church autonomy with the recognition of papal authority and infallibility. This marked a conceptual transition from understanding the church primarily as a hierarchical institution to a more inclusive view that acknowledges the entire faithful as integral to the Church’s identity.

12.1.4.2. Changes in Theology

1) The Council affirmed that various Protestant communities embody genuine elements of holiness and truth, acknowledging that no single tradition holds a monopoly on Christ’s grace.
2) It reiterated that the unity Christ desires for His followers is not only possible but also necessary, laying a theological foundation for ongoing dialogues among Christian denominations.

12.1.4.3. Shifts in Attitude

1) There emerged a spirit of humility and a genuine receptivity for open discussions. The declaration from *Unitatis Redintegratio* emphasised that without a fundamental change of heart, any attempts at ecumenism would lack authenticity and depth.[403]
2) The Catholic Church expressed a newfound willingness to learn from and engage with Protestant theology and practices, recognising that fruitful exchanges can enrich all faith traditions involved in ecumenical outreach. Through these developments, Vatican II fundamentally reshaped the Catholic Church’s approach to ecumenism, fostering a spirit of cooperation, understanding, and shared mission among Christians.

Conclusion

The historical division between Roman Catholics and Protestants, once characterised by profound distrust and rigorous theological disputes, has progressively transitioned into a more conciliatory and collaborative relationship, particularly in the aftermath of Vatican II. The Decree on Ecumenism and other conciliar documents have redefined the Catholic Church’s perspective towards Protestant communities, acknowledging the presence of elements of sanctification and truth beyond its institutional framework.

---

[403] See Couto, *May They All be One*, 143.

Despite the persistence of substantial doctrinal differences, especially regarding ecclesiology, sacramental theology, and authority, the ecumenical advancements initiated by Vatican II have facilitated enduring avenues for dialogue and collaboration. Understanding the evolution from conflict to communion not only sheds light on the intricacies of Christian history but also underscores the ongoing necessity for patience, humility, and a deep commitment to unity within the diverse body of Christ.

Chapter 13

Indian Expressions of Ecumenism

The Indian subcontinent presents a distinctive and dynamic expression of ecumenism shaped by its diverse religious, cultural, and social contexts. Unlike many Western ecumenical endeavours that primarily addressed doctrinal divisions, Indian ecumenism has been deeply interwoven with nation-building, social justice, interfaith engagement, and the search for Christian unity amidst pluralism. This chapter explores major institutional and theological developments that reflect Indian ecumenical initiatives - from the formation of the National Missionary Council and the South India United Church (SIUC), to the historic union of churches forming the Church of South India (CSI) and Church of North India (CNI). It also engages with post-union efforts such as the Communion of Churches in India and ecumenical academic institutions like the United Theological College and the Ecumenical Christian Centre. Each section highlights not only achievements but also the complex challenges encountered in realising visible unity and contextual relevance in ministry and mission. Together, these initiatives testify to India's vibrant contribution to the global ecumenical movement.

13.1. Formation of National Missionary Council

In 1855, a pivotal gathering of Bengal missionaries from various denominations converged in Calcutta for the inaugural Provincial Conference. This landmark event was designed to address their shared challenges and foster collaboration among different missionary societies. Following this precedent, similar conferences were organised across India, signifying a growing commitment to cooperative efforts in the mission field. In 1857, the Northwest Provincial Conference was held in Banaras, bringing together missionaries from the northern regions. The following year, in 1858, South India hosted its conference in the picturesque hill resort of Ootacamund,[404] where missionaries convened to discuss regional issues and strategies.

In 1862, the Punjab followed suit by holding its Provincial Conference in Lahore, further extending the network of missionary cooperation. A significant milestone was reached in 1872 with the first National General Missionary Conference held in Allahabad. This ambitious initiative not only united missionaries from across the country but also set the stage for future gatherings, which were repeated in 1882 and 1892.[405] These regional and national conferences laid the groundwork for the establishment of the National Missionary Council, along with its local branches, creating a structured and cohesive environment for mission work throughout India.

In 1897, a diverse group of Anglican, Lutheran, Congregationalist, Baptist, and Methodist missionaries in South India came together to form the South India Missionaries Association. This association was established to facilitate consultation and enable unified action to enhance the effectiveness of mission work across the region. A significant outcome of this collaborative endeavour was the establishment of the United Mission Tuberculosis Hospital at Arogyavaram, as well as the renowned Christian Medical College in Vellore,[406] both of which stand as testaments to the power of mission cooperation.

In the meantime, the 4th All India Missionary Conference was convened in 1902 in Madras. This conference was distinct as it featured delegates who were officially designated by their respective missions, marking it as the first authentic ecumenical gathering in India. A pivotal resolution from this conference was the establishment of a Board of Arbitration that would oversee mission activities throughout the country. The primary aim of this Board was to promote united efforts in evangelisation. Scholars like Baago[407] assert that this Board can be accurately viewed as a foundational step toward the eventual formation of a National Council.

The National Missionary Society, founded in 1905, was another significant milestone in the movement towards unity among Indian

---

[404] See Baago, *National Christian Council*, 5.

[405] See Baago, National Christian Council, 5.

[406] See D. Isaac Devadoss, "An Historical Survey of Ecumenism in India," https://studylib.net/doc/8008188/a-historical-survey-of-ecumenism-in-india (5 Jun 2025). Hereafter cited as Devadoss, "An Historical Survey."

[407] See Baago, *National Christian Council*, 6.

Christians from various denominations. This spirit of collaboration was further exemplified by the establishment of the United Theological College in Bangalore in 1910, as well as the reorganisation of Serampore College during the same year,[408] reinforcing the commitment to a unified approach in theological education and mission efforts.

In 1912, John R. Mott visited India as a representative of the Edinburgh Conference, aiming to promote the establishment of local bodies that could enhance cooperation among missions. The following year, 1913, saw the formation of 8 Provincial Councils in regions including Bengal, Bihar, Orissa, Bombay, Punjab, Mid-India, Upper Provinces, Madras, and Burma. A landmark event occurred on 4th and 5th February 1914, with the inaugural National Missionary Council held at the YWCA building in Calcutta, attended by 28 delegates.[409]

During this historic meeting, the Constitution of the Council was adopted, officially marking the establishment of the National Missionary Council. The first Secretary of this Council was Rev. H. Anderson, who served as the India Secretary of the Baptist Missionary Society. With the formation of the National Missionary Council, a pathway was opened for joint missionary enterprise, signalling the dawn of a new era in mission work. This development was pivotal as it positioned the Indian mission field alongside other significant global spheres such as China and Japan, fostering a meaningful movement toward cooperation[410] and fellowship in the vital mission of spreading the teachings of Christ.

In its inaugural 9 years, the National Council functioned primarily as a council of missions rather than a collective of churches. The council members predominantly comprised representatives from various missionary societies, most of whom were missionaries themselves. In January 1923, the Council convened in Ranchi for its final meeting as a 'missionary council.' Before this meeting, a conference of Indian Christians, orchestrated by Oldham, had taken place at the same location. This gathering provided strong support for the proposed changes and, likely influenced by Oldham, initiated discussions regarding the concept of indigenisation. With this endorsement, Oldham successfully guided the Council to adopt a revised constitution, which resulted in a new designation: the National Christian Council of India, Burma, and Ceylon. Subsequently, regional councils were established in various states. As of 1956, full membership in the NCC was limited exclusively to Indian churches and their corresponding regional

[408] See Baago, *National Christian Council*, 7.

[409] See Baago, *National Christian Council*, 15, 16.

[410] See Baago, *National Christian Council*, 15, 16.

councils. Moreover, in 1979, the NCC was rebranded as the National Council of Churches in India (NCCI).[411]

13.2. South India United Church (SIUC)

Intense consultative efforts have been undertaken to address denominational disagreements since the inception of the Bombay Missionary Union in 1825, with a trajectory of discussions extending through a series of regional and national conferences. These sustained endeavours have not only facilitated mutual respect among diverse missionary societies but have also cultivated a deeper understanding, enhanced cooperation, and invaluable advisory relationships. The interdenominational fellowship received a significant boost through the tireless travels of John R. Mott between 1896 and 1913, culminating in the establishment of pivotal organisations such as the Student Christian Movement and the National Missionary Council in India.[412]

Prior to the formation of the South India United Church (SIUC) in 1908, there existed a framework of confessional unions, collaborative union institutions, and intermission efforts that laid the groundwork for future ecumenical endeavours. The 19th century saw the emergence of a robust ecumenical foundation within Indian churches, marked by decennial and national conferences, regional meetings, and the establishment of missionary societies in major urban centres. A notable aspect of this movement was the influential role of the Confessional Union of Reformed Churches. In particular, the concerted activity of 3 distinct Presbyterian churches—the American Arcot Mission, the Church of Scotland, and the Free Church of Scotland—operated extensively in the Arcot region, including Madras and its neighbouring districts. This cooperative effort culminated in the formation of the South India United Church in 1901, which was characterised by a confessional basis. Three years later, the Presbyterian Church of India was founded when this organisation merged with 8 Presbyterian missions based in North India, further solidifying the interdenominational landscape.

In the year 1904, a significant development occurred in the landscape of Indian Christianity with the formation of a federal union among the Congregational Churches operating under the American Missions in the regions of Madura and Jaffna, alongside the Congregational Churches affiliated with the London Mission in South Travancore. This union marked a pivotal moment in the pursuit of greater unity among Protestant denominations in India.[413] Following this initial consolidation, an avenue

---

[411] Cf. Devadoss, "An Historical Survey," 2.

[412] See Snaitang, *A History*, 84.

[413] See J. W. Gladstone, *United to Unite: History of the Church of South India 1947-1997* (Chennai: CSI Synod, 1997), 10. Hereafter cited as Gladstone, *United*.

for broader union efforts between Presbyterians and Congregationalists began to materialise.

Between 1905 and 1907, extensive negotiations took place, as representatives from both traditions sought common ground. These discussions were rooted in a shared desire to transcend entrenched denominational differences, focusing instead on an agreed basis that emphasised their "essential oneness" in Christian faith. Through these collaborative efforts, the goal of fostering unity among differing Christian practices and beliefs became increasingly attainable.[414] Following the collaboration of the Presbyterians and Congregationalists in South India, as well as in the Jaffna District of Sri Lanka, the reorganised and interdenominational South India United Church was officially established in 1908. The SIUC gained further impetus in 1919 when it joined forces with the Basel Mission,[415] enhancing its capabilities and outreach.

Notably, the negotiation process leading to the establishment of the Church of India involved participation from three distinct traditions: Calvinism, Episcopalism, and Revivalism. Each of these traditions brought with it narratives of conflict and strife from their places of origin while concurrently establishing roots in India. Both the Congregationalists and the Presbyterians originate from the Calvinist tradition, which traditionally questioned the use of liturgy and the hierarchical structure of episcopacy. In contrast, Anglicanism in South India, rooted in the Anglo-Catholic tradition, retained many of the medieval church's characteristics, apart from a rejection of papal authority in Rome. Moreover, the Methodists, influenced by their commitment to the Evangelical Revival, opted to maintain their distinctive identity,[416] even though they share a common heritage with the Anglican tradition.

In May 1919, a significant informal gathering occurred in Tranquebar (referred to as Tharangambadi in Tamil), bringing together representatives from the Lutheran, Methodist, Anglican, and South India United Church (SIUC) denominations. This assembly of Indian clergy convened to address the critical issue of Church Union, which held substantial significance in the context of the growth and unity of Indian Christianity. On that historic occasion, the participants made a heartfelt appeal, clearly reflecting their collective concern for enhanced cohesion among the diverse Christian traditions.[417] They articulated a compelling argument that ecclesiastical separation constituted not only an obstacle to effective evangelisation but

---

[414] See Gladstone, *United*, 10.

[415] See Snaitang, A History, 86, 87.

[416] See Snaitang, A History, 86, 87.

[417] See Snaitang, *A History*, 87.

also an artificial barrier imposed by Western influences, thereby impeding the authentic expression of faith within the Indian context.

To address the complexities related to the governance of a united church, doctrinal creeds, the establishment of ministries, matrimonial issues, intercommunion practices, and the equitable standing of pastors, a joint committee was formed. This committee was entrusted with the responsibility of exploring a framework for unity, and it was resolved that the Lambeth Quadrilateral would serve as a foundational basis for their efforts. The Quadrilateral delineated four essential principles: the holy Scriptures, the creeds as a sufficient articulation of the Christian faith, the sacraments of baptism and Eucharist, and the historic episcopate, locally adapted.[418] All participating denominations consented to uphold these four cardinal tenets as they commenced their journey towards union.

Despite encountering numerous disappointments, setbacks, and bureaucratic challenges over the ensuing years, the vision of a united church gradually took form. Ultimately, a span of 28 years of dedicated efforts and persistent negotiations culminated in the union of 3 prominent South Indian churches - the South India United Church, the Methodist Church, and the Anglican Church - realised on 27th September, 1947. This historic union officially established what is now recognised as the Church of South India (CSI). At its inception, the CSI encompassed 14 dioceses and boasted a membership of approximately 10,17,184 individuals of whom 2,63,680 were communicants,[419] representing a significant milestone in the history of Indian Christianity and exemplifying the spirit of interdenominational cooperation and unity.

13.3. The Church of South India

The year 1947 marked a pivotal moment in the history of Christianity in South India, culminating the lengthy and intensive series of discussions focused on church unification. This effort aimed to create a more cohesive Christian community in the region, bridging diverse denominational lines. The Methodist leader J.S.M. Hooper, a prominent advocate for the Church Union Movement, delivered the inaugural sermon for this significant event. In his address, he articulated the profound importance of the year in shaping a unified Christian identity in South India. As a result of these concerted efforts, the Church of South India (CSI) was officially formed through the merger of various ecclesiastical bodies.

---

[418] See A. E. J. Rawlinson, *The Church of South India: the Lichfield Cathedral Divinity Lectures 1950* (London: Hodder and Stoughton, 1950), 22, 23.

[419] See Gladstone, *United*, 23.

This unification encompassed a diverse array of organisations, including the Madras, Madura, Malabar, Jaffna, Kannada, Telugu, and Travancore Church Councils of the South India United Church. Furthermore, the South Indian branch of the Methodist Church contributed significantly, encompassing the districts of Madras, Trichinopoly, Hyderabad, and Mysore. Alongside this, the Madras, Dornakal, Tinnevelly, Travancore, and Cochin branches of the Church of India, Burma, and Ceylon also played a crucial role[420] in this historical amalgamation.

At the time of the unification, the constituent groups represented a substantial number of adherents: approximately 220,000 Methodists, 290,000 Presbyterians and Congregationalists (from the South India United Church), and a significant 500,000 Anglicans (from the Church of India, Burma, and Ceylon). This monumental effort received backing from various missionary organisations, including the Church of England Zenana Missionary Society, the Church Missionary Society, the Church of Scotland Foreign Mission Committee, the London Missionary Society, along with the British Methodist Missionary Society, the Reformed Church, the American Board of Commissioners for Foreign Missions, and the Society for the Propagation of the Gospel in Foreign Parts.[421]

The inauguration ceremony took place at St. George's Cathedral in Madras, a key venue symbolising the historical significance of this event. On the morning of 27th September 1947, attendees began gathering early, and most were seated by 7:45 AM. The presiding bishop for the ceremony, the Rt. Rev. C. K. Jacob was supported by two presbyters: the Rev. Dr. Wierenga from the South India United Church and the Rev. Paul Ramaseshan from the Methodist Church, reflecting the collaborative spirit of this unification. Following a heartfelt prayer of thanksgiving offered by Rev. Ramaseshan, Bishop Jacob solemnly declared the union, an act that brought the congregation to their feet[422] in a collective acknowledgement of this historic event.

The First Synod of the CSI was held in Madurai from 6-10th March 1948. During this gathering, several key leaders were elected to serve as officers of the Synod:

Moderator: The Most Rev. A. Michael Hollis
Deputy Moderator: The Rt. Rev. C. K. Jacob

---

420 See Gladstone, *United*, 23.

421 See Rajaiah D. Paul, *Ecumenism in Action: A Historical Survey of the Church of South India* (Madras: Christian Literature Service, 1972), 6. Hereafter cited as D. Paul, Ecumenism.

422 See Gladson, *United*, 28.

General Secretary: Mr. G. V. Job
Treasurer: The Rev. J. S. M. Hooper

The Synod made a compelling appeal to all its members to actively engage in the further union of churches. It emphasised evangelism and witness as the church's highest priority. In a forward-looking decision, the Synod committed to joining the World Council of Churches (WCC), which was set to be inaugurated later that same year, and decided to send a delegation to represent the CSI. Additionally, believers from Nandyal and Cuddapah were encouraged to become members of the CSI, with an exhortation to all dioceses to ensure better representation for women and to initiate Women's Fellowship groups[423] within every congregation.

13.3.1. Challenges

13.3.1.1. Recognition of Episcopal Authority

Despite this momentous occasion, the Anglican communion faced immediate challenges concerning the recognition of episcopal authority within the newly formed CSI. The conference participants grappled with the legitimacy of bishops, presbyters, and deacons consecrated or ordained in the CSI following the inauguration. Two contrasting perspectives emerged during discussions. One viewpoint contended that these bishops, presbyters, and deacons should be recognised as valid ministers in the broader Church of Christ and accepted across all branches of the Anglican communion, adhering to existing regulations established by relevant authorities[424] in each region.

The opposing perspective cautioned that it was premature to reach a conclusive determination regarding the specific status of such appointments in the Church of Christ or to recommend their acceptance within the Anglican Communion. The conference participants concurred that there was a collective refusal to outright condemn or invalidate the episcopally consecrated and ordained ministry of the Church of South India. Bishop A.M. Hollis poignantly remarked that "the failure of the conference to reach a consensus on the status of those consecrated and ordained within the Church of South India highlights that the Anglican communion still has significant progress to make in achieving real unity."[425]

---

[423] See Gladstone, *United*, 34.

[424] Rajaiah D. Paul, *The First Decade: An Account of the Church of South India* (Madras: CLS, 1958), 197. Hereafter cited as D. Paul, *The First Decade.*

[425] See D. Paul, *The First Decade*, 197.

13.3.1.2. Personal Jealousies

Another significant issue facing the church is the existence of personal jealousies and the pursuit of selfish interests among its members. This has hindered attempts to unify diverse traditions into a single church community, resulting in failures in various regions. A notable example of this is Rayalaseema, where some factions of continuing Anglicans and individuals from the London Mission chose not only to withdraw from the proposed union but also instigated a complete breakdown of fellowship by initiating litigation concerning property disputes. Similar tensions were observed in Secunderabad, Mavelikara, and Trivandrum, where the disunity was marked by the involvement of a single Anglican congregation in each location. Furthermore, rivalry within the church has often undermined the very unity that was sought.[426] Members themselves have betrayed this newfound solidarity, leading to further complications.

13.3.1.3. Problems Identified by Bishop Chellappa

Bishop Chellappa identified 3 critical elements within the life of the Church of South India that impede its ability to express the spirit, thought, and life of the universal Church in a manner that is truly reflective of Indian conditions and traditions:[427]

1) The most uncharacteristically Indian, or perhaps the least representative of Christian values, aspect of the CSI is its convoluted organisational framework, which is heavily laden with committees and stringent constitutional guidelines.
2) The slow pace of devolution remains a significant hurdle, with ongoing overseas control perpetuated by the influx of foreign financial support, which correlates directly with the amount of external funding received.
3) The CSI continues to function as an unintegrated church, lacking a cohesive identity.

13.3.2. Towards Wider Union

The pursuit of wider union remains a foundational concern for the CSI. In 1953, the Joint Theological Commission highlighted the doctrinal agreements between the CSI and the Lutheran Churches, recommending concrete measures for fostering closer fellowship. These included: (1) enhancing collaboration in evangelical and social work; (2) establishing local organs of fellowship such as pastors, fraternals, joint retreats, and conferences; (3) facilitating the exchange of preachers on appropriate

[426] See D. Paul, *Ecumenism*, 57, 58.

[427] See D. Paul, *Ecumenism*, 57, 58.

occasions; and (4) inviting members of other churches to partake in the Lord's Supper during special circumstances. The CSI Synod accepted these proposals during its assembly in 1954.[428]

13.3.3. Worship

Regarding worship, the Executive Committee of the Synod convened in March 1949 and instructed the Synod Liturgy Committee to create a comprehensive Holy Communion service. This service was designed to incorporate the best elements from all the varied liturgical traditions within the CSI, to use it at the upcoming Synod meeting and develop a form for confirmation or admission to communicant membership that could be employed by Bishops as required. The inaugural Service of the Lord's Supper was celebrated on January 8, 1950, during the Synod session, and was subsequently approved in final form by the 1954 Synod,[429] establishing a distinctively CSI approach to Eucharistic worship.

13.3.4. Women in the Church

Within six months of its formation, the CSI witnessed its female members - previously part of separate women's organizations - desire to unify in a manner resonant with even the village women. In February 1948, a conference for leaders in women's ministry was convened in Trichy, culminating in the first Synod's approval to establish a Women's Fellowship on a national level. Deaconess Carol Graham was appointed to oversee the initiative, which rapidly expanded into a substantial organisation. The fellowship is characterised by its organisation into various groups across villages and urban parishes, hosting meetings on a weekly, bi-weekly, or monthly basis. They also hold retreats and conferences to enrich their collective spiritual journey. This fellowship significantly contributes to the life and witness of the Church, particularly in contexts filled with diverse faiths, as they actively assist in the creation of genuinely Christian homes[430] among their Hindu and Muslim neighbours.

After years of advocacy and dialogue, the Synod resolved in 1984 to ordain women.[431] This historic decision marked a gradual acceptance of the vision and practice of female ordination among the wider congregation.

---

[428] See Gladstone, *United*, 50.

[429] See D. Paul, *Ecumenism*, 33, 34.

[430] See D. Paul, *Ecumenism*, 45, 46.

[431] See Gladstone, *United*, 56.

13.3.5. Statement on Baptism

Concerning baptism, there has been a troubling trend where several members of the church have been misled into participating in the rite known as the Second Baptism, which involves re-baptism by immersion for those previously baptised in infancy. Bishop Legg recognised the need to address this concern and prepared a formal statement that was received and endorsed by the 1968 Synod,[432] which subsequently disseminated it to the dioceses for study and implementation.

13.4. The Church of North India

The series of round-table conferences and negotiating committees held between 1929 and 1970 chronicle the intricate negotiations that ultimately led to the establishment of the Church of North India (CNI). This journey toward church union was far from straightforward; it involved deep and complex discussions that extended beyond the confines of committees. The need for a cohesive union necessitated a delicate balancing act among the diverse church traditions present in the region, each with its own rich heritage and theological nuances.

These committees were composed of a diverse mix of Western missionaries and Indian church leaders, reflecting both the urgency to preserve longstanding customs and the aspiration to create a locally rooted church community. The interplay of these perspectives created a dynamic environment where the challenges of reconciling differing doctrinal positions and worship practices were continually navigated.[433] The commitment to fostering unity among varied Christian denominations was a profound undertaking, requiring not only negotiation but also mutual respect and an understanding of the diverse cultural contexts in which these churches operated.

13.4.1. Round Table Conferences

The 1st Round Table Conference was held on 10-11th April 1929 in Lucknow. The churches represented were Australian Churches of Christ Mission, Australian Methodist Church, Baptist Church, Church of the Brethren Mission, India Mission Disciples of Christ, Methodist Episcopal Church, United Church of Northern India, and Wesleyan Methodist Missionary

---

432 See Gladstone, *United*, 57, 58.

433 See Dhirendra Kumar Sahu, *The Church of North India: A Historical and Systematic Theological Inquiry into an Ecumenical Ecclesiology* (Frankfurt: Peter Lang, 1994), 106, 107. Hereafter cited as Sahu, *The Church of North India*.

Society. The visitors were S.P.G. and the Evangelical Synod of North America.[434]

In 1924, the Presbyterian and Congregational churches in India united to create the United Church of North India, a significant milestone aimed at fostering greater ecumenical collaboration. This new entity issued formal invitations to several other churches and missions across North India, seeking a more comprehensive amalgamation of faith communities. Key discussions during this formative period included the intricate dynamics of church politics, which shaped governance and decision-making within the newly formed body. Another focal point was the theological and liturgical practices surrounding the Sacrament of the Lord's Supper,[435] emphasising the diverse interpretations and rituals associated with this sacred rite.

Furthermore, the inclusion of organisations such as the Friends (Quakers), which operate without formal external rituals, sparked dialogue on how to integrate varying spiritual expressions within a unified church framework. An equally important theme was the recognition of the inherent connections that exist with churches worldwide, underscoring the vital links of fellowship and mission that transcend geographical and cultural boundaries.[436] This desire for unity reflects a broader commitment to fostering collaboration and mutual understanding among global Christian communities.

The 2nd Round Table Conference was held in Delhi on 18-20th November 1930. Churches represented were the Australian Methodist Church; Baptist Church; Church of the Brethren; Church of India, Burma and Ceylon; Methodist Episcopal Church; Society of Friends; United Church of Northern India, and Wesleyan Methodist Church. The visitors were the United Presbyterian Mission of the Punjab and the delegates of the Joint Committee from South India.[437]

A broad doctrinal statement was adopted as a guide for the discussion among the uniting churches:[438]

1) The acknowledgement of the Father, the Son and the Holy Spirit, one God blessed for evermore.
2) The acceptance of the Holy Scripture of the Old and New Testaments as containg all teaching necessary for salvation and as the ultimate standards of our faith.

---

434 See Sahu, *The Church of North India*, 107.

435 See Sahu, *The Church of North India*, 107.

436 See Sahu, *The Church of North India*, 107.

437 See Sahu, *The Church of North India*, 107.

438 See Minutes of the second Round Table Conference, page 10.

3) The commendation of the historic creeds known as the Apostles' and the Nicene as containing valuable statements of Christian doctrine.

The 3rd Round Table Conference was held in Lucknow during 6-8th April 1937. The churches represented were The Church of India, Burma and Ceylon; the Methodist Church (UK); the Methodist Church (Australia); the Methodist Episcopal Church; the Society of Friends and the United Church of North India.[439]

The 4th Round Table Conference was held in Lucknow during 22-23rd November 1939. Churches represented were The Church of India, Burma and Ceylon; the churches connected with BMS; the churches connected with LMS; The Methodist Church (UK); the Methodist Church in Southern Asia; the Methodist Church (Australia); the United Church of North India. Canon T. D. Sully presented the results of a subcommittee that was established at the previous round table conference to examine whether any suggestions in the Joint Council Plan were likely to obstruct a larger union project. It pointed out that the Joint Council had left out all allusions to the Apostles' and Nicene Creeds, which was a departure from the RTC's foundation[440] and outline and may potentially make future attempts at broader unification more challenging.

The 5th Round Table Conference was held in Allahabad from 31st July to 1st August 1941, attended by The Church of India, Burma and Ceylon; the Methodist Church; the Methodist Church in South Asia and the United Church of North India. A proposal regarding ordination and consecration by mutual laying of hands with prayer, using a formula that leaves no room for any scepticism or doubt regarding the unification of the episcopates of the Anglican and Methodist Episcopal churches,[441] was the catalyst for the breakthrough during this conference.

The 6th Round Table Conference was held in Allahabad during 23-24th July 1947. It was attended by the Church of India, Burma and Ceylon, the Methodist Church (British and Australian), the Methodist Church in Southern Asia, and the United Church of North India.[442]

The 7th Round Table Conference was held in Allahabad during 20-22nd February 1948. It was attended by the Church of India, Pakistan, Burma and Ceylon, the Methodist Church (British and Australian), the Methodist Church in Southern Asia, and the United Church of North India.[443]

---

[439] See Sahu, *The Church of North India*, 114.

[440] See Minutes of the fourth Round Table Conference, pages 3-4.

[441] See Minutes of the fifth Round Table Conference, pages 3.

[442] See Sahu, *The Church of North India*, 118.

[443] See Sahu, *The Church of North India*, 119.

13.4.2. Issues and Challenges

In the pursuit of reconciliation and consensus, the Negotiating Committees convened on numerous occasions to address and resolve points of contention. The remarkable commitment displayed by various churches to achieve mutual understanding and harmony can only be described as extraordinary, especially given the considerable obstacles presented during the union negotiations. One of the foremost challenges was the episcopacy issue, which highlighted the divergent governance structures within different denominations. For example, both the Methodist Church of Southern Asia and the Anglican Communion adhere to the episcopal system of governance; however, their approaches differ substantially. The Methodist Church embraces a constitutional form of episcopacy, characterised by a system where church authority is derived from a constitution and collective agreements, while the Anglican Church firmly believes in the Petrine Apostolic succession,[444] maintaining that spiritual authority is passed down through an unbroken line of bishops tracing back to Saint Peter.

Despite this deeply rooted doctrinal divide, a significant breakthrough occurred when representatives from both denominations acknowledged the necessity of accommodating the Church of North India's episcopal framework. They reached a consensus that this structure could effectively fulfil both apostolic traditions and constitutional mandates.[445] This pivotal agreement not only demonstrates the potential for collaborative dialogue but also signifies a crucial step forward in unifying the churches under shared governance principles.

The second difficulty was on the question of ministry. The CNI had set aside the CSI method of gradual unification and had chosen a rite of mutual laying-on of hands with prayer.[446] This was done as an unconditional act of the United Church after the inauguration, and in no way did it imply re-ordination.

The baptism problem emerged as the third significant challenge faced by the CNI. In an effort to unify the varying baptismal traditions and perspectives within its community, the CNI decided to acknowledge both adult and infant baptism as legitimate practices within the United Church framework. For adult members seeking baptism, the process involved a formal ceremony, during which a bishop or presbyter would administer the rite of baptism. Following this sacramental act, confirmation or admission into church membership would take place, signifying their full integration into the faith community. Conversely, individuals who were baptised as

---

[444] See Snaitang, *A History*, 95.

[445] See Snaitang, *A History*, 95.

[446] See Sahu, *The Church of North India*, 123.

infants would undergo a different pathway. At the time of their confirmation, these members would be expected to publicly declare their faith and commitment to the church, effectively affirming the promises made on their behalf during the infant baptism.[447] This approach not only respects the diverse baptismal traditions but also emphasizes the importance of personal affirmation within the CNI.

On the morning of Sunday, 29th November 1970, a momentous event took place as the Church of North India was officially inaugurated in the historic All Saints' Cathedral Compound in Nagpur. The ceremony was presided over by the Rt. Rev. Gurbachan Singh, who was serving as the retiring Moderator of the United Church of Northern India (UCNI) General Assembly. This significant occasion marked the culmination of efforts from 6 diverse and unifying churches that came together to form a single, visible fellowship under the CNI banner. The gathering was characterised by spirited worship, prayers, and a profound sense of unity, reflecting the aspirations of the congregations to foster inclusivity and collaboration in their mission. This day not only symbolised the merging of congregations but also represented a pivotal moment in the history of Indian Christianity, as it aimed to create a more cohesive and dynamic church that could address the spiritual and social needs of the community. The Church of India, Burma and Ceylon had 3,40,000 members, the United Church of North India 1,88,000, the Council of the Baptist Churches in North India 1,10,000, the Church of the Brethren 18,000, the Methodist Church (British and Australian) 10,000 and the Disciples of Christ 7,500.[448]

13.5. Communion of Churches in India

The founding churches - the Church of North India (CNI), the Church of South India (CSI), and the Malankara Mar Thoma Syrian Church (MTC) - collectively established the Communion of Churches in India (CCI) as a visible and dynamic organ that embodies their shared commitment to the expression of life and witness within the Christian community in India. These churches acknowledge their collective identity as part of the singular Church of Jesus Christ in India while retaining their distinct identities, traditions, and organisational frameworks.

The journey towards collaboration began when the CNI extended an invitation to the CSI and Mar Thoma Syrian Church to assemble delegates from each church. This initiative led to the formation of 3 dedicated committees tasked with exploring methods to enhance cooperation and unified participation among the churches in India, setting the foundation for

---

[447] See Snaitang, *A History*, 96.

[448] See Sahu, *The Church of North India*, 137.

a deeper relationship rooted in shared faith.[449] This effort was recognised and celebrated during a meeting of the CSI and MTC Negotiation Commission held on 17th May 1974. Each of these churches then appointed a representative to participate in their respective theological commissions, which subsequently began operating as a unified theological commission,[450] a stepping stone towards greater ecclesiastical unity.

In January 1975, the Joint Theological Commission convened for its inaugural meeting in Madras. The commission's primary objectives included engaging in meaningful discussions around ecclesiology and order, examining relevant theological concerns, and investigating avenues for closer collaboration between the CNI, CSI, and MTC. This endeavour was envisioned to promote unity among diverse congregations while remaining steadfast to the Church's core mission - one that calls all followers of Christ in India to act in solidarity for the Gospel. Following the endorsement of a new model of union among the participating churches, the Joint Council was formally established in Nagpur in July 1978, after the Joint Theological Commission's third meeting in September 1976.[451]

13.5.1. Aims and Objectives of the Communion

The Communion of Churches in India serves several crucial aims and objectives:[452]

1) Unity Representation

To act as the collective body for member churches in pursuit of a visible manifestation of the unity that characterises the whole Church of Jesus Christ in India.

2) Evangelisation Mission

To empower the churches in their mission of evangelising the people of India and witnessing to the righteousness of God, which is revealed in the Gospel of Jesus Christ, while advocating for social justice and a fair society.

3) Peace and Justice

To collaborate with all individuals of goodwill to foster peace anchored in justice and to uphold the integrity of creation.

---

[449] See Snaitang, *A History*, 173.

[450] See "The Communion of Churches in India," https://communionofchurchesinindia.org.in/history.html (7 June 2025). Hereafter cited as "The Communion."

[451] See "The Communion," 1.

[452] See "The Communion," 1.

4) Common Action Exploration

To investigate and explore potential avenues for joint action aimed at fulfilling the mission of the Church both within India and in the global context.

For the churches to foster deeper mutual understanding, strengthen their experience of unity in Christ, and visibly demonstrate this unity, critical considerations of faith, worship, and order, alongside other essential issues stemming from their full communion, must be addressed. They are committed to providing thoughtful recommendations based on these considerations. According to Russell Chandran, the Joint Council was established under the premise that the 3 churches, united through shared sacraments and ministry as well as common doctrinal beliefs,[453] constitute one church in essence.

This Council was intended to serve as a tangible manifestation of the inherent unity that already exists among them. One significant aspect of this visible unity was the adoption of a common name; however, this idea faced resistance due to concerns about preserving the distinct identities of the three churches.[454] Although the potential for biological unity under a shared name was ultimately set aside, the effort to illustrate unity through a collaborative framework began while ensuring the autonomy of each church remained unimpeded.

At a meeting of the Executive Committees of the Church of North India, Church of South India, and the Mar Thoma Church, held in Charal Kunnu, Kerala, from 11-14th November 1999, it was unanimously proposed to adopt the name "The Communion of Churches in India" (CCI) to better reflect the deepening unity experienced among these 3 bodies. The name change was officially accepted and declared during the 10th Joint Council Meeting, conducted in Calcutta on 13-14th November 2000. As outlined in the CCI's Constitution, the General Assembly convenes approximately every 4 years to discuss and strategise[455] on matters of common interest.

The inaugural General Assembly of the Communion of Churches took place in Cochin on March 10, 2004. This was followed by the second General Assembly, which occurred from during 3-5th July 2006, at the CSI Centre in Chennai. The third General Assembly was held at CNI Bhavan in New Delhi on 2-3rd March, 2010. During the second meeting of the Joint Council's Executive Committee on 5th May 1979, it was resolved to designate the second Sunday in November as the annual Festival of Unity, promoting solidarity and mutual support among congregations. This

---

[453] See "The Communion," 1.

[454] See Snaitang, *A History*, 173.

[455] See "The Communion," 2.

Festival of Unity, also known as the CCI Week, includes a special united worship service, fostering a spirit of togetherness and collaboration among the members.

13.5.2. Challenges

The leaders of the Joint Council approached the idea of church unity with earnest commitment. At their second meeting in Shantigiri, Aluva, Kerala, representatives from the CSI, Mar Thoma Church, and CNI reaffirmed their dedication to the founding principles of the CCI and engaged in ongoing discussions regarding actionable strategies to realise true unity among the churches.[456] The CCI has identified several challenges that need to be addressed:

1) Fostering unity at the grassroots level, particularly in the context of community struggles for social justice.
2) Making tangible the unity already present among various congregations, promoting a visible manifestation of this solidarity.
3) Transitioning from being mere institutions to becoming dynamic movements that actively engage in society's pressing issues.
4) Empowering congregants as a form of service that promotes justice, encouraging individual and communal actions that reflect Christian teachings.
5) Shifting from bureaucratic structures to more people-centred approaches, emphasising the importance of community engagement.
6) Focusing from a national perspective to localised actions that resonate with individual congregations and their unique needs. In his keynote address, the Moderator of the CNI articulated a profound call to introspection: "We need to learn lessons from our past, from our mistakes, and also from the wisdom of our ancestors, and be guided by the Holy Spirit toward the Unity that God desires. Let us journey together anew and make a fresh beginning in our pursuit of walking united in faith and action."[457]

The implications of these efforts are significant. With the ultimate goal of unity among all Indian followers of Christ, there is hope for the eventual merging of various churches. Presently, the CNI, CSI, and MTC enjoy a relationship of complete communion, acknowledging and accepting one another's clergy, doctrines, baptisms, sacraments, ministries, and interpretations of scripture. This profound acceptance allows congregations

[456] See Paominlen Kipgen, "Church Union Movement in India and its Contributions," Academia.edu.

[457] See "The Communion," 1.

and individuals to regularly utilise a common lectionary and liturgical calendar developed by the CCI, facilitating a synchronised worship experience across member churches.

13.6. United Theological College

One of the first and most notable examples of collaboration and ecumenism in theological education is the United Theological College (UTC). The College was established on 8th July 1910, and it was initially housed in the Mission Road LMS Seminary facilities. For Rs. 10,500.00, the current college location behind the Cantonment Railway Station was acquired in 1912. Rev. Dr. Robert F. Horton placed the cornerstone for the Chapel on 22nd November 1912, and Dr. John R. Mott lay the cornerstone for the Library[458] on the same day. The UTC was accorded autonomous status in 1976 for the BD programme by the Senate of Serampore College (University). Besides the B.D. course, the College offers M.Th., D.Th., and various other programmes under the Senate of Serampore system.

The integrity of every area of study is accorded the weight it deserves in the College's multidisciplinary programs. One of the distinctive aspects of theological education at UTC is the emphasis on critical, creative, and rigorous study in the educational process. The College is still cognizant of the different contextual issues that society as a whole faces. The ecumenical ethos of theological education at UTC is evident in the manner in which theological thought is expressed and reflected, as well as in how people coexist.[459] An essential part of this curriculum is practical ministry, which gives students exposure to a variety of religious and non-religious environments.

The college's staff and students are from all around India and overseas. A community that is so multicultural and interdenominational provides a singular cross-cultural experience[460] as well as chances to develop ecumenical understanding.

13.6.1. Mission of the College[461]

The College is founded of the faith that God has given new life and hope for the entire world in Jesus Christ, and that God has called the Church

---

[458] See S. Manickam, *United Theological College: A Brief History of Change and Continuity*, 1910-2000 (Bangalore: UTC, 2000), 39. Hereafter cited as Manickam, *United*.

[459] See Chilkuri Vasantha Rao, "The Continuing Legacy of UTC in the Field of Ecumenical Theological Education," in *Bangalore Theological Forum*, LIV/1, (June, 2022), 116 (115-131). Hereafter cited as Rao, "Continuing Legacy."

[460] See *The United Theological College Bangalore: Handbook 2024-2025* (Bangalore: UTC, 2045), 6. Hereafter cited as *The United Theological College*.

[461] See *The United Theological College*, 8, 9.

into being to share this life and hope with all humankind through worship, witness and purposeful action. The College recognizes that as a community it is set in the midst of neighbours of other faiths and diverse ideological conviction with whom it shares the mystery of human existence, and that its calling cannot be fulfilled apart from the ferment of renewal in society.

The College believes that for the fulfilment of the Church's calling God has given to the Church various forms of ministry and differing gifts appropriate to each, in order the whole Church may be involved in God's mission of liberation and reconciliation in the world. In the light of this understanding, the College seeks to be a community committed to active discernment of and participation in God's mission through a common life of disciplined study and devotion to God. To this end the College provides programmes of study, devotional life and practical experience for men and women to prepare themselves for the different ministries to which they are called, it seeks to provide students with the conceptual tools, spiritual discipline and practical skills which will equip them for a radical relevant ministry in the Church and in society, responding critically and creatively to the religio-cultural heritage and socio-politico-economic reality of India.

The College constantly seeks new ways to reflect, teach, learn, evaluate, and grow together as a Christian community. It is committed to wholeness in theological education, bringing together people of different confessional traditions, languages, regions, and countries. Its programme of education is inter-disciplinary in character, while recognising the distinctive contribution and integrity of each discipline. It seeks seriously the task of theological research, seeing such theological reflection as a necessary means of enrichment of the Church's faith and life. The College seeks to provide opportunities for theological education to people in the congregations who seek an informed understanding of the Christian faith in order to serve Christ more effectively in the world.

The College continues to cooperate with other theological colleges as well as with centres of learning of other religious persuasions or of secular convictions, and it will open its facilities of study and research to all who come in search of truth and fullness of life.

13.6.2. Theological Courses of Ecumenical Nature Offered at UTC

UTC offers courses for the Bachelor of Divinity, Master of Theology, and Doctor of Theology degrees to promote ecumenical theological viewpoints and to fortify ecumenical partnerships. Additionally, Martin Luther Christian University offers Master of Arts courses in Counselling and Pastoral Psychology, a Postgraduate Diploma in Counselling Proficiency, a Diploma in Christian Studies, an Online Diploma in Eco-Justice Ministries in collaboration with CWM, and a Diploma in Counselling Proficiency.

Through its Distance Learning department, it also provides lay theological courses, specifically the Bachelor of Christian Studies and Diploma in Christian Studies[462] programmes.

13.6.3. Ecumenical Ecclesial Exposure

In addition to helping the local Presbyters celebrate the Eucharist and lead youth groups or Sunday School ministries, students have the chance to take part in the Sunday worship services. This allows students to participate directly in running different programmes in their churches. The BD students are exposed to the worship styles and denominational differences[463] of other churches through this curriculum.

13.6.4. Intensive Field Education

For three weeks each year, participants in the Intensive Field Education program spend time with people in their natural environments. Throughout India, UTC has partnerships with 35 organisations, including diaconal, people's movements, chaplaincy, rehabilitation, palliative care, and urban and rural integrated development centres. Every year, as a component of the field education program, a professor who is actively involved with people's concerns gives a diaconal lecture to foster an integral and innovative motivation and help students come up with suitable ways to deal with social issues.[464] All of these exercises help students develop their theological and ecumenical viewpoints.

For both staff and students, the College's ecumenical, theological, national, and worldwide ethos held theological and sociological relevance. In terms of theology, both students and faculty learn firsthand how the Gospel was frequently misrepresented when examined solely from the perspective of a specific denomination or society through communal living, shared worship, and study. They gain a profound understanding of Christian faith within the collective experience of the Church as a whole, thanks to the diversity exhibited in the classroom and on campus.[465]

In order to counteract the limiting consequences of a narrow dogmatism, UTC seeks to extend Christian perspectives. Additionally, UTC cultivates a theology that strives for social change. For all Christians, the College seeks to instil a fresh outlook and a fresh vision. The Indian Church has historically been seen as a self-centred group that is committed to safeguarding our rights as a minority. Manickam, however, correctly

---

[462] See Rao, "Continuing Legacy," 117.

[463] See Rao, "Continuing Legacy," 119.

[464] See Rao, "Continuing Legacy," 120.

[465] See Manickam, *United*, 107, 108.

claims that the UTC reminds the Church of the necessity of a "radical" understanding of our religion in opposition to this way of thinking.[466] The Church is expected to dedicate herself in service to and identification with others, and UTC emphasises this point.

The College's academic program was designed to interact with the new difficulties and challenges of the changing society. The pastoral ministry has suffered greatly as a result of the sole focus on academic accomplishments and intellectual prowess, with little attention paid to pastoral training. Teachers are therefore encouraged to periodically assess their knowledge[467] of pastoral problems, scholarly proficiency, pedagogical skills, etc.

In addition, the establishment of the Young Men's Christian Association (YMCA) Training School in 1913 represents a significant milestone in the organisation's commitment to ecumenism, education, and community service. By September 1950, in response to the growing demand for accommodations, the YMCA Council undertook an expansion of the hostel facilities, adding 8 additional rooms to better serve its student population.[468] This development underscores the organisation's dedication to fostering a supportive environment conducive to both personal and professional growth.

The Christian Institute of Management (CIM), in collaboration with the YMCA, has been overseeing the YMCA's Secretary Training Programme in UTC. This comprehensive training initiative is designed not only as a professional endorsement for individuals aspiring to become YMCA secretaries but also serves as a crucial step in their career advancement. Spanning 1 year, the program is a well-coordinated effort among 3 esteemed institutions: the United Theological College, which provides rigorous training on theological subjects; the YMCA, which imparts its core vision and policies; and CIM, which emphasises essential leadership and management competencies.[469]

All training sessions are conducted in the serene environment of the United Theological College campus in Bangalore, renowned for its conducive atmosphere for learning. This unique collaboration guarantees that candidates receive a well-rounded education that equips them for effective leadership roles within the YMCA community and beyond.

The YMCA Secretarial Training Program has made considerable advancements thus far. Mr. Rajiv Kunwar John, Director of the YMCA

---

[466] See Manickam, United, 108.

[467] See Manickam, *United*, 113.

[468] See The United Theological College, 7.

[469] See "Training Leaders and Visionaries," https://www.cimindia.in/post/training-leaders-and-visionaries (3 June 2025). Hereafter cited as "Training Leaders and Visionaries."

Training and Leadership Department at the National YMCA Institute, emphasises that this collaboration has yielded valuable insights into various management disciplines, such as Organisational Behaviour and Resource Mobilisation.[470] These focal areas are critical for enhancing the skills and competencies of participants in the program.

13.7. Ecumenical Christian Centre

Ecumenical Christian Centre was established in 1963 by the Late Rev. Dr. M. A. Thomas with the vision of promoting "unity of humankind as an expression of radical obedience to Christ." He said,[471]

> Ecumenical and church unity are not identical terms. There is nothing specifically Christian about the word ecumenism. It concerns humanity, all aspects of their life and concerns, the unity of all mankind, irrespective of religion, race, sex, or political ideology. Therefore, justice and peace political, economical, social and cultural aspects of life are all integral to ecumenism.

The ECC (Ecumenical Community Centre) serves as a dynamic and inclusive space where individuals from diverse faith backgrounds and those with sceptical views can convene to engage in meaningful discussions focused on moral values, ethical standards, and collaborative efforts aimed at societal change and unity. Encompassing an expansive area of 29 acres, the ECC features 27 meticulously designed structures. These include comfortable accommodations for staff, state-of-the-art facilities for hosting conferences and conventions,[472] and dedicated spaces for workshops and community gatherings.

The Centre prides itself on its unwavering commitment to environmental conservation, actively promoting the preservation of both local flora and fauna, which reflects its core values of stewardship and sustainability. As an international entity, the ECC operates in accordance with its comprehensive governing documents and holds official registration as a charitable organization under the Indian Companies Act of 1956, ensuring compliance with established regulations and standards. The ECC Council is composed of 22 dedicated representatives hailing from a variety of Christian traditions, including Protestant, Orthodox, Roman Catholic, and Mar Thoma backgrounds.[473] This diverse representation fosters a rich

---

[470] See "Training Leaders and Visionaries," 1.

[471] As cited by Chunakara, *Ecumenism in Asia*, 205.

[472] See "Ecumenical Christian Centre," https://ecumenicalchristiancentre-iset.blogspot.com (3 June 2025). Hereafter cited as "Ecumenical Christian Centre."

[473] See "Ecumenical Christian Centre," 1.

tapestry of perspectives, enabling meaningful dialogue and collaboration on pressing social issues while promoting a culture of mutual respect and understanding among different faith communities.

13.7.1. ECC's Programmes

13.7.1.1. The Ecumenical Christian Centre organises seminars and workshops that encompass a broad spectrum of topics, including human rights, spirituality, ecology, and the environment, as well as integrity in public life. The objective of these initiatives is to promote appropriate ethical and moral responses to these critical issues.

13.7.1.2. The Indian School of Ecumenical Theology, a branch of ECC, conducts programmes that underscore the unity of humanity and the integrity of creation.

13.7.1.3. Another division, the International Institute of Horticulture Management (IIHM), offers specialised training in advanced floriculture, precision farming, and the cultivation of medicinal and aromatic plants, among other subjects.

13.7.1.4. Furthermore, ECC provides free educational opportunities for the children of migrant workers residing in adjacent villages.

In 2013, the Ecumenical Christian Centre commemorated its 50 years of dedicated service to the nation, the churches in India, and the wider community.[474] Over these 5 decades, tens of thousands of individuals, irrespective of their religion, caste, class, age, race, gender, or nationality, have benefited from the diverse programs offered by ECC.

The Ecumenical Christian Centre (ECC) is dedicated to fostering a spirit of peaceful coexistence and harmonious living among individuals of diverse religious beliefs and systems. To achieve this, the ECC actively engages in addressing pressing social issues through a comprehensive approach. Throughout the year, the Centre organizes a variety of conferences, seminars, and interactive discussions that examine pertinent and significant topics. These discussions often include advocacy for human rights, during which distinguished thought leaders and activists propose strategies for the protection and promotion of fundamental freedoms, especially for marginalised groups.

The ECC also explores the intersection of ecology and faith, emphasising the moral responsibility of spiritual communities in environmental stewardship and sustainable practices. It highlights actionable measures that faith-based organisations can adopt to contribute to ecological preservation and climate justice. Furthermore, the ECC provides training in

[474] See "Ecumenical Christian Centre," 1.

conflict resolution, equipping participants with essential skills to mediate and amicably resolve disputes, thereby fostering peaceful relationships within their communities. Moreover, the Centre underscores the importance of effective communication as a means to bridge cultural divides, facilitating dialogue that enhances understanding and respect among diverse groups. It prioritises development education tailored to empower marginalised communities, thereby offering them resources and opportunities to express their concerns and advocate for their rights. The discussions frequently focus on peace and reconciliation efforts in post-conflict settings, promoting healing and collaboration across various divides.

A crucial aspect of the ECC's mission is its commitment to examining and advocating for the rights of individuals with disabilities and sexual minorities, ensuring their inclusion in societal dialogues. Through these initiatives, the Ecumenical Christian Centre aspires to cultivate a culture characterised by understanding, respect, and collaboration among all community members, thereby promoting a more inclusive society. Over the years, the ECC has evolved into an essential forum for dialogue concerning India's socio-economic and political developments. It has developed a range of programs designed to strengthen the unity movement among churches, while also exploring opportunities for different religious traditions to collaborate on pressing social concerns and innovate solutions. Since its establishment, the ECC has built a robust network of contacts and constructive associations with both secular and religious organisations, along with leaders of secular ideologies. As articulated by M. A. Thomas, the founding of the ECC represents a transformative quest for a new style of Christian obedience that addresses the myriad challenges presented by socio-political and economic realms,[475] thereby paving the way for meaningful engagement with contemporary societal issues.

The experiences of M. A. Thomas facilitated the implementation of innovative methods of dialogue and interaction with individuals from diverse faith backgrounds through ECC programs. While interreligious dialogue was often regarded as a contemporary approach within the church's mission, M. A. Thomas actively engaged with individuals from various religions at the ECC to facilitate important discussions on issues pertinent to the Indian social and political context. He articulated his position by stating that "dialogue does not necessarily imply reaching a mutual agreement," and that "in an interfaith dialogue, we may opt to agree to disagree."[476]

---

[475] See Chunakara, *Ecumenism in Asia*, 206, 207.

[476] Chunakara, *Ecumenism in Asia,* 208.

13.7.2. Contributions to Nation-Building and Social Change

In response to the urgent challenges associated with nation-building and social change in India, the ECC initiated a series of training programmes commencing in the late 1960s. Notable initiatives such as the National Citizenship Academy, the School of Politics, the School of Economics, and Vicharodaya College were established to offer young individuals from diverse backgrounds, irrespective of their religion or caste, opportunities to engage with the ECC.[477] These programs facilitated learning, knowledge exchange, and meaningful interactions among participants, thereby promoting a sense of unity and collective advancement.

Participants of the training programs and courses offered by the ECC transformed into active advocates for social and human rights within their communities. Their experiences equipped them with the tools and knowledge needed to serve both the church and society in multifaceted ways. As a result, the ECC played a pivotal role in broadening the understanding of ecumenism, demonstrating that it transcends the confines of being solely a church or Christian concern. This approach highlights that ecumenism encompasses a wider spectrum of human experience and social justice, inviting diverse perspectives and fostering collaboration across various faiths and cultures.[478] Through these efforts, the ECC not only nurtured spiritual unity but also championed a more inclusive vision of social responsibility and ethical engagement in the world.

13.7.3. The Indian School of Ecumenical Theology (ISET)

The ISET serves as a pivotal programmatic arm of the Ecumenical Christian Centre (ECC), having been established in 1988. Its foundation was laid to provide a robust theological framework through a diverse array of educational initiatives. The primary objective of ISET is encapsulated in its mission to "evolve and share a Common Faith Vision," which symbolises a profound commitment to the Reign of God. This vision underscores a collective journey of solidarity with the entire cosmic community, aimed at realizing the fulfillment of this divine purpose. ISET actively organizes regional institutes in collaboration with various centres and organisations that operate in different linguistic and cultural contexts. These institutes are designed to disseminate broader ecumenical concerns, reinforcing the collective mission of God across diverse communities. The ecumenical vision championed by ISET is grounded in three fundamental thrusts:

---

[477] See See Chunakara, *Ecumenism in Asia*, 212.

[478] See Chunakara, *Ecumenism in Asia*, 213.

1) Inter-Church Relations

Facilitating dialogue and collaboration among various Christian denominations to promote unity and understanding.

2) Inter-Religious Engagement

Engaging with diverse religious traditions to foster respect, dialogue, and cooperative action.

3) Cosmic Awareness

Recognising the interconnectedness of all creation and advocating for a holistic approach to theology that acknowledges ecological and cosmic dimensions.

These thrusts collectively represent the comprehensive ecumenical process that ISET endeavours to promote. In alignment with these objectives, ISET is committed to:

- Viewing the entirety of the world as both "the text" and "the context" for theological reflection, emphasising the importance of engaging with real-world issues.
- Actively involving all churches and the broader human community in the collective process of theologising, thus encouraging participatory approaches to theology.
- Discovering, celebrating, and promoting the rich diversity and heritage found within all Christian and religious traditions, recognising that such diversity enhances the understanding of faith.
- Fostering the unity of humankind and all creation by critically analysing the divisive and destructive forces that permeate our world. This includes identifying root causes of conflict and proposing pathways toward healing, reconciliation, and peace grounded in justice.

13.7.4. ECC Neighbourhood Interactive Forum

In addition, the ECC Neighbourhood Interactive Forum (ENIF) was launched in 2007 with the intent of creating a vibrant platform for residents in the vicinity of the ECC. This initiative encourages residents to gather periodically for fellowship and mutual interaction. ENIF fosters a communal atmosphere where participants can candidly discuss pressing issues of common interest while also exploring and implementing community development programs tailored to address specific needs. The forum serves as a collaborative space where all residents' associations within Whitefield unite at the ECC, contributing to and embodying the overarching vision of the Centre. Through engagement in ENIF, community members can work together towards building a more cohesive and supportive neighbourhood, rooted in shared values and collective responsibility.

13.8. Christian Medical College and Hospital, Vellore

Founded in 1900, the Christian Medical College and Hospital (CMC) in Vellore stands as a cornerstone of India's ecumenical movement, dedicating itself to a mission rooted deeply in the healing ministry of Christ. CMC exemplifies excellence through an unwavering commitment to research, high-quality medical service, and comprehensive education. Embracing the vision of its founder, Dr. Ida Scudder, the institution cultivates compassionate, skilled, and ethically principled individuals who embody the role of servant leaders.[479] CMC strives to be a shining example of Christ's healing for both local and international communities, collaborating with churches and organisations to foster outreach, education, service, and research.

As one of India's premier medical, educational, and research institutions, CMC has earned a reputation for academic excellence and innovative healthcare. In 1918, it pioneered the introduction of the Licentiate Medical Practitioner degree, aimed specifically at empowering women in medicine. The medical college became coeducational in 1947, following the commencement of the MBBS degree program in 1942. CMC celebrated significant milestones, including the centenary of medical education in 2018, the 100th anniversary of the Town Campus in 2024, and the 125th anniversary of the institution as a whole in 2025.

13.8.1. Hospital Network

CMC boasts an extensive healthcare network comprising six campuses in and around Vellore, featuring a total of 3,675 beds across primary, secondary, tertiary, and quaternary care teaching hospitals. Each facility is recognised globally for its advanced multispecialty medical care. Originating from a modest single-room clinic founded by Dr. Ida Sophia Scudder, daughter of second-generation American missionaries, the institution has transformed into a multifaceted medical college offering a wide array of courses in medicine, nursing, and allied health sciences. As a strictly non-profit organization, CMC allocates all generated funds towards supporting student education dand providing free or heavily subsidized medical care to underprivileged patients. Additionally, the institution invests in charitable outreach initiatives and infrastructure projects to expand its capacities and fulfill its mission. CMC is dedicated to social and environmental

[479] See Victor James, "Indian Expressions of Ecumenism," https://www.scribd.com/document/712933047/Indian-Expression-of-Ecumenism-by-Victor-James, p. 12 (5 June 2025).

responsibility, ensuring transparency and accountability in managing the resources entrusted to it.

13.8.2. Mission and Vision

The Christian Medical College in Vellore aims to exemplify the healing ministry of Christ by striving for excellence in teaching, research, and service,[480] thereby making a significant impact on community health.

The primary mission of CMC Vellore is to educate, train, and nurture compassionate, highly skilled, and ethically grounded individuals who will lead healthcare teams and communities as servant leaders. Graduates are equipped to engage in various facets of healthcare, including research, education, prevention, treatment, rehabilitation, and palliative care. With a steadfast dedication to professional excellence, CMC creates a culture of compassion in healthcare delivery. It prioritises the adoption of innovative, suitable, affordable, and empathetic technologies to improve patient care.

By fostering a spirit of inquiry and commitment to truth, CMC aims to understand and address God's purposes and intentions within the realm of research. This involves exploring the root causes of health and illness, refining therapeutic interventions, and optimising resource utilization. CMC remains resolute in its dedication to promoting health and wholeness for individuals and communities, with a particular focus on vulnerable, marginalized, and disabled populations. Through a collaborative approach, the institution actively seeks partnerships with like-minded organisations both within India and globally to enhance its outreach, educational, service, and research programmes.[481] As a living embodiment of Christ's healing ministry, CMC aspires to collaborate closely with both Indian Church institutions and the broader global Church community to extend its impact.

13.8.3. Motto

The motto is, "Not to be served, but to serve." The motto of CMC Vellore is inspired by the teachings of Jesus Christ from the Bible, "Not to be ministered unto but to minister," emphasising the principle of serving others rather than seeking to be served. This foundational ethos underpins the entire organisation, which is committed to improving healthcare in India. CMC Vellore, as a philanthropic institution, has a profound impact on the health landscape of the nation.[482] While millions of patients directly benefit from the hospital services, the ripple effect of training countless healthcare

---

[480] See "Vision and Mission," https://www.cmcvellore.ac.in/vision-mission/ (5 June 2025).

[481] See "Vision and Mission," https://www.cmcvellore.ac.in/vision-mission/ (5 June 2025).

[482] See "Motto," https://www.cmcvellore.ac.in/motto/ (5 June 2025).

professionals has an even more extensive influence, as these individuals go on to treat, educate, and uplift communities across the country.

Although many patients can pay for their medical care, CMC Vellore employs a model where surplus revenue generated from paying patients is reinvested into training programs and educational initiatives. This surplus also funds subsidies and free care for those unable to afford treatment. Importantly, this mission transcends religious affiliations, as both Christians and individuals from other faiths receive uncompromised care. The institution operates without financial support from the government or external entities for its essential functions; however, research endeavours, the development of new programs and infrastructure, the expansion of free and subsidised healthcare for the underprivileged, and outreach initiatives are often made possible through external funding.[483] CMC Vellore aspires to ensure that nobody is denied care due to financial constraints, irrespective of their religious background.

13.8.4. Department of Community Health

At the heart of CMC Vellore's efforts to promote community health is the Community Health and Development Programme (CHAD), which was established in 1955. CHAD serves as a training nexus for medical, nursing, and paramedical students, postgraduate trainees, and healthcare professionals by providing robust educational opportunities through its training centre, outpatient clinic, and secondary care hospital. The programme has gained international recognition for its outstanding contributions to epidemiology and translational research in healthcare.

13.8.5. Rural Unit for Health and Social Affairs (RUHSA)

Situated 25 kilometres from Vellore, RUHSA was founded in 1944 to address the healthcare needs of rural populations. This initiative offers a comprehensive array of primary healthcare services, inpatient treatment, mobile health services, and vocational training programmes. It also actively promotes income-generating enterprises and enhances agricultural practices, fostering sustainable community development.

13.8.6. Low Cost Effective Care Unit & Shalom Family Medicine Centre

Established in 1982, the Low Cost Effective Care Unit (LCECU) is dedicated to providing essential healthcare services to impoverished urban neighbourhoods. As a division of the Family Medicine Department, LCECU offers primary and secondary care to low-income individuals. The unit has 48 beds and operates both inpatient and outpatient services at the Schell Campus. Moreover, it organises outreach clinics in seven economically

---

[483] See "Motto," https://www.cmcvellore.ac.in/motto/ (5 June 2025).

disadvantaged neighbourhoods in Vellore. LCECU is instrumental in advancing primary care research and offers valuable training for interns and postgraduate students specialising in family medicine.

13.8.7. The Department of Ophthalmology

One of the most esteemed annals of CMC Vellore, the Department of Ophthalmology was founded in 1900. It occupies the 40-bed Mary Taber Schell Memorial Hospital for Women and Children, named in honour of the donor's wife. The Eye and ENT division was initiated in 1928 under the leadership of Dr. Pauline Jeffery at Schell Hospital. By 1938, plans emerged to modernise the hospital facilities and enhance the MBBS curriculum. Given the rising demand for ophthalmic services, a dedicated department for eye care was deemed essential, leading to the establishment of the 14-bed Schell Eye Hospital in 1941, utilising resources from the former Schell Hospital.

13.8.8. College of Nursing Community Health (CONCH)

In 1987, the Community Health Nursing Department launched the College of Nursing Community Health (CONCH) programme to meet the urgent healthcare needs in rural regions. CONCH extends its services to 25 villages, catering to a combined population of approximately 72,000, alongside a town population of 27,000 across two Community Development blocks in the Vellore and Ranipet districts.[484] This initiative works collaboratively with local communities while leveraging existing infrastructure provided by both governmental and private entities.

CMC Vellore's dedication to academia and society is exemplified through various initiatives, including the Annual Virtual Ecumenical Leadership Forum.[485] This forum aims to foster collaboration among the foundation's affiliated faith-based organisations, facilitating exploration of divine purposes and transformative changes in the context of global missions.

Conclusion

The Indian expressions of ecumenism reflect a courageous journey of faith communities seeking unity in diversity and relevance in mission. From ecclesial unions to educational and medical institutions, Indian ecumenical initiatives have consistently prioritised inclusivity, dialogue, and social transformation. While structural unification has seen significant milestones,

---

[484] See "Outreach," https://www.cmcvellore.ac.in/about-us-outreach/ (5 June 2025).

[485] See "2nd Annual Ecumenical Leadership Forum Takes Place Virtually," https://vellorecmc.org/uncategorized/2nd-annual-ecumenical-leadership-forum-takes-place-virtually/ (5 June 2025).

such as the formation of CSI and CNI, the deeper goal of fostering a shared Christian witness in a multi-religious and socio-economically complex society continues to face both theological and practical challenges. Institutions like UTC, ECC, and CMC Vellore illustrate how ecumenism in India extends beyond church polity into realms of education, health, and community engagement. Ultimately, Indian ecumenism stands as a testament to the persistent hope for Christian unity grounded in contextual theology, common mission, and an unwavering commitment to justice, peace, and reconciliation.

Chapter 14

Council of Churches in Mizoram

The church union movement in Mizoram has its roots dating back to 1949, shortly after the end of World War II, when prominent leaders from the Presbyterian and Baptist churches came together for a significant dialogue on church unity in the town of Thenzawl. This landmark meeting marked the beginning of a series of efforts aimed at fostering a sense of unity among various Christian denominations in the region.

Nevertheless, despite at least 10 meetings held at diverse venues over the years, substantial progress towards a unified front remained elusive. In a notable development, the 2 southern Mizoram churches - the Evangelical Church of Maraland (ECM) and the Congregational Church of India Maraland (CCIM) - finally reconciled after being separated for three and a half decades. The trying times of the COVID-19 pandemic have now faded into the past, paving the way for a divinely ordained opportunity for reconciliation and the formation of a church council. This culminated in the establishment of the Council of Churches in Mizoram (CCM) on 27th October 2024, at the Mission Veng Presbyterian Church in Aizawl. This date is not just symbolic; it also commemorates 130 years since the advent of Christianity in Mizoram.

The CCM comprises the largest and most influential Christian denominations in the state, including the Mizoram Presbyterian Church, the Baptist Church of Mizoram, the Evangelical Church of Maraland, the Lairam Jesus Christ Baptist Church, the Church of Jesus Christ, the Evangelical Free Church of India, the Independent Church of India, and the Wesleyan Church of Mizoram. The Zomi Baptist Church, although its membership application has been tentatively approved, is still awaiting final confirmation to join this collaborative body.

14.1. Mizoram's Ecclesiastical History can be Broadly Categorised into 4 Distinct Periods

14.1.1. The First Period (1894-1948)

This era saw the establishment of 3 primary church denominations within Mizoram: the Evangelical Church of Maraland, the Baptist Church of Mizoram, and the Mizoram Presbyterian Church. During these formative years, the relationship between the Presbyterian and Baptist churches flourished, marked by collaboration and shared initiatives. They jointly published a periodical named *Kristian Tlangau,* which served as a platform for disseminating church news and information. Furthermore, they co-created a cherished hymn book still utilised in worship today. Each year, during their apex body meetings, they honoured their connection by assigning fraternal delegates to one another,[486] acting under the pretence of belonging to a singular denominational entity.

14.1.2. The Second Period (1949-1983)

This phase commenced in 1949 when leaders from the Baptist and Presbyterian churches gathered in Thenzawl to deliberate on mechanisms for achieving church unity. Over the next three decades, those involved conducted around 10 meetings at various locations with the same objective. The Mara Independent Evangelical Church joined this movement in 1970. A remarkable moment came during the 6th meeting in 1972, where a groundbreaking resolution was adopted to form a "Zoram Christian Council,"[487] laying the groundwork for future union efforts. By the 9th meeting in 1981, a draft constitution was also approved, signalling a serious intent to formalise the union.

14.1.3. The Dark Period (1884-2010)

A challenging era commenced in 1984 when the two principal churches, the Baptists and the Presbyterians, violated established geographical boundaries, leading to a complete breakdown in their relationship. Each church began to operate independently, often encroaching on the territory and congregations of the other. This fractious period had dire repercussions for the wider community, sparking concern among church officials and members of the

---

486 See Lalhmangaiha, "Brief History of Council of Churches in Mizoram," in *Presbyterian Review,* 30/2, (July-December, 2024) in 21-27. Hereafter cited as Lalhmangaiha, "Brief History of Council of Churches in Mizoram."

487 See Lalhmangaiha, "Brief History of Council of Churches in Mizoram," 21, 22.

Mizo Theological Association,[488] who sought to reignite discussions on a church merger to address the deteriorating situation.

14.1.4. The Brighter Period (2011-2023)

In this transformative phase, leadership inspired by the Holy Spirit cultivated an environment conducive to reconciliation and unity among the churches. During its 92nd Session in December 2015, the Synod, the highest authority in the Mizoram Presbyterian Church, received a proposal to explore the formation of a church council. Proposed by the Champhai South Presbytery, Aizawl Bethel Presbytery, and Aizawl East Presbytery, the Synod endorsed this proposal and instructed the Synod Executive Committee to pursue it diligently.

In 2021, the Baptist Church of Mizoram Assembly made a decisive resolution to investigate the formation of a council, while the Evangelical Church of Maraland initiated steps to facilitate joint participation between the Baptist Church of Mizoram and the Mizoram Presbyterian Church in their respective annual meetings.[489]

In 2022, the Mizoram Synod dispatched 2 delegation teams to engage with the headquarters of the Baptist Church of Mizoram in Serkawn, Lunglei, and the Lairam Isua Krista Baptist Kohhran headquarters in Lawngtlai. The meetings yielded positive results, underscoring a renewed commitment to unity. However, the COVID-19 pandemic posed a challenge, preventing the MPC and BCM from conducting their scheduled joint meeting on May 21, 2022. Despite this setback, they reconvened on 26th August 2022, at the BCM headquarters in Serkawn, Lunglei, where they passed several important resolutions, including a priority focus on organising a gathering of all churches in Mizoram to further consolidate their efforts towards unity and collaboration. The resolutions were:[490]

1) The responsibility for convening a gathering of all churches in Mizoram is to be assigned to the Mizoram Presbyterian Church.
2) The Baptist Church of Mizoram is designated as the host for the meeting and shall also appoint the recording secretary for the event.
3) The initial gathering will invite representatives from the Salvation Army, the Baptist Church of Mizoram, the Evangelical Church of Maraland, the Mizoram Presbyterian Church, Lairam Isua Krista Baptist Kohhran, and IKK Bualpui (Ng), with each church requested to send 7 representatives.

---

[488] See Lalhmangaiha, "Brief History of Council of Churches in Mizoram," 23.

[489] See Lalhmangaiha, "Brief History of Council of Churches in Mizoram," 24.

[490] See Lalhmangaiha, "Brief History of Council of Churches in Mizoram," 24, 25.

To implement this resolution, the Mizoram Presbyterian Church convened a meeting for the aforementioned 6 churches on 24th January 2023, wherein it was unanimously agreed to establish a Joint Committee as follows:

Chairman: Moderator of the Mizoram Presbyterian Church;

Secretary: General Secretary of the Baptist Church of Mizoram;

Recording Secretary: Mr. Lalruatkima, Administrative Officer, Baptist Church of Mizoram.

Before the formal inauguration of the Council of Churches in Mizoram, the Joint Committee for Church Union convened 5 meetings. These meetings occurred sequentially at various locations, including the Baptist Church of Mizoram office in Serkawn, Lunglei, the Synod office of the Mizoram Presbyterian Church, and the Booth Mansion Hall at the Salvation Army India Eastern Territorial Headquarters in Tuikual, Aizawl.

The inaugural meeting of the Joint Committee took place on 24th January 2023, at the Baptist Church of Mizoram headquarters office in Serkawn, Lunglei, specifically within Sap Upa leh Pu Buanga Hall. This meeting was presided over by Rev. Dr. C. Chawnghmingliana, Moderator of the Mizoram Presbyterian Church, and was attended by 29 representatives from the Mizoram Presbyterian Church, Baptist Church of Mizoram, Evangelical Church of Maraland, Salvation Army India Eastern Territory, and Lairam Isua Krista Baptist Kohhran.[491]

The 2nd meeting of the Joint Committee was held on 19th May 2023, at Booth Mansion Hall in Aizawl. This session, chaired by Rev. Dr. C. Chawnghmingliana, was attended by 43 members from the Mizoram Presbyterian Church, Baptist Church of Mizoram, Evangelical Church of Maraland, Salvation Army, Lairam Isua Krista Baptist Kohhran, the Evangelical Free Church of India, and IKK Bualpui (Ng).[492]

The 3rd convening of the Joint Committee occurred on 3rd April 2024, at J. M. Lloyd Hall in the Mizoram Presbyterian Church Synod Office, Aizawl, presided over by Rev. R. Vanlalnghaka, the Moderator of the Mizoram Presbyterian Church, and included 38 members from the respective churches.[493]

On 11th June 2024, the 4th Joint Committee meeting was conducted at J. M. Lloyd Hall in the Mizoram Presbyterian Church Synod Office, Aizawl, again led by Rev. R. Vanlalnghaka, with 35 attendees[494] from the participating churches.

---

[491] See *Inpumkhatna, Council of Churches in Mizoram Lo Pian Dan* (Aizawl: Mizoram Kohhrante Inpumkhatna Joint Committee, 2024), 9-11. Hereafter cited as *Inpumkhatna.*

[492] See *Inpumkhatna*, 23-35.

[493] See *Inpumkhatna*, 36, 45.

[494] See *Inpumkhatna*, 46-59.

The 5th meeting of the Joint Committee took place on 13th September 2024, at the Baptist Church of Mizoram Hall in Serkawn, Lunglei. Chaired by Rev. R. Vanlalnghaka, Chairman of the Joint Committee, this gathering involved 43 representatives from the Mizoram Presbyterian Church, Baptist Church of Mizoram, Evangelical Church of Maraland, Lairam Isua Krista Baptist Kohhran, Evangelical Free Church of India, IKK Bualpui Ng, the Independent Church of India, and the Wesleyan Methodist Church of Mizoram. During this meeting, a budget totalling Rs. 32,40,000 was approved[495] for the period from October 2024 to March 2025.

14.2. First Business Session

On Saturday, 26th October, 2024, the first business session convened to address matters related to the Council of Churches in Mizoram. This session predominantly focused on ratifying the proposed structure, constitution, executive members, office holders, and interim budget of the Joint Committee. The session saw the participation of 552 official delegates representing each of the eight churches.[496] The Joint Committee deliberated and unanimously ratified the constitution, executive committee members, office bearers, and additional agenda items.

14.3. Inauguration of the Council of Churches in Mizoram

The official inauguration of the Council of Churches in Mizoram was hosted on Sunday, 27th October 2024, at 10:30 AM, by the Mission Veng Presbyterian Church in Aizawl. This ceremony was officiated by Rev. R. Vanlalnghaka, Moderator of the Mizoram Presbyterian Church Synod and Chairman of the Joint Committee. Rev. Dr. H. Remthanga, a member of the Joint Committee, was responsible for the installation of the new leadership. The office bearers of the Council comprise:[497]

President	:	Rev. Dr. R. Lalbiakliana (Baptist Church of Mizoram);
Vice Presidents	:	Rev. B. Zazawna Lai (Lairam Isua Krista Baptist Kohhran), Rev. Lalrodinpuia L. S. Nghaling (IKK, Bualpui Ng);
General Secretary	:	Rev. Dr. Lalhmangaiha (Mizoram Presbyterian Church);
Joint Secretary	:	Rev. T. Salaw (Evangelical Church of Maraland);
Treasurer	:	Upa R. Lalmalsawma (Mizoram Presbyterian Church);

495 See *Inpumkhatna*, 60-87.

496 See Lalhmangaiha, "Brief History of Council of Churches in Mizoram," 25.

497 See Lalhmangaiha, "Brief History of Council of Churches in Mizoram," 26, 27.

Finance Secretary : Rev. Jessai L. Neitham (Evangelical Free Church of India, Mizoram Region).

14.4. Mission Statement[498]

1) This Council aims to foster the unity of churches in Mizoram, as aligned with the teachings of Jesus Christ regarding church unity.
2) We endeavour to collaboratively promote the Gospel, and
3) We aim to engage in initiatives that contribute to the restoration of both the land and society.

14.5. Membership[499]

Membership is open to churches with a minimum of 3,000 members that maintain either a headquarters office or a regional headquarters within Mizoram and that acknowledge Jesus Christ as Lord and Saviour.

---

[498] See *Inpumkhatna*, 91.

[499] See *Inpumkhatna*, 91.

Chapter 15

Women in the Ecumenical Movement

Women have historically played a vital role in shaping the Christian Ecumenical Movement, which seeks to promote reconciliation among the diverse Christian denominations. Despite their significant contributions, women have often been marginalised in church and theological discussions, rarely receiving recognition as transformative figures who advocate for equality, equity, and harmony within the ecumenical vision. Nevertheless, several notable women have made impactful contributions to the movement. Key ecumenical partnerships have been pioneered by various women's movements, including the Sisterhood Movement, the Young Women's Christian Association (YWCA), and the Women's World Day of Prayer, along with numerous auxiliary organisations that supported women in missionary work.

Although the 1910 International Missionary Conference had limited female representation, the discussions surrounding women's contributions to mission work highlighted the necessity of including women's voices in ecumenical conversations. The publication of the influential study "The Place of Women in the Church in the Mission Field" in 1923 brought attention to the role of women in the church and advocated for their increased involvement. Throughout history, the Church has seen women serving in various capacities - whether in lay ministry, monastic orders, diaconates, or as missionaries - while also being strong advocates for women within congregational life.[500] The transformative social changes of the 20th century

---

[500] See Pauline Webb, "Women in Church and Society," in *Dictionary of the Ecumenical Movement*, edited by Nicholas Lossky et.al., (Geneva: WCC Publications, 1991), 1069. Hereafter cited as Webb, "Women."

propelled women into broader roles in secular society, challenging their long-standing subservient status and initiating a struggle for full citizenship rights, including equitable employment opportunities and collaborative roles with men across family and community spheres.

15.1. Theological Contributions

Women theologians have enriched ecumenical theology by emphasising crucial themes such as interconnectedness, empathy, and the link between faith and social justice. Their contributions extend beyond mere doctrinal reconciliation, as feminist and womanist, introduce essential discussions around patriarchy, gender justice, and comprehensive redemption. By critically examining androcentric traditions, scholars like Mercy Amba Oduyoye, Kwok Pui-lan, and Letty M. Russell have fostered a more inclusive and contextually relevant understanding of ecumenical theology.

15.1.1. Letty M. Russell

Letty M. Russell's advocacy for marginalised groups stemmed from her personal experiences of exclusion, first as a Christian educator and later as a woman pastor in East Harlem. Here, she directly observed how systemic oppression and injustice profoundly affected her parishioners. Russell dedicated her life's work to advancing fairness and embodying God's kingdom on earth, leading her to prioritise education as a means for achieving justice.[501] For over 5 decades, Russell has illuminated the relationship between Christian education and the justice initiatives pursued by Christian communities.

In her early writings, she outlined this connection through what she referred to as "three perspectives." The first perspective emphasises that God's mission and the Church's role are to "participate in God's mission of reconciling the world to Godself through Jesus Christ." The second perspective acknowledges that God's mission unfolds within historical contexts, indicating that God is actively at work in the world. The third perspective underscores the urgency for new structures and institutions within church activity,[502] firmly asserting that existing denominational frameworks and local congregational organisation are inadequate for meaningfully engaging with the world or fulfilling God's calling.

15.1.2. Mercy Amba Oduyoye

Often recognised as the "mother of African women's theologies," Mercy Amba Oduyoye has made significant strides as a distinguished theologian,

---

[501] See Letty M. Russell, *Christian Education in Mission* (Philadelphia: Westminster Press, 19671), 4. Herefater cited as Russell, *Christian Education.*

[502] See Russell, *Christian Education,* 4.

educator, author, and mentor. As the director of the Institute of Women in Religion and Culture at Trinity Theological Seminary in Legon, Ghana, she has focused her professional life on pressing issues such as women's rights, poverty alleviation, healthcare access, and youth empowerment. Her career began in Christian education and youth ministry with the WCC, followed by her role as a youth secretary for the All Africa Conference of Churches (AACC).[503]

A committed member of the Methodist Church, Oduyoye has shown remarkable leadership, having served as the first female president of the Ecumenical Association of Third World Theologians (EATWOT) and as the Deputy General Secretary of the WCC. Oduyoye's innovative efforts to uplift African women in theological discourse are exemplified by her founding of the Circle of Concerned African Women Theologians, a platform aimed at supporting African women in publishing their theological works.[504] Her deep commitment to ecumenism fosters an environment where students from diverse backgrounds can thrive collectively, engaging in critical dialogue and mutual understanding as they explore the intersection of faith and social challenges.

15.1.3. Kwok Pui Lan

Kwok Pui Lan stands out as a distinguished scholar, innovative educator, and paradigmatic leader within the realm of theology, particularly noted for her in-depth exploration of the intersections between Asian feminist theology and postcolonial theological thought. Throughout her remarkable 25-year career at the Episcopal Divinity School, she held the prestigious title of William F. Cole Professor of Christian Theology and Spirituality.[505] In this capacity, she profoundly shaped the academic discourse, mentoring countless students and fostering a rich environment for theological inquiry.

Her educational influence further extends to several prestigious institutions, including the Chinese University of Hong Kong, Auburn Theological Seminary, Union Theological Seminary, and Yale Divinity School, where her expertise and dedication to theological education have left an indelible mark. In 2011, Kwok Pui Lan's exceptional leadership was recognised through her appointment as the president of the American Academy of Religion, a leading organisation that promotes scholarly

---

[503] See Yolanda Smith, "Mercy Amba Oduyoye" https://www.biola.edu/talbot/ce20/database/mercy-amba-uduyoye (6 June 2025). Hereafter cited as Smith, "Mercy Amba Oduyoye."

[504] See Smith, "Mercy Amba Oduyoye."

[505] For more information on her groundbreaking scholarship rooted in communities, see "Kwok Pui Lan: Groundbreaking Scholarship, Grounded in Community," https://candler.emory.edu/kwok-retirement/ (11 June 2025). Hereafter cited as "Kwok Pui Lan."

discourse on religious studies. Beyond her presidency, she co-founded the Pacific, Asian, North American Asian Women in Theology and Ministry (PANAAWTM) network. This initiative has emerged as a vital forum for women theologians from diverse backgrounds to engage in meaningful dialogue[506] and collaborative efforts, fostering a sense of community and shared purpose within the field.

Her influence extends into several key organisations, including the Association of Theological Schools (ATS) and the Wabash Centre for Teaching and Learning, where she has been instrumental in shaping educational practices in theological studies. As a prolific author, Kwok has contributed significantly to theological literature, writing or editing 23 impactful books in both English and Chinese.[507] Her works address critical issues in theology and spirituality, contributing to an enriched discourse and providing essential resources for students, academics, and practitioners alike.

15.2. Administrative Role

Over the years, women have gradually ascended to prominent positions within ecumenical organisations, overcoming historical barriers that limited their official representation in these spaces. Women have increasingly claimed leadership roles in influential bodies such as the National Council of Churches in India (NCCI), the Christian Conference of Asia (CCA), and the World Council of Churches (WCC). Notably, the WCC's "Women in Church and Society" program has emerged as a significant platform for addressing and combating gender disparities not only within ecclesiastical contexts but also in broader societal frameworks.

15.3. Equity Work

Women's roles have proven essential in forging connections between ecumenism and pressing issues such as ecological justice, human rights, and peacebuilding initiatives. Their advocacy efforts have focused on ensuring fair participation in church decision-making processes, combating gender-based violence, and promoting the ordination of women in various denominations. By underscoring social justice as a vital element of Christian unity, their involvement in interfaith and intercultural dialogues has strengthened and expanded ecumenical relationships.

A historical figure that stands out in this narrative is Anne Hutchinson, who, in the 1630s, challenged the male-dominated religious authorities of Massachusetts by convening women for discussions about her pastor's

---

[506] See "Kwok Pui Lan," 2.

[507] See "Kwok Pui Lan," 2.

sermons. Hutchinson's courageous acts led to her trial, resulting in a conviction and subsequent exile to Rhode Island. Historically, legal ordination for women in Christian leadership remained an elusive goal until the mid-1800s, even though many women had assumed leadership roles within their communities during that time. In 1853, Antoinette Brown made history as the first woman to be ordained as a minister in the Congregationalist tradition after being called to serve at a church in New York. A decade later, in 1863, Olympia Brown received her ordination within the Unitarian Universalist movement, and in 1898, Mary Jane Small became an ordained preacher[508] in the African Methodist Episcopal Zion Church.

These ordinations marked significant milestones reflective of the profound transformations occurring in women's roles in public and religious life during the 19th and early 20th centuries. However, these shifts were met with considerable controversy, evident in the fervent debates that ensued among organisations that vocally supported or opposed women's ordination.[509] Such discussions not only highlighted the evolving landscape of ecclesiastical roles but also underscored the continuing struggle for gender equality within religious institutions.

15.4. Fostering Down-to-Earth Movement

Women have played a vital role at the grassroots level, contributing to community development through a variety of service-oriented projects and ecumenical prayer movements. These initiatives have been instrumental in promoting cross-denominational solidarity, especially within women's ecumenical fellowships and networks. Such efforts have been particularly impactful in regions grappling with systemic discrimination, persistent poverty, or ongoing conflict, highlighting the resilience and commitment of women to effect change in their communities.

15.5. Historical Study of Women's Engagement in the Ecumenical Movement

By the time the WCC was being established, the global network of women connected through the YMCA had already begun exploring women's roles within the Church on a worldwide scale. A significant study, conducted specifically for women, was presented during one of the addresses at the inaugural assembly in Amsterdam in 1948.[510] This study inspired the

---

[508] See "The Women's Ordination Movement, Theology, Religion, Essay," https://www.ukessays.com/essays/theology/the-womens-ordination-movement-theology-religion-essay.php?vref=1 (11 June 2025). Hereafter cited as "The Women's."

[509] See "The Women's," 3.

[510] See Webb, "Women," 1070.

WCC to proactively engage in assessing the global ministry of women, acknowledging their contributions and the necessity of their voices within ecclesiastical contexts.

In 1954, during the Evanston assembly, the WCC recognised the need for greater emphasis on cooperation between genders by renaming the department that addressed women's issues. It was rebranded as the Department of the Cooperation of Men and Women in Church and Society, reflecting a theological understanding that the connection between genders signifies a divinely ordained order. This rebranding was further underscored in a theological consultation held in Herrenalb in 1956, which examined the implications of closer collaboration between men and women as a crucial element for the renewal of the Church.

The All Africa Conference of Churches, founded in 1963, saw enthusiastic participation from women across various denominations, who were invited to a preparatory meeting to ensure their full engagement in the burgeoning ecumenical organisation. A consultation on Changing Patterns of Men/Women Relationships held in Madras, just before the New Delhi assembly in 1961, played a vital role in expanding the mission of the women's department to address issues directly related to family dynamics.[511]

The Uppsala assembly in 1968 highlighted a concerning trend: the underrepresentation of women in the Church's official delegations. It became evident that the Church was not immune to the widespread societal sexism that permeated various institutions. This new terminology of "sexism" was employed to describe such discrimination and was prominently featured in the title of an all-female consultation that the WCC convened in Berlin in 1974. This gathering was intended to prepare churches for the International Year of Women, which was proclaimed by the United Nations in 1975,[512] marking the beginning of a decade where issues of justice, poverty, and abuse faced by women were propelled to the forefront of international discussions.

The women who participated in the WCC assembly in Nairobi in 1975, where a full plenary session was dedicated to women's issues for the first time, gained significant momentum from the Berlin consultation. It was here that a decision was made to advance theological investigations and biblical studies through the lens of feminine insights and experiences,[513] closely examining social justice issues affecting women.

---

[511] See Webb, "Women," 1069.

[512] See Yingli Omei, "A Feminist Historical Assessment on "The Ecumenical Decade of the Churches in Solidarity with Women, 1988-1998,"" D.Th. assessment paper, 2024, United Theological College, Bengaluru.

[513] See Webb, "Women," 1071.

15.6. The Zenana Mission

The Zenana Mission emerged primarily as a Christian missionary effort focused on reaching women residing in the secluded areas, or "zenanas," of Indian households during the late 19th and early 20th centuries. While the mission originated from a Christian context, its impact extended far beyond that, positively affecting women from diverse religious backgrounds, including Sikh, Muslim, and Hindu communities. In a society governed by the purdah custom, women were isolated from all men except their husbands and immediate male family members, effectively confining them to their zenanas. Many women suffered dire consequences, including health complications and preventable deaths, due to a lack of access to medical care[514] in a male-dominated society where the practice of medicine was exclusively male.

The pressing question arose: how could the gospel penetrate such cultures? The answer became clear - only Christian women, equipped to provide nursing care, education, and essential health support, could effectively engage with these women in critical need. Until the 1840s, almost all Protestant missionaries were men, limiting outreach to these secluded spaces. The formal call for training women as missionaries to visit the Zenanas was made public in 1840 by Thomas Smith, a Christian math teacher from Symington in Lanarkshire. His appeal signalled the beginning of a new chapter in missionary work, emphasising the necessity of women's involvement[515] in reaching out to the otherwise inaccessible spheres of female life.

The Zenana Mission played a crucial role in facilitating access to basic literacy and education for women from diverse religious backgrounds, including Hindu and Muslim communities, who otherwise would have been excluded from formal educational opportunities due to stringent societal and cultural norms. Many of these women were restricted by purdah practices, which mandated strict gender segregation, limiting their ability to seek medical attention from male healthcare providers. The Zenana Mission addressed this gap by providing essential medical care and health education specifically tailored for women, thereby improving their overall well-being. By prioritising the education of women and addressing their healthcare needs, the Zenana Mission contributed to a gradual transformation of traditional gender norms. Women engaged in these programs became more self-aware and confident, breaking barriers that had long constrained them.

---

[514] See "Thirty Years of Women's Ordination in India," https://lutheranworld.org/news/thirty-years-years-womens-ordination-india (11 June 2025). Hereafter cited as "Thirty Years."

[515] See "Thirty Years," 2.

Some branches of the Zenana Mission expanded their efforts to include vocational training in areas such as handicrafts, sewing, and embroidery. This vocational instruction empowered many women of other faiths to achieve economic independence, earn respect in their communities, and effectively navigate responsibilities beyond their domestic confines. Furthermore, the Zenana Mission fostered cross-cultural communication through the interactions of missionaries with women across different faiths. While evangelism remained a fundamental objective, these exchanges promoted mutual respect and understanding among diverse groups, particularly within the educated urban elite.[516] The ripple effects of the Zenana Mission's initiatives also influenced broader social reform movements in India, contributing to the gradual evolution of societal attitudes towards women's education and rights.

15.7. A Postcolonial Reading of the Contributions of Women in the Ecumenical Movement

During the formative years of the Ecumenical Movement, which began in the late 19th and early 20th centuries, women often found themselves relegated to supportive roles while the movement was largely led by male church leaders from the Global North. These leaders operated within a framework steeped in colonial ideologies that reinforced Western cultural and theological supremacy. As a result, the substantial contributions of women, particularly those from colonised regions, were frequently overlooked or rendered invisible, mirroring the broader systemic issues of patriarchy and imperial domination that pervaded both church and society.

For instance, at the 1910 World Missionary Conference held in Edinburgh, women played crucial roles in the missionary movement, yet their representation was strikingly minimal; only a fraction of the delegates were female, even though many women were actively involved on the ground in mission fields as teachers, nurses, and social reformers. Their significant contributions to educational programs, healthcare initiatives, and social justice efforts were often dismissed as ancillary activities rather than recognised as integral to the missionary mandate. Furthermore, women's theological insights and leadership capabilities remained largely unacknowledged within ecclesiastical discussions and decision-making bodies, where male voices predominated.[517]

This marginalisation highlights the need to critically examine and re-evaluate the historical narrative of the Ecumenical Movement to include

---

516 See "Thirty Years," 2.

517 See Dana L. Robert, *Christian Mission: How Christianity became a World Religion* (West Sussex, UK: Blackwell, 2009), 118, 119.

the experiences and contributions of women. Thus, understanding the role of women in this context is essential for appreciating the full scope and impact of the Ecumenical Movement, as it reveals the intersections of gender, race, and colonialism within the formation of modern Christianity. Women's participation in ecumenism can be interpreted as acts of resistance from a postcolonial perspective. The establishment of the WCC in 1948 marked a significant turning point in the ecumenical movement; however, it was not until the 1960s and 1970s, spurred by feminist movements and decolonisation efforts, that women began to more emphatically assert their rightful roles within ecumenical discussions.

One prominent figure in this transformative landscape is Mercy Amba Oduyoye from Ghana, who has been instrumental in articulating African women's theology. Oduyoye critically examined the cultural blind spots of Western feminist theology, arguing that it often fails to resonate with the lived realities of women in Africa.[518] Her work with the Circle of Concerned African Women Theologians[519] exemplifies a decolonial reclamation of women's voices within and outside ecumenical discourse. Oduyoye's writings emphasise core values such as community, oral tradition, and personal experiences, actively challenging both colonial legacies and the male-centred narratives prevalent in religious contexts.

Ecumenical platforms have frequently mirrored imperial hierarchies, as revealed by postcolonial studies. In many cases, women from the Global South have been compelled to conform to Western ecumenical norms or risk being dissected in discussions that should represent a broader diversity of voices. Nonetheless, these women have persistently disrupted these unequal dynamics by: 1. Presenting contextual theologies grounded in local cultures, contemporary conflicts, and the unique spiritual expressions of their communities. 2. Shedding light on critical issues often overlooked in mainstream ecumenical discourse, such as gender-based violence, systemic poverty, indigenous spirituality, and ecological justice. 3. Opposing hierarchical models of theology and advocating for relational, inclusive approaches that prioritise justice and genuine unity among diverse groups.

Postcolonial feminism highlights the intersectionality of race, class, and gender as key factors that shape women's experiences within ecumenism. Theologically engaged women who identify as Black, Dalit, Tribal, or indigenous assertively critique both colonial oppression and the multifaceted discrimination associated with caste, class, and gender. Their

---

[518] Her work, *Introducing African Women's Theology,* UK: Continuum International Publishing, 2001, is a good example of her concern for the African women.

[519] The Circle of Concerned African Women Theologians is a pan-African ecumenical organisation that supports scholarly research of African women theologians.

theological interpretations lay bare the multilayered marginalisations that persist within church institutions and ecumenical frameworks. In India, for instance, Dalit Christian women have courageously challenged the entrenched male dominance and upper-caste biases that characterise Indian ecumenism. They advocate for a distinct form of ecumenism rooted in the narratives of suffering, resistance, and survival that arise from their experiences.

Among the prominent Tribal feminist thinkers, Lalrinawmi Ralte emerges as a significant figure, known for her innovative concept of crab theology. This theological framework serves as a critical lens through which she examines and critiques the gender bias prevalent in Tribal society. By drawing on the metaphor of crabs, Rini Ralte illustrates the struggles and societal constraints faced by women, highlighting how cultural norms often impede their progress and autonomy. Her work not only sheds light on the intersection of gender and culture but also encourages a re-evaluation of traditional roles and seeks to empower marginalised voices within these communities.

Their stories, rituals, and liturgical practices not only reclaim their agency but also serve as transformative forces within the church. From a postcolonial feminist standpoint, women in the ecumenical movement are seen as transformative agents rather than mere participants. Their contributions advance the movement towards solidarity, justice, and wholeness, moving it beyond mere concepts of abstract unity. These women passionately demand that ecumenical theology and language undergo decolonisation to reflect diverse cultural realities. They also see to it that grassroots and lived expressions of faith receive prioritisation in discussions and decisions. Lastly, they demand that inclusive spaces be created where marginalised voices can actively shape the agenda and influence the broader discourse on ecumenism.

Conclusion

The influence of women on the Christian Ecumenical Movement has been profound and transformative, impacting theological, administrative, social, and grassroots domains. Despite facing systemic challenges and marginalisation, women have persistently advanced the ecumenical vision by advocating for justice, inclusivity, and reconciliation within both the Church and society. The contributions of pioneering theologians such as Letty M. Russell, Mercy Amba Oduyoye, and Kwok Pui Lan have significantly enriched ecumenical theology, incorporating insights from lived experiences, feminist and postcolonial perspectives, and a strong commitment to social justice.

The increasing leadership of women in prominent ecumenical organisations, including the WCC, CCA, and NCCI, underscores the growing recognition of their essential role in fostering Christian unity. Their emphasis on equity, spanning gender justice, peace initiatives, and ecological advocacy, has expanded the relevance and impact of ecumenism in a rapidly evolving global context. Initiatives such as the Zenana Mission exemplify how women's ministry transcends ecclesiastical boundaries, significantly enriching lives across diverse religious and cultural settings by promoting dignity, education, and mutual respect.

Historically and contemporarily, women have not only participated in but often led movements that challenge exclusionary practices and redefine the Church's mission. As they continue to mend divides, build cohesive communities, and articulate inclusive theologies, the ecumenical movement becomes increasingly enriched, providing a more authentic representation of the Gospel's messages of love, justice, and unity. Their legacy emphasises that the pursuit of comprehensive Christian unity is intricately linked to the ongoing struggle for gender equality and the recognition of women's voices in all facets of church life.

Chapter 16

Edinburgh 2010

The Edinburgh 2010 Conference constituted a significant centennial milestone in the evolution of global Christian mission. Building upon the foundational achievements of the 1910 World Missionary Conference, this initiative sought not only to commemorate a historical assembly but also to re-evaluate Christian mission in the context of major global transformations. Emerging from the "Towards 2010" initiative, planning for the conference commenced in 2000 and was shaped through extensive collaboration across various ecumenical bodies.

The conference aimed to reflect the shifting centre of Christianity toward the Global South and to address contemporary issues in mission theology and practice. By uniting a diverse array of participants, spanning Orthodox to Pentecostal backgrounds and representing both Western and Global South contexts, Edinburgh 2010 fostered an inclusive, multi-centred, and action-oriented engagement with the theme, "Witnessing to Christ Today." Through its myriad sessions, celebrations, and reflective discussions, the conference not only honoured the legacy of Edinburgh 1910 but also paved new pathways for Christian witness in a divided and troubled society.

16.1. An Overview

The planning for the Current and Future Mission Conference commenced as early as 2000 under the initiative titled "Towards 2010," initiated by a small group in Edinburgh. In 2002, this group organised a series of seminars aimed at leveraging the missionary connections of the global church. These seminars conducted a comprehensive examination of the eight commissions arising from the 1910 conference, establishing links to the ongoing mission of the church. This exploration led to the development of a novel research approach, addressing various contemporary mission challenges, culminating in a centennial conference held in Edinburgh in June 2010. Unlike the 1910 conference, which primarily involved Western Protestant missionaries, Edinburgh 2010 embraced an ecumenical framework that included diverse global perspectives,[520] acknowledging that the global South has emerged as an important centre of Christianity.

The Edinburgh 2010 event was characterised by its complexity, as it brought together the principal branches of the Christian tradition, including Catholic, Evangelical, Orthodox, Pentecostal, and Protestant communities, in a unique collaboration. An unprecedented ecumenical study process was established, which underwent considerable breadth and depth across major Christian centres. To ascertain contemporary mission challenges and delineate relevant topics for the study process, an international assembly was convened during 2005 and 2006. The Church of Scotland provided substantial support for the initiative, while the University of Edinburgh consented to host the event. The appointment of an International Director took place in April 2007, and the formation of a General Council, comprising twenty stakeholders, occurred in September of the same year during its inaugural meeting in Edinburgh. The study process officially commenced in 2008, characterised by collaboration and a polycentric approach, with a small support team being assembled at the beginning of 2009.[521]

16.2. The Conference

Initially, participation was projected at approximately 1,000 individuals, akin to the attendance at the 1910 conference. However, owing to funding limitations stemming from the global economic downturn and additional factors, the General Council decided to conduct a smaller yet symbolically significant convening featuring 300 delegates. The primary focus of the conference was articulated as "Witnessing to Christ Today." The conference took place in the well-appointed Pollock Halls at the University of Edinburgh, the institution's residential and conference facility, under favourable summer conditions in June. It convened representatives from various research entities and delegates appointed by stakeholders to deliberate on potential challenges that the study process may pose to churches in the forthcoming

---

[520] See Kirsteen Kim and Andrew Anderson, "Introduction," in *Edinburgh 2010 Mission Today and Tomorrow,* edited by Kirsteen Kim and Andrew Anderson (Oxford: Regnum Books International, 2011), 4. Hereafter cited as Kim, "Introduction."

[521] See Kim, "Introduction," 4.

years. These 300 delegates represented 202 organisations and entities, corresponding to 115 national churches or denominations, travelling from across the globe to Edinburgh, embodying 75 different nationalities and communicating in 61 distinct mother tongues.[522]

The objective of the significantly larger event, which attracted thousands of participants on Sunday, 6th June,[523] was to commemorate, express gratitude, seek forgiveness, and reaffirm commitments. This gathering was held at the Church of Scotland Assembly Hall, the same venue that hosted the 1910 conference.[524] The initiative employed contemporary communication tools, including a website, Facebook, and Twitter, to encourage global church engagement.

The concluding celebration was broadcast live online, and an accompanying online conference was also conducted. Opening remarks at the Pollock Halls Opening Celebration, held on 3rd June 2010, were delivered by Rev. Dr. Olav Fykse Tveit and Rev. Dr. Geoff Tunnicliffe. Cardinal Keith O'Brien provided the welcoming address on Wednesday, 2nd June 2010.[525]

A noteworthy aspect of this initial welcoming session was the considerable representation of diverse nationalities, unified by the rhythmic beats of drums and the singing of songs from various cultures, including the refrain, "Everyone is welcome in God's presence." The opening prayer acknowledged the changing circumstances, the challenges confronting Christian witness today, and expressed hope for renewed vision and vigour for the churches, recalling the gathering of missionaries in the same city a century earlier. Delegates had the opportunity to introduce themselves, sharing their names, nationalities, church affiliations, and aspirations for the conference.[526] Subsequently, representatives from the city's historic university and various national churches provided brief welcome addresses as members convened.

However, an important question arose: Where were the female leaders and speakers during the meeting? The delegates were predominantly welcomed by white Western men, raising concerns regarding representation. Emotions overshadowed facts and rationalisations, reflecting a spectrum of perspectives on the necessity for discourse regarding challenging realities

---

[522] See Kim, "Introduction," 4.

[523] See Raj Bharat Patta, "Mission Moorings: Ecumenical Experiences from Edinburgh 2010," in *NCC Review,* CXXX, (June, 2010), 15-20. Hereafter cited as Patta, "Mission Moorings."

[524] See Kim, "Introduction," 5.

[525] See Kim, "Introduction," 7.

[526] See Elizabeth Moran, SSC, "Spiritual Life of the Conference," in *Edinburgh 2010 Mission Today and Tomorrow,* edited by Kirsteen Kim and Andrew Anderson (Oxford: Regnum Books International, 2011), 16. Hereafter cited as Moran, "Spiritual Life."

and the pursuit of reconciliation.[527] This context raises the question of whether such discussions would yield sources of despair or pathways to renewed hope, vitality, and collaboration.

The survey was conducted within the framework of the conference's spiritual life in Edinburgh from 2-5th June 2010. The overarching goals of the conference's study process included:[528]

- Establishing a new vision and spirituality of mission to inspire Christians in churches and mission organisations;
- Promoting networks and partnerships across regions, particularly concerning the North-South divide, to enhance unified witness;
- Providing guidelines on mission practices while identifying priorities for church and mission leaders;
- Highlighting topics for further exploration and reflection. The anticipated tangible outcomes of the conference's research process were:
- Shared ownership of calls and commitments for the Sunday celebration;
- A record of key issues and priorities identified, along with indications of their perceived urgency;
- A report generated by a listening group;
- Reflections on the conference from 3 invited delegates;
- Audio-visual materials utilised during the conference that can be uploaded to the website;
- A comprehensive conference report summarising presentations and discussions. The objectives of the conference's study process were accomplished over nine scheduled sessions across three full days at Pollock Halls.

These sessions consisted of 3 plenary discussions and 6 parallel workshops wherein delegates were organised into groups.

Plenary 1, titled "Mission in Long Perspective," took place on Thursday, 3rd June 2010, featuring a keynote address delivered by Dr. Dana L. Robert, Truman Collins Professor of World Christianity and History of Mission at Boston University School of Theology, USA. Plenary 2, titled "Mission Worldwide," occurred on Friday, 4th June 2010, and included a case study, "Christian Spirituality and the Diakonic Mission of the Yoido

---

[527] See Moran, "Spiritual Life," 17.

[528] See Kirsteen Kim, "Conference Study Process," in *Edinburgh 2010 Mission Today and Tomorrow,* edited by Kirsteen Kim and Andrew Anderson (Oxford: Regnum Books International, 2011), 51, 52. Hereafter cited as Kim, "Conference."

Full Gospel Church," presented by Rev. Dr. Lee Young-Hoon, Senior Pastor of the Yoido Full Gospel Church in Seoul.[529]

16.3. Hopes Beyond Edinburgh 2010

In its endeavour to explore relevant, praxis-oriented missiologies that enable the Church to effectively bear witness to Christ, Edinburgh 2010 undertook a critical examination of various mission models. The imperative of fostering a united common witness that addresses the injustices of our era, irrespective of denominational and confessional distinctions, constitutes one of the most pressing needs of our time. As a mission is inherently dynamic and not static, it is essential to adopt innovative and contemporary mission strategies.[530] The Church aims to elevate its mission and witness, aspiring for them to be more impactful and meaningful, rather than merely seeking historical markers.

According to the situation currently unfolding in India, the livelihoods and well-being of the average citizen are under severe threat due to protracted crises in regions such as Manipur and Kashmir, compounded by religious and social conflicts, challenges faced by minority groups, and widespread migration issues across the country. To ensure that our missiological discourses regarding the witness of Christ are pertinent in the modern context, it is crucial to engage more profoundly with these ongoing crises. Reports of genocide, torture, eviction, and displacement, often justified under the guise of development, are prevalent throughout India.[531] In particular, Tribal and Adivasi populations are being forcibly removed from their land. We must collaborate to address and resolve these urgent challenges.

One of the significant challenges faced by Christian Churches today is the move from "Disunity to Unity." Despite the vital discussions that took place during the Edinburgh Conference of 1910, there remains a pressing need for churches to seek forgiveness for past grievances and to engage in substantial efforts aimed at relational healing and reconciliation. This call for unity is not merely an ideal but a critical necessity for effective ministry and collective witness in the diverse cultural landscape of India. Wati Longchar[532] believes that the aspiration of "Witness to Christ in Unity" remains largely unfulfilled among the Christian communities in India.

---

[529] See Kim, "Conference," 85.

[530] See Patta, "Mission Moorings," 20.

[531] See "Editorial," in *NCC Review,* CXXX, (June, 2010), 1.

[532] See Wati Longchar, "Edinburgh 2010: Challenges for Witnessing to Christ Today in India," in *History of Ecumenical Movement: Issues, Challenges and Perspectives,* edited by Watimongla Jamir, (Kolkata: SCEPTRE, 2014), 345. Hereafter cited as Longchar, "Edinburgh 2010."

Another formidable challenge lies in the transition from a state of passivity to one of active, collective resistance. This requires a concerted effort to confront and oppose the existing institutions and systemic structures that perpetuate injustice and undermine God's divine intention for humanity and creation. True justice cannot be realised unless there is a radical transformation of power structures that prioritise uplifting the marginalised and the oppressed in society. Thus, advocating for justice becomes not only a matter of faith but also a necessary missiological imperative that shapes one's lifestyle and community engagement.[533] It is ultimately futile to profess a commitment to following Christ without simultaneously advocating for justice, as the two are inherently intertwined in the Christian calling to love and serve others.

16.4. Postcolonial Reading of Edinburgh 2010

16.4.1. Edinburgh 1910s Legacy: Persistence and Disintegration

The primary objective of the Edinburgh 2010 conference was to honour and critically assess the legacy of the Edinburgh 1910 gathering, noted for its significant role in fostering collaboration among Protestant missionary organisations.[534] However, the foundational colonial mindset underpinning this first conference remained inadequately addressed. While Edinburgh 1910 represented a crucial turning point in global missionary efforts, it was predominantly orchestrated by Western Protestant entities and largely neglected the perspectives of colonised territories, especially the voices of indigenous communities and people of other faiths.[535]

In response, Edinburgh 2010 aimed to broaden the dialogue by incorporating diverse viewpoints from Africa, Asia, and Latin America, as well as engaging representatives from the Catholic Church, Orthodox Churches, and Pentecostal movements. Nevertheless, a postcolonial critique reveals that such inclusivity often functioned within existing frameworks dominated by institutional agendas and Western theological paradigms. While attempts were made to involve these varied voices, representation did not invariably translate into genuine authority[536] or meaningful influence over theological discourse and decision-making.

---

[533] See Longchar, "Edinburgh 2010," 347.

[534] See Longchar, "Edinburgh 2010," 341.

[535] See Gladson, *Decolonising*, 8-10.

[536] See Kapya J. Kaoma, "Post Edinburgh 2010 Christian Mission: Joys, Issues and Challenges," Academia.edu (15 June 2025). Hereafter cited as Kaoma, "Post Edinburgh 2010."

16.4.2. Western Domination

Despite an emphasis on mutuality and partnership, Edinburgh 2010 exhibited lingering Northern ecclesiological and missiological preoccupations. Although the thematic discussions aimed to be inclusive, many focal points heavily reflected global issues framed through the lens of Western organisations. A postcolonial perspective sees the insufficient space afforded to indigenous theological frameworks or decolonial epistemologies that challenge traditional Western models of mission theology. Crucial topics relevant to postcolonial contexts - such as economic imperialism, climate justice, militarism, and migration - were often underrepresented or treated in a manner that spiritualised them, thereby diluting their political significance. The overall discourse remained structured to privilege academic theology, leaving grassroots voices from the Global South sidelined and marginalised.

16.4.3. Representation and Counterfeiting

A postcolonial reading argues that many participants from the Global South were invited symbolically rather than meaningfully engaged. Despite ongoing claims of inclusivity in Edinburgh 2010, a significant imbalance was evident: approximately 160 delegates hailed from the global North, with the United States alone accounting for more official representatives than all of Africa combined. Alarmingly, women comprised only 32% of the total delegates, while a mere 6% were under the age of 30.[537]

This demographic distribution raises concerns about the representation and agency of marginalised voices. As decision-making authority remained predominantly in the hands of Western organisers and funders, many critical intellectuals from Asia, Africa, and Latin America found themselves relegated to the periphery of theological and missiological conversations. Furthermore, the conference's emphasis on Western modes of knowledge generation often marginalised the oral, experiential, and narrative-based traditions prevalent in numerous postcolonial societies. This stylistic and linguistic preference for Western documentation practices risked sidelining the rich, diverse knowledge systems of these communities.

A significant incident underscored these tensions during the conference's final day, when many African delegates vocally protested the dismissal of Dr. Balia, the key organiser and co-editor of the conference's study guide, who was removed from his position and barred from the premises for undisclosed reasons. The planning committee framed the issue surrounding Dr. Balia as an administrative concern; however, African participants perceived it as indicative of a broader systemic problem within global Christianity - the persistent undervaluation of the Global South,

---

[537] See Kaoma, "Post Edinburgh 2010," 1, 2.

particularly Africa.[538] As the conference concluded, African delegates firmly articulated their opposition to Dr. Balia's mistreatment, illuminating underlying fractures within the global church.

16.4.4. Colonial Shadows and Missiological Vocabulary

Despite efforts to redefine mission as holistic, dialogical, and incarnational at Edinburgh 2010, certain terminologies and assumptions continued to bear the weight of colonial connotations. For example, the conference's call for a global "missional identity" risks glossing over the specific experiences of oppression, cultural trauma, and resistance encountered by previously colonised communities. The phrase "mission is from 'anywhere to anywhere'"[539] remains prevalent. While this may appear to advocate for inclusivity and balance, it obscures the historical and structural inequalities that continue to affect access to mission resources, mobility, and theological representation. Such language perpetuates the dominance of Western theological narratives, challenging the conference's aims of creating an equitable and representative platform for global dialogue.

Conclusion

Edinburgh 2010 transcended the notion of a mere commemorative gathering; it served as a prophetic call to renew Christian witness grounded in unity, justice, and contextual relevance. The event underscored the imperative for churches to evolve from historical fragmentation to reconciliation, and from passive observation to active resistance against systemic injustice. In the contemporary world, particularly in contexts such as India, where communal violence, socio-political turmoil, and economic displacement threaten the lives of vulnerable populations, the Church's mission must be firmly underpinned by theological foundations while remaining socially engaged.

The conference's emphasis on collaboration, contextual theology, and missional spirituality provides a compelling framework for the Church's ongoing mission. Nevertheless, key challenges remain, particularly in addressing gender inequality, reconciling divisions, and empowering marginalised communities. The enduring legacy of Edinburgh 2010 will ultimately be assessed not solely by the ideas articulated or examined but by the extent to which its vision is embodied through a united, faithful, and justice-oriented witness to Christ in today's world.

---

538 See Kaoma, "Post Edinburgh 2010," 2.

539 Kwok Keung Chan, "The First Mark of Mission: To Proclaim the Good News of the Kingdom of God," in *Life-Widening Mission: Global Anglican Perspectives*, edited by Cathy Ross (Oxford: Regnum Books, 2012), 19.

The conference strongly encouraged participants to craft more imaginative and engaging statements of faith, emphasising the importance of keeping Christian beliefs relevant, practical, and significant in today's rapidly changing world. It highlighted the ongoing efforts of the Edinburgh 2010 initiative, which aimed to revitalise Christian mission and collaboration globally. However, the organisers acknowledged that this initiative is far from complete; they stressed the necessity of fresh, innovative interactions and approaches to effectively connect with diverse communities and respond to contemporary challenges.

Bibliography

Books

__________ *Inpumkhatna. Council of Churches in Mizoram Lo Pian Dan.* Aizawl: Mizoram Kohhrante Inpumkhatna Joint Committee, 2024.

__________ *Sharing in One Hope: Commission on Faith and Order, Bangalore 1978, Reports and Documents.* Geneva: WCC, 1979.

__________ *The United Theological College Bangalore: Handbook 2024-2025.* Bangalore: UTC, 2045.

A History of the Ecumenical Movement 1517-1948. Edited by Ruth Rouse and Stephen Charles Neil. London: SPCK, 1954.

Baago, K. *A History of the National Christian Council of India 1914-1964.* Madras: NCC, 1965.

Backholer, Mathew. *Revival Fires and Awakenings: Thirty-Six Visitations of the Holy Spirit.* United Kingdom: Faith Media, 2009.

Bate, H. N. *History of the Church to A.D. 325.* 2nd ed. London: Rivingtons, 1943.

Beaver, R. Pierce. *Ecumenical Beginnings in Protestant World: A History of Comity.* New York: Thomas Nelson & Sons, 1962.

Becker, C. *History of the Catholic Missions in North East India (1890-1915).* Translated & edited by S. Stadler and S. Karotemprel. Shillong: Vedrame Missiological Institute, 1980.

Bhuyan, S. K. *Early British Relations with Assam.* Shillong: Department of Historical and Antiquarium Studies in Assam, 1949.

Bosch, David J. *Transforming Mission: Paradigm Shifts in Theology of Mission.* Bangalore: Omega Book World, 2021.

Brown, Robert McAfee. *The Ecumenical Revolution: An Interpretation of the Catholic-Protestant Dialogue.* London: Burns & Oates, 1969.

Brown, Robert McAfee. *The Ecumenical Revolution: An Interpretation of the Catholic-Protestant Dialogue.* London: Burns and Oates, 1967.

Bruce, F. F. *The Spreading Flame.* Exeter: Paternoster Press, 1964.

Butler, Rex D. *The New Prophecy and New Visions: Evidence of Montanism in the Passion of Perpetua and Felicitas.* Washington D.C.: The Catholic University of America Press, 2006.

Christie-Murray, David. *A History of Heresy.* Oxford: O.U.P., 1990.

Chunakara, Mathews George. *Ecumenism in Asia: Prospects and Challenges.* Tiruvalla: Christava Sahitya Samithi, 2014.

Clark, Elizabeth and Herbert Richardson. *Women and Religion.* New York: Harper & Row Publishers, 1977.

Clark, N. G. *True and False Economy in Missions.* Boston: American Board of Commissioners for Foreign Missions, 1891.

Couto, Anil J. T. *May They All be One: Ecumenism in Catholic Perspective.* Bangalore: Conference of Catholic Bishops of India, 2021.

Debbarma, Sukhendu. *Origin and Growth of Christianity in Tripura with Special Reference to the New Zealand Baptist Missionary Society 1938-1988.* New Delhi: Indus Publishing Company, 1996.

Dena, Lal. *Christian Missions and Colonialism: A Study of Missionary Movement in North East India with Particular Reference to Manipur and Lushai Hills 1894-1947.* Shillong: Vendrame Institute, 1988.

Dena, Lal. *Christian Missions and Colonialism: A Study of Missionary Movement in North East India with Particular Reference to Manipur and Lushai Hills 1894-1947.* Shillong: Vendrame Institute, 1988.

Downs, Frederick S. *History of Christianity in India, Volume V, Part 5 – Northeast India in the Nineteenth and Twentieth Centuries.* Reprint. Bangalore: CHAI, 2003.

Downs, Frederick S. *The Mighty Works of God.* Revised ed. Guwahati: Christian Literature Centre, 2014.

Dyck, Cornelius J. and Dennis D. Martin, eds. *Mennonite Encyclopaedia, Volume 5.* Scottsdale, PA: Herald Press, 1990.

Fitzmyer, Joseph A. S.J. *Essays on the Semitic Background of the New Testament.* USA: Sources for Biblical Study & Society of Biblical Literature and Scholars Press, 1974.

Foundations of Ecumenical Social Thought. Edited by J. H. Oldham. Philadelphia: Fortress Press, 1966.

Gladstone, J. W. *United to Unite: History of the Church of South India 1947-1997.* Chennai: CSI Synod, 1997.

Goodall. *The Ecumenical Movement.* 2nd ed. Oxford, New York, 1964.

Gutierrez, Gustavo. *A Theology of Liberation: History, Politics and Salvation.* Maryknoll, New York: Orbis Books, 1973.

Haokip, M. Thankhosei. *A History of Ecumenical Movement in Northeast India with Special Reference to the Northeast India Christian Council.* Delhi: ISPCK, 2015.

Hoakip, M. Thongkhosei. *Ecumenism among the Kukis of North East India.* Secunderabad: The Author, 2016.

Hogg, William Richie. *Ecumenical Foundations: A History of the International Missionary Council and its Nineteenth Century Background.* New York: Harper and Brothers Publishers, 1952.

Hooft, Willem Adolf Visser't. "The Word 'Ecumenical' Its History and Use." In *A History of the Ecumenical Movement 1517-1948.* 3rd ed. Edited by Ruth Rouse, Stephen Charles Neil. Geneva: WCC, 1993.

Horton, F. L. *The Melchizedek Tradition.* England: Cambridge University Press, 1976.

Hughes, Philip. *The Church in Crisis: A History of the Twenty Great Councils.* London: Burns & Oates, 1961.

James, Woba. *History of Christianity in India: A Reader.* Delhi: Christian World Imprints, 2019.

Jathanna, Gladson. *Decolinising Oikumene.* Delhi: ISPCK, 2020.

Jayakumar, A. *History of Christianity in India: Major Themes.* Kolkata: Sceptre, 2013.

Koshi, Ninan. *A History of the Ecumenical Movement in Asia, Vol. I.* Hongkong: CCA, 2004.

Lalduhsaka, Samuel. *Striving for a Missional Mandate: Tripura Baptist Christian Union from Missional Church Perspective.* Agartala: Tripura Academy of Integrated Christian Studies, 2016.

Latourette, Kenneth Scott. *A History of Christianity, Vol. I: AD 1500.* New York: Harper & Row Publishers, 1953.

Latourette, Kenneth Scott. *A History of the Expansion of Christianity, Vol. I, The First Five Centuries.* New York and London: Harper & Brothers Publishers, 1937.

Lawmsanga. *Theology of Mission: Postcolonial Perspective.* Aizawl: Lalmuanpuii, 2016.

Lazareth, William H., Nikos Nissiotis, *Baptism, Eucharist and Ministry, Faith and Order Paper No. 111.* Geneva: World Council of Churches, 1982.

Lebreton, Jules, S.J. and Jacques Zeiller. *Heresy and Orthodoxy.* USA: Macmillan Company, 1962.

Manickam, S. *United Theological College: A Brief History of Change and Continuity*, 1910-2000. Bangalore: UTC, 2000.

Morris, John Hughes. *The Story of our Foreign Mission.* Liverpool: Hugh Evans & Sons Ltd, 1930.

Mott, John Raleigh. *The Decisive Hour of Christian Missions.* London: BMS, 1910.

Nash, Ronald H. *Christianity and the Hellenistic World.* Michigan: Zondervan Publishing House, 1984.

Newbigin, Lesslie. *The Reunion of the Church: A Defence of the South India Scheme.* London: SCM Press, 1948.

Nigg, Walter. *The Heretics.* New York: Alfred A. Knopf, 1962.

Pathil, Kuncheria. *Future of the Ecumenical Movement.* Delhi: ISPCK, 2017.

Pathil, Kuncheria. *Models in Ecumenical Dialogue.* Bangalore: Dharmaram Publications, 1981.

Paul, Rajaiah D. *Ecumenism in Action: A Historical Survey of the Church of South India.* Madras: Christian Literature Service.

Paul, Rajaiah D. *The First Decade: An Account of the Church of South India.* Madras: CLS, 1958.

Philip, T. V. *Edinburgh to Salvador: Twentieth Century Ecumenical Missiology: A Historical Study of the Ecumenical Discussions on Mission.* Delhi: ISPCK, 1999.

Puthenkurakal, Joseph. *Baptist Missions in Nagaland: A Study in Historical and Ecumenical Perspective.* Shillong: Vendrame Missiological Institute, 1984.

Ralte, Lalfakawma. *Ni leh Thla Betute Zinga Pathian Hnathawh Ropui (Wondrous Works of God in Arunachal Pradesh).* Reprinted. Aizawl: Lalchamliana, 2013.

Rawlinson, A. E. J. *The Church of South India: the Lichfield Cathedral Divinity Lectures 1950.* London: Hodder and Stoughton, 1950.

Report of the Centenary Conference on the Protestant Missions of the World, Held in Exeter Hall (June 9th - 19th), London, 1888, Vol. I. Edited by James Johnston. London: James Nisbet & Co., 1888.

Robert, Dana L. *Christian Mission: How Christianity became a World Religion.* West Sussex, UK: Blackwell, 2009.

Rossing, Barbara R. "(Re)-claiming Oikumene?: Empire, Ecumenism, and the Discipleship of Equals." In *Walk in the Ways of Wisdom: Essays in Honour of Elisabeth Schuessler Fiorenza.* Edited by Shelly Matthews, et.al. Harrisburg, London, New York: Trinity Press International, 2003.

Rouse, Ruth, Stephen Charles Neill, eds. *A History of the Ecumenical Movement 1517-1948.* 3rd ed. Geneva: WCC, 1986.

Rouse, Ruth, Stephen Neill, eds. *A History of the Ecumenical Movement, Vol.I – 1517-1948,* 3rd revised ed. Geneva: WCC, 1948.

Russell, Letty M. *Christian Education in Mission.* Philadelphia: Westminster Press, 1967.

Sahu, Dhirendra Kumar. *The Church of North India: A Historical and Systematic Theological Inquiry into an Ecumenical Ecclesiology.* Frankfurt: Peter Lang, 1994.

Sangma, Milton S. *History of American Baptist Mission in North East India: Vol.I.* Dibrugarh: NEIHA, 1981.

Sangma, Milton S. *History of the American Baptist Mission in North-East India (1836-1950): Vol.I.* New Delhi: Mittal Publications, 1987.

Shillington, George. *The New Testament in Context.* New York: T&T Clark, 2008.

Singh, K. M. *History of Christian Missions in Manipur and other Neighbouring States.* New Delhi: Mittal Publications, 1991.

Snaitang, O. L. *A History of Ecumenical Movement: An Introduction.* Bangalore: BTESSC, 2016.

Stanley, Brian. *The History of the Baptist Missionary Society 1792-1992.* Edinburgh: T&T Clark, 1992.

Swartzendruber, H. Dwight. *Forty Years of Service Beyond our Borders.* Morgantown: Masthof Press, 2012. Fey, Harold C., ed. *A History of the Ecumenical Movement, Volume 2.* Eugene: Wipf and Stock, 2004.

Tabbernee, William. *Fake Prophecy and Polluted Sacraments Ecclesiastical and Imperial Reactions to Montanism.* Leiden, Boston: Brill, 2007.

Thomas, Pradip. *An Ecumenical Wordsmith: the Writings of T. K. Thomas.* Tiruvalla: Christava Sahitya Samithi, 2002.

Trevett, Christine. *Montanism: Gender, Prophecy, and the New Authority.* U.K.: Cambridge University Press, 1996.

Vaiphei, Kim. *The Coming of Christianity in Manipur with Special Reference to the Kukis.* Delhi: Joint Women's Programme, 1995.

Vischer, Lukas. *A Documentary History of the Faith and Order Movement, 1927-63.* USA: WCC, 1963.

Vischer, Lukas. *Faith and Order, Louvain, 1971: Study Reports and Documents.* Geneva: WCC, 1971.

W. H. T. Gairdner. *Edinburgh 1910: An Account and Interpretation of the World Missionary Conference.* Edinburgh and London: Oliphant, Anderson and Ferrier, 1910.

Articles on Books

Brown, William Adams. *Toward a United Church: Three Decades of Ecumenical Christianity.* New York: Charles Scribner's Sons, 1946.

Chan, Kwok Keung. "The First Mark of Mission: To Proclaim the Good News of the Kingdom of God." In *Life-Widening Mission: Global Anglican Perspectives.* Edited by Cathy Ross (Oxford: Regnum Books), 2012.

Chia, Edmund Kee-Fook. "Asian Ecumenism from Roman Catholic Perspective." In *History of Ecumenical Movement: Issues, Challenges and Perspectives.* Edited by Watimongla Jamir. Kolkata, SCEPTRE, 2014.

Gaikwad, Roger. "Churches Together in God's Mission." In *History of the Ecumenical Movement: Issues, Challenges and Perspectives.* Edited by Watimongla Jamir. Kolkata: SCEPTRE, 2014.

Kim, Kirsteen and Andrew Anderson. "Introduction." In *Edinburgh 2010 Mission Today and Tomorrow.* Edited by Kirsteen Kim and Andrew Anderson. Oxford: Regnum Books International, 2011.

Kim, Kirsteen. "Conference Study Process." In *Edinburgh 2010 Mission Today and Tomorrow.* Edited by Kirsteen Kim and Andrew Anderson. Oxford: Regnum Books International, 2011.

Koshey, Ninan. "The Ecumenical Movement in Asia." In *History of Ecumenical Movement: Issues, Challenges and Perspectives.* Edited by Watimongla Jamir. West Bengal: SCEPTRE, 2014.

Lianzuala, C. "America Khawmualpuia Harhna." In *Harhna: Mizoram Revival Centenary Souvenir, 1906-2006.* Aizawl: Synod Revival Committee, 2006.

Longchar, Wati. "Edinburgh 2010: Challenges for Witnessing to Christ Today in India." In *History of Ecumenical Movement: Issues, Challenges and Perspectives.* Edited by Watimongla Jamir. Kolkata: Sceptre, 2014.

Massey, James. "Whither Ecumenical Movement? 10th WCC Assembly." In *History of Ecumenical Movement: Issues, Challenges and Perspectives.* Edited by Watimongla Jamir. Kolkata: Sceptre, 2014.

Moran, Elizabeth, SSC. "Spiritual Life of the Conference." In *Edinburgh 2010 Mission Today and Tomorrow.* Edited by Kirsteen Kim and Andrew Anderson. Oxford: Regnum Books International, 2011.

Newbigin, Lesslie. "Union, Organic." In *The Ecumenical Movement: An Anthology of Key Texts and Voices.* 2nd ed. Edited by Michael Kinnamon. Geneva: WCC, 2016.

Niles, D. T. "A Church and its Selfhood." In *A Decisive Hour for the Christian Mission.* London: SCM Press Limited, 1960.

Spivak, Gayatri C. "Can the Subaltern Speak?" In *Postcolonialism, Critical Concepts, Vol. IV.* Edited by D. Brydon. London and New York: Routledge, 2000.

Thomaskutty, Johnson. "Oneness in John 17:1–26 as a Paradigm for Wider Ecumenism and Dialogue." *HTS Teologiese Studies/ Theological Studies*

78/3, (Oct, 2022), a7838. https://doi.org/10.4102/hts.v78i3.7838 (16 May 2025).

Thomas, V. V. "Historical Models of Church Unity." In *History of Ecumenical Movement: Issues, Challenges and Perspectives.* Edited by Watimongla Jamir. Kolkata: Sceptre, 2014.

Tissington, Tatlow. "The World Conference on Faith and Order." In *A History of the Ecumenical Movement (1517-1948).* Edited by Ruth Rouse and Stephen Neill. Philadelphia: The Westminster Press, 1986.

Articles on Dictionaries and Journals

"Editorial." In *NCC Review*, CXXX. June, 2010.

"The Importance of the Conciliar Process in the Ancient Church for the Ecumenical Movement." In *Councils and the Ecumenical Movement.* Geneva: World Council Studies, 1968.

"The Unity of the Church-Next Steps: The Report of Salamanca Consultation of Faith and Order, September 1973." In *The Ecumenical Review*. 26/2, April 1974.

Ariarajah, S. Wesley. "Wider ecumenism." In *Current Dialogue.* Issue 47, June, 2006.

Beaver. "Comity." In *Concise Dictionary of the Christian World Mission.* Edited by Stephen Neill, Gerald Anderson, and John Goodwin. New York: Abingdon Press, 1971.

Behera, Marina Ngursangzeli. "Ecumenism in Theological Education." In *Bangalore Theological Forum* LIV/1, June, 2022.

Best, Thomas F. "Union, Organic." In Nicholas Lossky. *Dictionary of the Ecumenical Movement*, 2nd ed. Edited by Nicholas Lossky, Jose Miquez Bonino, John Poboe, and Tom F. Stransky. Geneva: WCC, 2002.

Devadoss, Isaac. "A Historical Survey of Ecumenism in India." In *History of Ecumenical Movement: Issues, Challenges, and Perspectives.* Edited by Watimongla Jamir. Kolkata: Sceptre, 2014.

Downs, F. S. "Early Christian Contacts with North East India." In *ICHR* V/1, June, 1971.

Downs, Frederick S. "Rangammati: A Christian Community in North-East India During the Seventeenth and Eighteenth Centuries." *ICHR,* XII/2, 1972.

Drake, Harold. "The Emperor as a Man of God: the Impact of Constantine the Great's Conversion on Roman Ideas of Kingship." In *Historia*. Vol. 35, 1 Jan., 2016.

Eade, M. J. "Beginnings." In *Towards the Sunrise: the Centenary History of the New Zealand Baptist Missionary Society*. Edited by Angus H. MacLeod. Wellington: NZBHC, 1985.

Gassmann, Gunther. "Faith and Order." In *Dictionary of the Ecumenical Movement.* Edited by Nicholas Lossky. Geneva: WCC, 1991.

Geewarghese, Mor Coorilos. "Mission towards Fullness of life." In *International Review of Mission* 103/1, (2014).

Gideon, Rohan. "Why Revisiting the Process of Nicene Creed is Important." In *The New Guardian.* 8/1, March, 2025.

Heller, Dogmar. "Baptism – the Basis of Church Unity? The Question of Baptism in Faith and Order." In *The Ecumenical Review*, 50/4, October, 1998.

Heuser, Frederick J. "'Woman's Work for Woman,' Cultural Change, and the Foreign Missionary Movement." In *The Journal of Presbyterian History (1997).* 75/2, 1997.

Jayaseelan, Lazar. "Christianity in Manipur." In *A Concise Encyclopaedia of Christianity in India.* Edited by Errol D'Lima. Pune: Jnana-Deepa Vidyapeeth, 2014.

Joseph, M. P. "Revisiting the Edinburgh Conference in the Context of Globalisation." In *Witnessing in Context, Essays in Honour of Eardly Mendis.* Edited by Monica J. Melanchton and George Zachariah. Tiruvalla: CSS, 2007.

Lalhmangaiha. "Brief History of Council of Churches in Mizoram." In *Presbyterian Review,* 30/2, July-December, 2024.

Latourette, Kenneth Scott. "Ecumenical Bearings of the Missionary Movement and the International Missionary Council." In *A History of the Ecumenical Movement 1517-1948,* edited by Ruth Rouse and Stephen Charles Neil. London: SPCK, 1954.

Mackenna, Stephen. "The Saintly Scholars of the Church." In *The Ecclesiastical Review*, August, 1942.

Newbigin, J.E. Lesslie. "Niles, Daniel Thambyrajah." In *Dictionary of the Ecumenical Movement.* Edited by Nicholas Lossky, José Míguez Bonino, et.al. Geneva: WCC Publications, 1991.

Pathil, Kuncheria. "Theological Reflections on the Church from India." In *Asian Horizons* 6/4, December, 2012.

Patta, Raj Bharat. "Mission Moorings: Ecumenical Experiences from Edinburgh 2010." In *NCC Review*, CXXX, (June, 2010).

Patta, Raj Bharat. "Nicene Creed: A Dalit-Decolonial Reading." In *The New Guardian.* 8/1, March, 2025.

Rao, Chilkuri Vasantha. "The Continuing Legacy of UTC in the Field of Ecumenical Theological Education." In *Bangalore Theological Forum*, LIV/1, June, 2022.

See Adakho Poji K, "Advent of Christianity in Manipur and its Impact on the Mao Naga Tribe," *Indian Church History Review,* 44/1, (June, 2010): 67.

Shullai, Pynhunlang N. M. "Colonialism, Christianity and Mission Activities In India: A Postcolonial Perspectives." In *International Journal of Humanities & Social Science Studies.* 3/5, (March, 2017).

Thomas, T. K. "WCC, Basis of." In *Dictionary of the Ecumenical Movement,* 2nd *ed. Edited by* Nicholas Lossky et.al. Geneva: WCC Publications and Grand Rapids: Eerdmans, 2002.

Thomaskutty, Johnson. "Faith and Theology in the Johannine Community and in the Reformation: A Paradigm in the Indian Context." In W. Kinzig & J. Winnebeck (eds.), *Glaube und Theologie: Reformatorische Grundeinsichten in der ökumenischen Diskussion, Evangelische Verlagsanstalt, Leipzig,* 2019.

Vischer, Lukas. "Faith and Order Reports: their Nature and Significance." In *A Documentary History of the Faith & Order Movement 1927-1963.* Edited by Lukas Vischer. USA: WCC, 1963.

Webb, Pauline. "Women in Church and Society." In *Dictionary of the Ecumenical Movement.* Edited by Nicholas Lossky et.al. Geneva: WCC Publications, 1991.

Unpublished Sources

Chinzah, Zadingluaia. "History of Christianity in Assam: A Subaltern Perspective." A paper presented at M.Th. class seminar, Aizawl Theological College, 1 February 2019.

Keshishian, Aram. "Conciliar Fellowship: A Model of Church Unity: the Emergence and Development of Conciliarity in the World Council of Churches." A dissertation submitted in partial fulfilment of the requirements for the degree of Doctor of Philosophy in the Department of Theology at Fordham University, New York, 1989.

Klawiter, Frederick C. "The New Prophecy in Early Christianity: The Origin, Nature and Development of Montanism A.D. 165–220." Ph.D. dissertation, University of Chicago, 1975.

Omei, Yingli. "A Feminist Historical Assessment on "The Ecumenical Decade of the Churches in Solidarity with Women, 1988-1998.'" D.Th. assessment paper, 2024, United Theological College, Bengaluru.

Ralte, Lalfakawma. "Revival in Mizoram as Resistance Movement from 1987 to the Present." D.Th. Dissertation, Senate of Serampore College, 2023.

Ralte, Lalfakawma. "The Impact of Christianity among the Adi Tribe of Arunachal Pradesh." M.Th. dissertation, Senate of Serampore College, 2004.

Other Sources

Kipgen, Paominlen. "Church Union Movement in India and its Contributions." Academia.edu.

Mallick, Sohan K. "The Northeast India Church Union Movement." Academia. edu.

Paominlen Kipgen, "Church Union Movement – Changing Approaches and Types of Union," Academia.edu.

Thomas, B. M. "Edinburgh 1910 and The International Missionary Council (IMC), with Special Reference to the IMC as Means of Involving Asian and African Christians in Ecumenical Movement up till 1961." Academia. edu.